Power,
Meaning,
and
Identity

Studies in the
Postmodern Theory of Education

Joe L. Kincheloe and Shirley R. Steinberg
General Editors

Vol. 109

PETER LANG
New York • Washington, D.C./Baltimore • Boston
Bern • Frankfurt am Main • Berlin • Vienna • Paris

Michael W. Apple

Power,
Meaning,
and
Identity

Essays in Critical
Educational Studies

PETER LANG
New York • Washington, D.C./Baltimore • Boston
Bern • Frankfurt am Main • Berlin • Vienna • Paris

Library of Congress Cataloging-in-Publication Data

Apple, Michael W.
Power, meaning, and identity: essays in critical
educational studies / Michael W. Apple.
p. cm. — (Counterpoints; vol. 109)
Includes bibliographical references and index.
1. Critical pedagogy. 2. Popular education.
3. Curriculum planning. 4. Educational sociology. I. Title.
II. Series: Counterpoints (New York, N.Y.); vol. 109.
LC196.A77   370.11'5—dc21   98-53525
ISBN 0-8204-4427-8
ISSN 1058-1634

Die Deutsche Bibliothek-CIP-Einheitsaufnahme

Apple, Michael W.:
Power, meaning, and identity: essays in critical educational
studies / Michael W. Apple. –New York; Washington, D.C./Baltimore;
Boston; Bern; Frankfurt am Main; Berlin; Vienna; Paris: Lang.
(Counterpoints; Vol. 109)
ISBN 0-8204-4427-8

Cover design by Nona Reuter

The paper in this book meets the guidelines for permanence and durability
of the Committee on Production Guidelines for Book Longevity
of the Council of Library Resources.

Printed in the United States of America

Table of Contents

Acknowledgments

More than two years ago, Shirley Steinberg suggested to me that I do this book. At first I hesitated. Like many other people, I was involved in too many other projects. I had just completed one book and was in the midst of doing the revised edition of another. Further, my political activities both nationally and internationally had escalated measurably as the growth of neoliberal and neoconservative platforms made it ever more necessary to "put one's money where one's mouth is" and to lend whatever support I could to those social movements contesting their arrogant policies. It was difficult to find time to breathe.

However, Shirley (rightly) persisted and I was able to find the time to think it through and to organize this volume. Shirley is a wise and committed person and I thank her for her patience.

The essays contained here were written over a number of years and the ideas behind them were tried out in many institutions on many continents. Two specific institutions, however, played important parts in the creation of this volume. First, the Department of Policy Studies at the University of London Institute of Education provided a hospitable environment for serious work and serious discussion during a period when this book was in its formative stages. Second, the University of Wisconsin, Madison has been my home for nearly three decades. It remains a remarkably open place where that rare combination of collective criticism and support exists. In this regard, let me add a special word of thanks to the Friday Seminar there. This group of my graduate students and visiting colleagues comes from all over the world. It shows how it is possible to hold strong, but sometimes differing, political and theoretical commitments and yet still form that "decentered unity" I talk about in this book and in others.

There have been a number of individuals who have helped me think more deeply about the issues I raise in the essays here. I especially want to thank Rima D. Apple, whose historical knowledge and technical assistance were crucial to the completion of this volume. Other friends and colleagues provided help along the way as well. Among them are James Beane, Barbara Brodhagen, Debbie Epstein, David Gillborn, Carl Grant, Gloria Ladson-Billings, Steven Selden, Tomaz Tadeu de Silva, William Tate, Hannah Tavares, Carlos Alberto Torres, and Geoff Whitty. I also wish to thank Allison Halpern for her editorial assistance and her work as a project assistant on this volume.

I want to dedicate this book to three people: my son Peter, for his honest and consistent ethical questioning about the world and his place in it; my son Paul, for his constant struggles against racism and for his affirmation of personal responsibility in the face of damaging social conditions; and my granddaughter Alyssa, whose school life has only recently begun.

*****

The original versions of a number of the essays included in this book have appeared elsewhere. These include:

"The Politics of Official Knowledge in the United States," *Journal of Curriculum Studies* 22 (July/August 1990): 377–83.

"There Is a River: James B. Macdonald and Curricular Tradition," *Journal of Curriculum Theorizing* 6 (Fall 1985): 9–18.

"Social Evaluation of Curriculum," in *The Curriculum: Problems, Politics, and Possibilities*, ed. Landon Beyer and Michael W. Apple. (Albany: State University of New York Press, 1988): 334–49.

"Power and Culture in the *Report of the Committee of Ten*," *New York University Education Quarterly* 14 (Winter 1983): 28–32.

"Do the Standards Go Far Enough?" *Journal of Research in Mathematics Education* 23 (November 1992): 412–31.

"Education, Culture, and Class Power," *Educational Theory* 42 (Spring 1992): 127–45.

"Power, Meaning, and Identity," *British Journal of Sociology of Education* 17 (June 1996): 125–44.

"Freire, Neoliberalism, and Education," in *Paulo Freire: Politica e Pedagogia*, ed. Michael W. Apple and Antonio Novoa (Lisbon: Porto Editora, 1998): 21–45.

"Between Neo and Post in Critical Educational Studies," in *Multicultural Research*, ed. Carl Grant (Philadelphia: Falmer Press, 1998).

INTRODUCTION

Chapter 1

The Personal and the Political in Critical Educational Studies

Personal Stories

Although some may deny it, we are not an equal society. Our social system is crisscrossed by axes of class, gender, race, age, nationality, region, politics, religion, and other dynamics of power. All of these produce differences, some of which are more strongly experienced than others depending on the situation. However, these sets of social differences are *not* isolated. They interact with each other in a complex nexus of power relations. And since social power is clearly not distributed equally throughout society, "any set of social relations necessarily involves power and resistance, domination, subordination, and even struggle."[1] Notice that the prior quotation begins with the words "any set of social relations." This phrase needs to be taken quite literally, I believe, especially when one is talking about the core institutions in this society—including schools. The recognition that schools—and the curricula, teaching, and evaluative policies and practices that structure the daily events that go on in them—are among the most central of our institutionalized sets of social relations is not new, of course. But our understanding of what this means has grown massively over the past decades. This growing recognition constitutes much of the core of this book.

A "simple" set of questions underpins a good deal of critical research in education. Who benefits from the ways education is organized? Whose knowledge and ways of knowing are considered legitimate or "official"? Whose knowledge is not? What is the relationship between the inner world of schools and the larger society? How is power constituted and how do we think about it? Obviously, this list of questions could and should be expanded. And just as obviously, these questions are anything but simple to ask or to answer. They require a considerable amount of conceptual and empirical sophistication. They require a detailed and complex understanding of the relationship among the economy, politics, and culture, and an equally detailed and complex understanding of the social movements and groups that constitute this society. They involve difficult issues of theory, ideology, and politics, about whom research is supposed to serve, and ultimately about one's own appraisal of the multiple struggles for social justice in an unequal world. And, not least of all, these questions should also be grounded in an unromantic—but still hopeful—sense of what actually goes on in those places we call schools.

Our understanding of all of this did not spring full-blown, nor is it now complete (as if this were possible in the first place). It has taken decades of theoretical, historical, empirical, and practical work of many kinds to come as far as we have. Indeed, what even counts as the "we" here is contested because there are multiple traditions of ways to construe these issues, including (but not limited to) structural/functional approaches, various kinds of Marxist and neo-Marxist theories, world system theories, postmodernisms and poststructuralisms, feminisms, theories of race and postcolonianism, and synthetic perspectives drawn from cultural studies. The plural forms are important here, because each of these approaches has differences within itself. Further, trying to gain a picture of this terrain is made even more difficult because none of these traditions is static. They are in constant motion, with new material appearing rapidly that often cuts across any neat boundaries that have been established to easily differentiate among them.

The above paragraphs give a sense of some of the intellectual issues that serve as a basis for much of what is included in this volume. However, this account fails to ground the concerns that are expressed in the essays collected in this book in lived experiences of a different kind, experiences that are also essential to the formation of the arguments you will find here. As some of you may know, I do not usually engage in the act of personal storytelling, but I trust that you will forgive me if I tell a number of stories here that relate to why I have taken many of the positions you will find in this book.

In the 1950s, many parts of the United States remained officially segregated by race. Black and white (and many Chicano/a) students were prevented from going to school together. After school segregation was supposedly officially abolished, many school districts, especially in the southern parts of the country (northern states often found even more creative "solutions" to the problem of putting children together, but not really together), closed many of their public schools and reopened them as private academies, so that black children could be legally excluded. My first experience as an educator was as a volunteer and as an activist, supporting literacy work in communities where schools had been closed to keep African American children out. I was still a teenager myself, but this experience had a lasting impression on me. Schooling had much to do with *power*.

Later on, when I became a paid teacher in inner-city schools in the poor neighborhoods where I, too, had grown up, the relationship between poverty and education, the struggles that people participated in when they fought bureaucratic inertia, and the class and race interests that characterized urban schools made the realities of power and inequality even more visible to me. Still later, when I became president of a teachers' union, the constant battles for sufficient funding, for unbiased curricular materials and textbooks, for better working conditions, and for schools that actually fulfilled the promises they made to working-class and poor communities convinced me that we had to examine our educational system much more critically than we had ever done before. I am certain that my experiences are not singular. Many others have been affected by similar experiences, including, I am certain, many of you who are reading this book.

In the next few years of my teaching career—after I had spent some time teaching in inner-city schools and well before I ever dreamed of becoming a "critical scholar"—I was an elementary school teacher in a small and strikingly conservative town in a rural area of a northeastern state. Although there was a middle-class population, most of the town was certainly considerably less affluent. My own classroom was filled with children who were relatively poor or working class; it also included a number of children whose parents were migrant laborers who worked on local farms picking crops for extremely low pay and under conditions that can only be described as inhuman and exploitative. The curriculum and the textbooks (they were one and the same) were not only completely out of touch with these children's cultures, histories, and daily lives, but they were simply *boring* both for me and the students in that class.

To try to overcome this, we reorganized the curriculum. We wrote and performed plays. We studied local histories, the relations between food production and the conditions of farm labor, and the hidden histories of the people who were invisible in the textbooks but who had lived in the area. (For example, the town at one time had a small black farming community near it that had been a stop on the Underground Railroad where escaped slaves had been safely housed as they made their way to the industrial cities in the northern part of the state.) We interviewed parents, grandparents, and others about their lives and histories there and elsewhere. These stories were written up into narratives. The texts of their lives became the texts of historical study and led to trips to the local archives to connect the lived versions of historical events with the "official news" that was published. Histories of racial tensions and racial subjugation were uncovered. Histories of racial segregation in the local area (which supposedly never happened in such northern states) were bared. Stories of the uncommon courage of people (African American, Chicano/a, and Euroamerican), in which people collectively and individually stood up to racist movements and policies, surfaced as well. The students put out an informal mimeographed newspaper to tell what they had learned.

Much of this was—how can I put this kindly?—unsettling to some people. The local Chamber of Commerce felt that these kinds of topics were "not appropriate for young minds" (the students in my class were 12 and 13 years old), but also that the kinds of issues my students were making public would put the town "in a bad light." This could be "bad for business." A local fundamentalist minister who believed that the Bible clearly showed that "God had made the white race superior" led a small but very vocal group that criticized what they felt were "radical" and "unchristian" methods. Either I was to stop doing this or pressure would be put on the school board to ensure that my contract would not be renewed.

Like many teachers, I suppose, I was initially shocked by the hostility of these groups to what seemed to me and the students to be simply an attempt to create the conditions for a *serious* education. But after the initial shock had worn off, I decided that I could not let the attacks go unchallenged. I spoke at meetings about the racism being exhibited. I publicly demonstrated the quality of the reading and writing that the students were doing and the open-mindedness with which they approached their historical research. I showed that the scores the students had achieved on the standardized tests (yeah, we all have to compromise, don't we?) were actually higher than before. (Is it so odd that when students are actually engaged in educational work that seems socially and personally serious to them, they tend to do better at it?)

The students themselves, and their parents, were not silent about these attacks. They also spoke out to members of the school board and to other members of the community, often more than a little eloquently. Colleagues of mine—even those who were more politically and educationally conservative than I was—lent support. They too knew that what was at stake was the loss of autonomy in creating curricula and teaching methods that were in any way critical. Soon, considerable counterpressure arose. The conservative ideologues had to back down. But for years teachers, administrators, and students looked over their shoulders whenever methods or content got a bit more "creative" than the norm.

I look back on this time with both joy and distress. The students, the parents, and my colleagues and I had gained—at least temporarily—some important educational space. We had collectively demonstrated that it *was* possible to engage in educational practices that were personally meaningful, that asked critical questions, that were grounded in a sense of critical literacy, and that connected the school to a wider community in serious ways. Yet the fact that it continues to be both professionally and personally risky to engage in this kind of pedagogic action—and in fact because of the power of the current conservative restoration, may now at times be even more risky not only at elementary, middle, and secondary schools, but even at universities—is not something that is the stuff of joy. But it does remind me constantly of what I think a significant portion of our work must be about.

These historical, yet intensely personal, reminders are complemented by some equally powerful ones much closer in time to the present. Fast forward in time for another, more recent, instance that helps explain why the essays included in this book take the position that they do.

A few years ago, I was giving a lecture at a university in (South) Korea. The police had surrounded the university to prevent students and faculty from leaving the campus to demonstrate against the repressive military government that was then in power. The vast lecture hall was crowded with people sitting everywhere—on the floor, in the aisles, even on the stage. The heat from the bodies pressed together and the lack of air circulation in that overcrowded hall were ignored by everyone. We were there to talk about the politics of education; and in the midst of such a politicized and galvanizing situation, physical discomfort seemed beside the point. I spoke about the crucial significance of critical education in the struggle for democracy. I began academically. I described the developing traditions of "critical educational studies" and how they provided tools for us to more fully understand and combat the complex relationship between education and unequal cultural, political, and economic power. I pointed to the police surrounding the campus and to the fact that many students, faculty, union members, dissidents, and so many other people—not only in their own nation, but in all too many places throughout the world—were fearful of speaking honestly and openly. I spoke of the recent firing of the teachers' union leaders in Korea who were trying to form a union that was independent of government manipulation and control. I said that all of this provided evidence of the deep fear that dominant groups had of a truly liberatory education. The tension and intensity that packed that lecture theater were palpable. The questions and discussions that followed my lecture were among the most compelling experiences I have had.

And then I and my Korean colleagues who had organized the lecture were arrested. Saying such things and engaging in serious discussions of them were not to be tolerated.

If ever I again needed confirmation of the power of critical ideas and of the understanding of dominant groups that teaching such critical ideas could be dangerous, this was it. For in that moment, the importance of critical education and the perils of doing it were crystallized in living form right before my eyes in even more powerful ways than the ways that the students and I had experienced in that small town.

Yet, as threatening as it was, it is not only the arrest that is crucial here. It may be of some interest to the reader to know that in this instance a number of the people behind the government that arrested me and my colleagues were ultimately sent to jail themselves for their corrupt, repressive, and sometimes murderous acts, thereby documenting the fact that action based on critical ideas can bring new possibilities into existence. This combination—the realities and dangers of differential power and the always existing possibility that dominant relations can be successfully challenged—provides the tension that drives critical work for me and others. In Aronowitz and Giroux's words, we must combine the "language of critique and possibility."[2]

The Roots of Relational Analysis

I have related these brief stories because they stand in direct contrast to the ways that all too many educators think about schooling. Even with the extensive international literature on the complex relationship between educational policy and practice and the recreation and sub-version of unequal relations of cultural, political, and economic power, a considerable number of educational researchers, administrators, government officials, teachers, and others look at the policies and practices of schooling with a remarkably uncritical eye. Or when they do cast a critical eye on educational institutions, they do so using the conservative discourses that now circulate so widely in the dominant media. They either accept the official pronouncements of educators or of government officials as the daily reality of education—or worse, they accept its role in fostering social stratification or in not challeng-ing dominance as "natural." In the process, we remain unable to more fully understand the contradictory ways in which schools function in societies riven with inequalities, such as the United States.

This is a very real problem, because how we think about something makes a considerable difference in how we act. Let me give an ex-ample that I used in an earlier volume of mine.[3] We are now quite accustomed to seeing pictures of disasters in which thousands of people lose their lives due to storms, mudslides, drought, and so forth. (The complicated politics of "pleasure" involved in "wanting" to see the pictures of death and destruction needs to be paid close attention to, I think.) We are told to think of these as "natural" disasters. But is this the appropriate way of understanding these situations or is it a form of category error?

Take the massive mudslides that occurred in parts of South America in which large numbers of people were killed as torrential rains washed their houses (usually shacks) down the mountainsides. A closer exami-nation of this case reveals nothing natural about this disaster at all. Every year there are rains and every year some people die. This year an entire side of a mountain gave way. "Only" the thousands of poor people living on it lost their lives. No one in the valley died. A few wealthy people own the land in the valleys, which contain the safe and fertile land. Poor people are forced to live on the dangerous hillsides. This is the only land they can find to eke out a precarious existence that is barely survivable. They crowd onto this land not because they want to, but both because of utter poverty and because of land own-ership patterns that are historically and grossly unequal.

Hence, the problem is not the yearly rains—a natural occurrence—but the economic and often racialized structures that allow a tiny mi-nority of individuals and families to control the lives of the vast majority of people in that region. Notice that this altered understanding of the problem would require a different kind of action. Not only would we send immediate aid to help the victims of the rains, but we would need to engage in a large-scale program of land redistribution to make it much more equal.

I want to use this as an instance of what has come to be called *relational analysis*.[4] That is, the institutions and events of our daily lives need to be understood not in an isolated way—separate from the relations of domination and exploitation of the larger society—but in ways that stress their interconnections with these relations. I take it as a given that this is especially important in education since, as I noted in the opening paragraph of this introductory chapter and in the personal vignettes I shared, education as a set of institutions and as a cultural and ideological practice is strongly connected to the maintenance and the possible subversion of unequal power.

For many of us, this has not been a solely intellectual issue. Rather, how and why one does relational analysis is directly related to a set of more general values that are taken very seriously by members of the critical educational community(ies).

Critical research in education is guided by a set of broad ethical and sociocultural commitments. Among these are: extending the *reality* of democracy to all of this society's groups and institutions, including all of its economic, political, and cultural life (as well as interrogating the contradictory meanings and uses of democracy in our political economy and in our lived culture); eliminating the basic causes of the massive and growing differences in wealth and power, in economic and cultural capital; investigating the ways in which education participates in maintaining these differences or may be employed to alter them; providing important aspects of the theoretical, historical, and empirical (both qualitative and quantitative) resources to help social movements challenge rightist offensives and to defend the gains that they have made over years of hard work. Finally, critical work is guided by a commitment to ask difficult questions that are open to radical answers. That is, it is not afraid to ask the most basic and substantive questions about how a society's economic, political, and cultural processes operate and to set about answering them in what may be uncomfortable—and at times personally risky—ways.

Because of these commitments, as many people have argued over the years, critical educators need to be "organic intellectuals" of a particular kind. They need to be connected to and actively participate in larger social movements that seek the transformation of the conditions that continue to have such tragic effects on the cultures, histories, economic possibilities, and the very lives and bodies of real people in real institutions in this and other nations. Only by bringing the margins to the center can this be done.

Obviously, these values affect how education is thought about. <u>Education is not seen as a neutral instrumentality. Rather it is seen as *inherently* political, as an arena in which various groups attempt to institutionalize their cultures, histories, and visions of social justice.</u> Yet, this general statement needs to be delved into more deeply, since education is political in a number of ways. Let me briefly mention a number of these, since they act as something of a set of first principles for relational analysis and underpin nearly all that is included in this book.

<u>First,</u> the curriculum is itself part of what has been called a selective tradition. That is, from that vast universe of possible knowledge, only some knowledge gets to be official knowledge, gets to be declared legitimate as opposed to simply being popular culture. There is a strong, but exceedingly complex, relationship between a group's social and cultural power and its ability to set the terms of curriculum debates and to have its values, culture, and histories seen as the backdrop against which all other values, culture, and knowledge are to be measured. The results of this are not preordained, however. The curriculum is always the result of constant struggle and compromise.[5] But this is not a level playing field; differential cultural and economic capital *do* count.

<u>Second</u>, this political structuring is not only seen at the level of content. It is also visible in the ways in which the curriculum is organized and evaluated. As Basil Bernstein, Pierre Bourdieu, myself, and others have demonstrated, curricular *form* also represents the social and cultural glue, the ways of being in the world, of particular classes and class fractions[6] and of dominant race and gender relations. Indeed, most of the debates about the form the curriculum should take and how it should be evaluated are really arguments within groups who already have considerable power.

<u>Third,</u> the politics of education is visible in the relationship between schooling as a set of institutions and the social, sexual, and racial divisions of paid and unpaid labor. Even though many educators actively work to promote the (individual) mobility of their students, it is still the case that education functions to roughly support or at least to not actively interrupt these larger social divisions. As nearly two decades of research have documented, this is neither a mechanistic

process in which education has no relative autonomy, nor are teachers and students passive in the face of this. Yet, this said, no matter how elegant our theoretical positions have become in understanding the complexities involved in these processes, it is still absolutely crucial to remember that on the whole the education system works much more effectively for those social groups that already have cultural and economic capital and that are able to convert one to the other.[7] This may be the result of differential funding, the economic and cultural advantages affluent groups have in guaranteeing that the cultural "gifts" their children possess are those that are both recognized in school and are connected to the changing dispositional and knowledge needs of dominant institutions, the histories of mistrust and alienation that dispossessed peoples rightly have when interacting with dominant institutions, the intricate politics of popular culture, and much, much more. The reasons are historically and culturally complicated; but the results are visible in what Kozol so correctly called the "savage inequalities" in this society's schools.[8]

These social divisions go beyond the relatively essentializing categories of class, race, and gender, to include sexuality, "ability," age, nation, bodily politics, and so on—each of which is in constant interaction with the others. These kinds of "things" are often separable only at an analytic level. In saying this, however, I do not wish to deflect attention from what I still take to be useful categories. Although we know, for instance, that people may have multiple identities and that categories such as the seemingly holy trinity of class, race, and gender may not always be sufficiently nuanced to capture the complex politics of identity or the shifting nature and mobilizations surrounding identity and its hybrid forms, we need to not lose sight of some quite basic sensitivities.

And this point leads me to the fourth way in which education is political. This involves the ways in which it participates as a workplace in the historic construction of teaching as classed, gendered, and raced labor. As I have shown in *Teachers and Texts*,[9] in many nations of the world the majority of teachers are women. This is especially the case at the elementary school level. We cannot understand why curricula and teaching are controlled in the ways they are unless we also recognize that work that is done by women (and what is or is not even defined as skilled work) is unfortunately often subject to lower pay, less respect and autonomy, and more social blame. The fact that, historically, working-class women and men saw teaching as a path to class mobility needs to enter into the argument as well. Also, the history of teachers of color, especially the fact that African American, Latino/a, Asian American, Native American, and other populations were historically often excluded from teaching jobs or placed in segregated underfunded schools and had to struggle for decades to gain recognition as *teachers* documents the fact that schools exist as part of a racialized and racializing state, a gendered state, and a classed state. The fact that gay and lesbian teachers are still at risk of losing their jobs in many communities documents that the state is part of a political apparatus that polices sexuality in its employment practices as well.[10] Schools, then, are not separate from political and moral economies, but are very much part of them. People *work* there, and struggling in schools both historically and in the present over employment practices, over policing actions, etc. *is* struggling in the larger society. In essence, the separation we make between the politics of education and the politics of the larger society is not all that useful. The separation is an artificial one, because schools are crucial parts of that larger society. Indeed, not only are they among the central institutions that make it up,[11] they have also played extremely important roles in providing arenas for the very formation of social movements that have challenged dominant power relations.[12]

That this occurs in and through the state leads me to my next first principle. Formal schooling by and large is organized and controlled by the government (the "State"). This means that, even aside from the role of schooling as an arena of class, gender/sex, and race mobilizations or as a place of paid employment, by its very nature the entire schooling process—how it is paid for, what goals it seeks to attain and how these goals will be measured, who has power over it, what textbooks are approved, who has the right to ask and answer these questions, and so on—is political.[13] Thus, as inherently part of a set of political institutions, the educational system will constantly be in the middle of crucial struggles about the meaning of democracy, about definitions of legitimate culture, and about who should benefit the most from government policies and practices. That this is not of academic interest alone is made more than a little visible in the current attempts to institute neoliberal "reforms" in education (such as attempts at marketization through voucher plans) and neoconservative "reforms" (such as national curriculum and national testing, a "return" to a "common culture," and the English-only movement).[14]

This fact points to the final part of my argument. Education is thoroughly political in an even more practical and gritty way. In order to change both its internal dynamics and social effects and the policies and practices that generate them—and in order to defend the more democratic gains that committed educators and activists have won over the years (after all, the right would not be so angry currently if there had not been gains won by progressive forces)—we need to act collectively. Multiple movements around multiple progressive projects having to do with education and its role in all of the complex politics I have only hinted at here are either already formed or are currently in formation. Collective dilemmas warrant collective political responses.

Struggles With and In Theory

Although I have described some of the ways in which I take education to be fundamentally political, this set of first principles can seem both overly taxonomic and deceptively simple. Yet, as I stated earlier, understanding what these claims imply actually requires some serious and quite detailed theoretical, historical, and empirical work if it is not to degenerate into slogans. This also requires that I position myself in relation to the debates currently under way about the politics of theory, about what it should do, and about the (often overly) divisive debates among the various strands of critical work now captured under the labels of, for example, neo-Marxist, postmodern, and poststructural approaches.

Let me say something about how I approach theory. I am not interested in theory as a subject in and of itself. Unfortunately, critical theory has become something of a substitute. The production of endlessly refined accounts of supposedly new perspectives has created a situation in which theory has become an academic pursuit of its own. Yet, in the process of "politicizing the academic," all too often what has happened has been a process of "academicizing the political." Let me hasten to add that there are positive moments to this. We absolutely need to constantly interrogate our accepted perspectives—including the perspectives that are accepted as given within the multiple critical communities in education. However, I am impatient with some of this activity. It is all too often not connected—except in the most ephemeral ways—to the most important political, economic, and cultural issues of our time. As Said says, "The question of oppression, of racial oppression, the question of war, the question of human rights—all of these issues ought to belong together . . . as opposed to the massive, intervening, institutionalized presence of theoretical discussion."[15] "Doing theory," especially in its most arcane forms, enables the knower to comment from on high, unmuddied by the pollution of and dangers from ongoing and concrete economic/political/cultural mobilizations in education or elsewhere.

As I shall say later on, theoretical interventions are important. And they do count as political work themselves at times. But I fear that for too many people within the critical educational studies communities, this may be the only political/educational work that is done. It is a bit reminiscent of Bakhtin's discussion of the function of balconies during carnival in Europe hundreds of years ago. The affluent were both attracted to and repelled by the cultural, political, and bodily transgressions that accompanied carnival. The smells, the noise, the possibility of loss of control, the undercurrent of danger, all of this was fascinating. But the bourgeoisie could not let go of their safe havens. The balcony was the creative solution. The carnival of the streets could be experienced—vicariously. The sights and smells and sounds could be safely lived—and commented upon, which also had its own politics of pleasure—from the balcony overhanging the street. One could be in and out, almost-participant but mostly observer, at the same time.[16]

The universalism of the intellectual who stands above it all, observes, and deconstructs the positions of others has of course a long tradition in education and elsewhere. Adorno's vigorous attack on such "innocuous skepticism" is telling here. As he put it, such a standpoint "calls everything into question and criticizes nothing."[17] Although there is much to question, my own position has little in common with such innocuous skepticism. Unlike, say, Karl Mannheim's view of the unattached intelligentsia in which the relative classlessness of free-floating intellectuals enables them to stand aside from the political and ideological struggles of the larger society and to look at the "interest of the whole,"[18] I believe that we are already deeply positioned. We must attach our criticisms to identifiable social movements that seek, expressly, to challenge the relations of exploitation and domination within the larger society.

This, of course, is easy to say but harder to do, given the multiplicity of emancipatory political projects and movements today. It is clear that there have been significant transformations in the political imaginary. At times, claims for the recognition of group differences have eclipsed claims for social equality. As Nancy Fraser clearly puts it in her description of the growth of identity politics and the decentering of class politics:

> We are witnessing an apparent shift in the political imaginary, especially in the terms in which justice is imagined. Many actors appear to be moving away from a socialist political imaginary, in which the central problem of

justice is redistribution, to a "postsocialist" political imaginary, in which the central problem of justice is recognition. With this shift, the most salient social movements are no longer economically defined "classes" who are struggling to defend their "interests," end "exploitation," and win "redistribution." Instead, they are culturally defined "groups" or "communities of value" who are struggling to defend their "identities," end "cultural domination," and win "recognition." The result is a decoupling of cultural politics from social politics, and the relative eclipse of the latter by the former.[19]

Fraser may be overstating the split in some ways, as many of us are familiar with and/or participate in groups correctly demanding recognition who also are deeply committed to a politics of economic justice. However, there is enough truth to what she is pointing to for us to take her worries seriously.

I believe that we are increasingly faced with a false antithesis between what might be called the "social left" and the "cultural left." One of its most recent iterations can be seen in the *Social Text* hoax, in which a social left writer parodied the language and concepts employed by many "post" authors in their analyses of the relationship between science and power. He got it published as a serious contribution to the debates in the journal and only after its publication did he admit that it was a hoax.

The fact that it made national and international news says something of great import about the eagerness of the dominant media to look for any excuse to pillory the left. But no matter what the merits of the case (as a former board member of one of *Social Text*'s editorial collectives, I have mixed emotions here), the entire incident points to a divide that I believe is not very useful. "While one side insists in retrograde accents that 'it's all the economy, stupid,' the other retorts in hypersophisticated tones 'it's the culture, stupid.'" [20] Both seem to evade what I and others take to be crucial tasks: interrogating the distinction between economy and culture; understanding how both work together in complex and sometimes contradictory ways to produce injustices; and, finally, figuring out how, "as a prerequisite for remedying injustices, claims for recognition can be integrated with claims for redistribution in a comprehensive political project."[21] The task before us is to combine the two, in essence to think "about" and "across" at the same time.

Because of this, I believe that we need to be very careful about how we theorize. There are gains and losses in new theories and in new approaches to understanding the complex power relations involved in education. Thus, just as earlier periods of educational discourse marginalized class and had little interest in political economy, we need now to be equally sensitive to the fact that—given this history—some of the major gains (and there are many) brought about by newer "post" theories may also function in ways in which their proponents may be unaware. They too may serve to distance critical understandings of the power and complexities of class relations, even though this may not at all be their intent.

In my mind, then, it is crucial that those who take "post" positions as full *replacements* of neo-Marxist perspectives remember that such post positions risk reproducing hegemonic relations, just as neo-Marxist theories did and do. Just as neo-Marxist theories were sometimes in danger of becoming the voice of white, male academics, postmodern and poststructural theories paradoxically can be captured by the new middle-class academic intent on engaging in status and mobility politics within the academy.[22] One set of balconies replaces another.

At the risk of overgeneralizing in the extreme, I am worried that although the arguments about the dangers of essentialism and reductionism advanced against neo-Marxist positions by some post theories are correct to a point, in some ways they can perform the function of mirroring—and perhaps even tacitly supporting—rightist claims. In nearly every part of the dominant cultural apparatus, we hear politicians, journalists, academic commentators, and business flacks blame unions and the labor movement for detracting from the competitiveness of "our" economy. Yet, where were they when workers were burned to death in a large North Carolina chicken processing plant because their employers locked the fire doors on them so that no employee "stole" a few pieces of chicken?[23] And where are they when hundreds of thousands—indeed, millions—of workers are laid off due to "restructuring" and the seemingly never-ending search for higher rates of return, and when lives and communities are destroyed in the name of the bottom line? And where are they when factories move outside the borders of the United States through capital flight, so that women and men (and thousands upon thousands of children) in other nations can suffer even more oppressive forms of exploitation as capitalism returns to "primitive models of accumulation"?[24] Any theory in critical educational and cultural analysis that doesn't allow for these phenomena to be included in truly constitutive ways needs to get a grip on reality.

Perhaps my point about the dangers of forgetting all that the neo-Marxist approaches taught us can be made clearer if you allow me to ask something of you. I'd like you to do a little thought experiment with me. Think of what would happen to those of you who do have "professional" paid work if I informed you that because of the stock-holders' need for higher returns on investment or the fiscal crisis of your city or state or school or college you no longer had a paying job or your pension funds had been lost or your health insurance (if you were actually lucky enough to have it) was now too expensive and had to be cut back. Think about what would happen in *this* economy to you and to those for whom you care. Think about what it might mean in terms of housing, medical bills, food, and all those things that some of us take for granted all too easily. Think about the psychological as well as the economic costs. And think about how one might person-ally and collectively mobilize to challenge such decisions in ways that might incorporate other employees across a range of differences who are suffering similar or even more destructive effects of these decisions.[25]

No matter what the shortcomings of state bureaucratic socialism or the orthodox Marxist or neo-Marxist traditions, it would be an act of utter foolishness to give capitalism a free ride, to not name it for what it is and for what it does. And no amount of theoretical elegance must allow us to distance ourselves from this. We must *never* excuse as somehow necessary or inevitable the suffering that its inequalities, exploitations, and alienations not only allow but constantly produce.[26] We make discourses about these sufferings and about the institutions, policies, and practices that create them, but it would be the height of arrogance to assume that these are other than grittily material. As I have said elsewhere, the linguistic turn may have reminded us to look at the world as a text, but some folks seem to have more power to write their words on our lives and bodies than others.[27]

Just as I want us to reject life on the balcony, so also the task is to reject the demand in critical educational and cultural theory that we make an either/or choice between a politics of recognition and a poli-tics of redistribution. Instead, the goal should be to locate the liberatory and emancipatory possibilities of both problematics—"neo" and "post," structural and poststructural—in what I elsewhere have called a *decentered unity.*[28] Once again, I agree with Fraser when she argues that critical approaches "must reject facile dismissals that throw the baby out with the bath." Rather, it is crucial to develop critical and reflexive theories of both recognition and redistribution that would distinguish between those claims for recognition of difference that advance the causes of social and economic equality from those that undermine and retard its growth (*and* vice versa, of course).[29]

What does all this mean in terms of doing critical educational stud-ies? In my mind, it means first that we need to *constantly* hold dominant perspectives and practices—in curriculum, in teaching, in evaluation, in policy (including both accepted and emerging critical positions)—up to the spotlight of honest, intense, and searching social and cultural criticism. This is nothing new, of course. But it also means that we must balance theoretical elegance with a commitment to do a number of other things. We need to have respect for the actual daily lives and insights of people in the institutions of schooling and in communities and in social movements who are often struggling mightily in tremendously difficult conditions. At the same time, we ourselves need to struggle to be as clear as possible.

Of course, there will be times when the complexities of issues and the need to develop entirely new vocabularies and ways of seeing will make this difficult. Yet some of the discourse of critical social and cultural analysis of education has been a bit too arrogant. It has tended at times to fall into a style of trendy arcane overtheorization, too often substituting rhetorical forms taken from newly emerging high-status academic areas for what bell hooks has called "plain talk."[30] When this trendiness is criticized as part of a class strategy for gaining mobility within the social field of the academy and as being unnecessarily obtuse, the response has sometimes been all too dismissive.

I am not alone in worrying that, for all of its insight, important power relations are revivified in practice by the growing arcane quality of such linguistic flourishes. Others too have claimed that, in essence, overly inaccessible language may not actually enable new perspectives to evolve, but instead may serve other functions about which we may wish to be cautious. It may latently serve "to distance researchers from those who might critique this scholarship on the grounds of reflective, direct experience."[31]

I do *not* want to be misunderstood here. As I noted above, I fully recognize the utter centrality of pushing our critical ideas as far as they can take us and that this may indeed require new, unfamiliar, and difficult concepts and elaborations. This is to be welcomed. As Ian Ramsey reminds us, new "disclosure models" are absolutely essential for reconstituting our very "being in the world."[32] What I am asking for, however, is an honest struggle to work against the dangers associated with this, to not in the process reconstitute the relations of power and authority we are supposedly fighting against, to understand that we too are not outside of the social fields of power in which dominance and subordination are reproduced. Writing in full recognition of the multiple arenas of power in which we operate is hard work. And we need to work even harder at it.[33]

Because of this, I also believe that to the extent that those of us who engage in critical social and cultural studies in education listen carefully and respectfully to the criticisms of our own discourses and practices, to that extent we can justify engaging in similar work ourselves. Thus, internal debates and a welcoming of criticism (and a loss of hubris) are crucial to any sort of progress we might be able to make.

To quote from my childhood in Paterson, New Jersey, "That ain't easy." And I certainly am no genius in pulling this all together myself. The essays that follow represent some of my attempts to balance all this: to be critical, but to ground the criticisms in a recognition of the complexities of schools and the actors within them; to think theoretically, but to struggle to be as clear as I can; to think critically about even the best of radical work in the field, but still be supportive of what others within the communities of critical educational studies are doing and what they are showing us that was hidden before. I don't think that I am fully successful in accomplishing this. Indeed, it may not be possible for any individual to do so. But, then, like so much else in this society, this too is a *collective* process and we (and certainly I) have so much to learn from each other, from colleagues in the academy whose social position gives them the space to reflect on the ways power works in education to educators and community activists whose social location demands that they critically reflect and act on the daily realities they face. The resources with which to do this are multiple, from the experiences of struggling daily to alter the relations of power in the institutions in which we work to the multiple traditions already in existence or now being formed that we can draw upon to critically reflect on these experiences. From this process of *mutual* critical education, there is real hope. As Raymond Williams, one of the very wisest writers on the connections between politics, economy, and cultural struggles so cogently reminded us,

> It is only in the shared belief and insistence that there are practical alternatives that the balance of forces and chances begins to alter. Once the inevitabilities are challenged, we begin gathering our resources for a journey of hope. If there are no easy answers there are still available and discoverable hard answers, and it is these that we can make and share.[34]

Organization

This book is divided into three sections. Each section is roughly organized in chronological order. The essays that establish a particular problematic come first, followed by chapters that deepen it or develop its initial concerns along new paths, although at times, as in the first section, the organization doesn't totally follow a strict chronological order. There the more general issues are followed by essays that center on similar issues, even though they may have been written earlier. The essays often parallel the arguments I have made in books I have written over the past two decades: *Ideology and Curriculum*, *Education and Power*, *Teachers and Texts*, *Official Knowledge*, and *Cultural Politics and Education*. Yet, sometimes the arguments go off in new directions historically or conceptually, or clarify and apply them to important past or current educational reforms.

The first section, "The State of the Field," is concerned with how we understand curriculum and evaluation. As some of you may know, I have constantly moved back and forth in my work between a more proximate concern with the field of curriculum studies and the study of the constitution and politics of teaching on the one hand and the larger issues of educational theory, policy, and practice on the other. This section deals with both of these levels. It challenges the process/product models that have historically dominated the field of curriculum and education in general. It demonstrates as well how the reliance on supposedly neutral technical models contributes to a misrecognition of how power actually functions in education. As you will also see, it raises objections to the notion that there has been any sort of "reconceptualization" of the field or any easily applicable categorization of people called "reconceptualists." All of what we now do and ask has a very long history and it is important to connect with it.

In the second section, "The Curriculum as Compromised Knowledge," the analysis gets more detailed. The focus turns toward how specific things such as the history of major curriculum reforms, the current attempts to "reform" teaching and to build national standards, and the social context of the justifications of current neoliberal and neoconservative approaches to educational policy and practice all embody a complex web of conflicts and compromises. These conflicts and compromises often pull curriculum decisions onto a terrain that favors dominant groups, but sometimes they also offer the possibility of continued progressive gains.

The third section, "Doing Critical Educational Theory," steps back and illuminates the ongoing debates about *how* we might better understand these conflicts and compromises and the ways in which power works in education. It traces my continuing attempt to lessen the effects of trendiness in critical educational studies in order to prevent the loss of many of the gains that I believe were made by neo-Marxist theories at the same time as we recognize the important insights of postmodern and poststructural advances, and ultimately to bring elements of "neo" and "post" theories together so that what each is best at illuminating can be mobilized.

The majority of chapters in the first and second sections were written not for those people who are already convinced of the correctness of critical positions. Rather, they were written with a more "mainstream" audience in mind. As the chapters move from the earlier ones to the later ones, they become somewhat more theoretically and politically nuanced; but never, I hope, so overly theoretical that the form of argument interferes with understanding. When they are read in this general sequence, the essays provide a picture both of some of the continuities and the developing complexities surrounding the political/educational concerns that have organized and disorganized critical curriculum studies and critical educational studies in general.

These essays have been lightly edited, but I have tried to keep their original flavor. In addition, I have not usually updated my original references, since it may be important for the reader to see what I was drawing upon when I first made particular arguments.

Let me say something more specific about each of the chapters collected in this book. Each has its own history and its own set of claims.

Chapter 2, "The Politics of Official Knowledge in the United States," was the result of an invitation to provide an assessment of the curriculum field and to answer the question of why its members supposedly are no longer listened to. It sets the stage for the chapters in the section that follows.

Chapter 3, "There Is a River," was presented at a memorial symposium to honor the contributions of the late James B. Macdonald, one of the most influential humanists in the curriculum field. It situates some of my own efforts in the context of the decades of criticisms of the overly technical orientation of the field made earlier by Dwayne Huebner (my own major professor when I attended graduate school in the late 1960s), his close friend James Macdonald, and their teacher at Wisconsin, Virgil Herrick.

Chapter 4, "Social Evaluation of Curriculum," was co-authored with Landon Beyer. It takes one of the primary foci of current curriculum work (evaluation), deconstructs it, and then reconstructs its emphases so that social justice becomes its guiding concern.

Chapter 5, "Power and Culture in the *Report of the Committee of Ten*," is an analysis of a critically important part of curriculum history, the *Report of the Committee of Ten*, which set the stage for a significant amount of curriculum deliberation for much of this century.

Chapter 6, "Do the *Standards* Go Far Enough?," was written as a result of a request from a number of my colleagues in mathematics education to provide a critical reading of the major documents that are the framework for widespread reform in mathematics teaching and curriculum. Although generally supportive of their efforts, I am less than sanguine about the processes and results that are likely to come out of them.

Chapter 7, "How the Conservative Restoration Is Justified," constitutes my reflections on some of the reasons why a tradition that, unfortunately, has such a long history in education and social policy—genetic determinism—is seen as acceptable today. It tries to answer why and how it is considered a legitimate explanation and how it is connected to issues of white identity, even though its basis has been undercut many times before. The chapter restates, and extends, arguments I made in *Cultural Politics and Education* and elsewhere.

Chapter 8, "Education, Culture, and Class Power," is organized around a critical, but still very appreciative, reading of one of the most generative social theorists in education in recent years, Basil Bernstein. I use my discussion of his work to urge us not to become so postmodern that we ignore the structural realities in which we exist. Yet, as the chapter also clearly indicates, I have always been against reductive forms of structuralism, ones that ignore complexity, agency, multiple identities, and the real lives of real people.

Although the previous chapter provides an appreciative essay about one major figure who has pushed the field forward for many years, Chapter 9, "Power, Meaning, and Identity," synthesizes much of the recent work in critical sociology of education and curriculum studies. It extends the discussion of the limits and possibilities of critical approaches begun earlier.

Even though Chapter 9 reviews the status of largely academic work in the critical sociology of education, I have argued that such theoretical and academic by itself is weak and insufficient. It needs to be constantly connected to concrete political/cultural/educational struggles. Chapter 10, "Freire, Neoliberalism, and Education," examines another powerful influence on me and so many other critical educators, someone whose entire life embodied these connections. Its genesis was an invitation to present a lecture to honor Paulo Freire on the occasion of his being awarded an honorary doctorate at the University of Lisbon. Although, tragically, he died just before the lecture was to be given in his presence, the essay shows how important it is to situate ourselves in the long tradition of critical work in education at a time when an education worthy of its name is under grave threat. It points to the utter import of living the connections between our political and educational lives in more than rhetorical ways.

Chapter 11, "Between Neo and Post," returns us to how I began this introductory chapter—to the personal and the political. It positions my own work over the past decade in the debates described in the previous chapters. By restating and then significantly expanding some of the arguments I have made in the prior chapters and in my most recent books, it gives a fuller picture of why I have taken the position that neither structural nor poststructural or postmodern arguments *alone* are sufficient. It connects the theoretical/political arguments I have advanced in a number of recent books with my more programmatic efforts to develop and make more widely available critical teaching and curricula on the ground.

Most of these essays included in this book are part of my attempt to build a language of critique. But, they are also best understood as paralleling the considerably more practical work in which I have been engaged at the same time as these essays were written. Some of this work is discussed in the descriptions of my activity with children as a filmmaker in *Official Knowledge*.[35] Or it is represented in the material about the struggles to build more democratic, responsive, and socially critical classrooms and schools collected in *Democratic Schools*.[36] Thus, although these essays don't speak to all of my past and present concerns—either about politics and theory or about the daily events surrounding life in classrooms—they do provide a measure of the critical concerns that accompanied the rejection of life on the balcony.

Notes

1   John Fiske, *Television Culture* (New York: Methuen, 1987), 17.

2   Stanley Aronowitz and Henry Giroux, *Education Still Under Siege* (Westport, CT: Bergin and Garvey, 1993).

3   Michael W. Apple, *Official Knowledge* (New York: Routledge, 1993).

4   This is a broad category that includes a number of different positions. See, for example, the similarities and differences in the ways relational analysis is used in Michael W. Apple, *Ideology and Curriculum*, 2d ed. (New York: Routledge, 1990) and Pierre Bourdieu, *The State Nobility* (Stanford: Stanford University Press, 1996).

5   I have discussed this in much greater detail in Michael W. Apple, *Ideology and Curriculum*, 2d ed. (New York: Routledge, 1990) and Michael W. Apple, *Official Knowledge* (New York: Routledge, 1993).

6   See for example, Basil Bernstein, *Class, Codes, and Control*, vol. 3 (London: Routledge, 1977); Pierre Bourdieu, *Distinction* (Cambridge: Harvard University Press, 1984); and Michael W. Apple, *Education and Power*, 2d ed. (New York: Routledge, 1995).

7   See Bourdieu, *Distinction* and Bourdieu, *The State Nobility* for further discussion of these relations and of how conversion strategies operate.

8   Jonathan Kozol, *Savage Inequalities* (New York: Crown, 1991).

9   Michael W. Apple, *Teachers and Texts* (New York: Routledge, 1988).

10   See, for example, Sue Middleton, *Disciplining Sexuality* (New York: Teachers College Press, 1998) and Debbie Epstein and Richard Johnson, *Schooling Sexualities* (Bristol, PA: Open University Press, 1998).

11   See R.W. Connell, *Schools and Social Justice* (Philadelphia: Temple University Press, 1993).

12   See, for example, the discussion of the place of struggles over schooling in the processes of class formation in the United States in David Hogan, "Education and Class Formation," in *Cultural and Economic Reproduction in Education*, ed. Michael W. Apple (New York: Routledge, 1982), 32–78. This is still one of the better analyses of the active role schools have played in the formation of oppositional social movements.

13   Roger Dale, *The State and Education Policy* (Philadelphia: Open University Press, 1989).

14   Michael W. Apple, *Cultural Politics and Education* (New York: Teachers College Press, 1996); Geoff Whitty, Sally Power, and David Halpin, *Devolu-*

tion and Choice in Education (Bristol, PA: Open University Press, 1998); and Ernest House, *Schools for Sale* (New York: Teachers College Press, 1998).

15   Edward Said, "Orientalism and After," in *A Critical Sense*, ed. Peter Osborne (New York: Routledge, 1996), 73.

16   See the discussion of carnival in Peter Stallybrass and Allon White, *The Poetics and Politics of Transgression*. Ithaca: Cornell University Press, 1986.

17   Theodor Adorno, quoted in "Philosophy and the Role of Intellectuals," in *A Critical Sense*, ed. Peter Osborne (New York: Routledge, 1996), xiii.

18   Ibid.

19   Nancy Fraser, *Justice Interruptus* (New York: Routledge, 1997), 2.

20   Ibid., 3.

21   Ibid.

22   See Pierre Bourdieu, *Homo Academicus* (Stanford: Stanford University Press, 1988) for an insightful discussion of the ways in which struggles over what counts as "critical" academic work can be part of conversion strategies at work in competing markets over cultural capital.

23   George Lipsitz, *Rainbow at Midnight* (Urbana: University of Illinois Press, 1994), 2.

24   See William Greider, *One World, Ready or Not* (New York: Simon and Schuster, 1997).

25   Some of the possible effects and costs can be seen in Bill Bamberger and Cathy Davidson, *Closing: The Life and Death of an American Factory* (New York: Norton, 1998).

26   Ibid., 10.

27   Michael W. Apple, *Official Knowledge* (New York: Routledge, 1993).

28   Michael W. Apple, *Cultural Politics and Education* (New York: Teachers College Press, 1996).

29   Fraser, *Justice Interruptus*, 5.

30   bell hooks, *Talking Back* (Boston: South End Press, 1989). See also Lois Weis, "Qualitative Research in Sociology of Education" in *Continuity and Contradiction*, ed. William Pink and George Noblit (Creskill, NJ: Hampton Press, 1995), 157–73.

31   Richard Westheimer and Kathryn Borman, "Introduction: Doing Emic Research in Education" in *Continuity and Contradiction*, ed. William Pink and George Noblit (Creskill, NJ: Hampton Press, 1995), 106.

32   Ian Ramsey, *Models and Mystery* (Oxford: Oxford University Press, 1963).

33   I have discussed this in more detail in Michael W. Apple, "The Shock of the Real: Critical Pedagogies and Rightist Reconstructions" in *Revolutionary Pedagogies*, ed. Peter Trifonas (New York: Routledge, in press).

34   Raymond Williams, *The Year 2000* (New York: Pantheon, 1983), 268–69.

35   Apple, *Official Knowledge*. See especially Chapter 7, "'Hey Man, I'm Good': The Art and Politics of Creating New Knowledge in Schools."

36   Michael W. Apple and James A. Beane, eds. *Democratic Schools* (Washington, DC: Association for Supervision and Curriculum Development, 1995).

THE STATE OF THE FIELD

Chapter 2

The Politics of Official Knowledge in the United States

Introduction

No matter what some of our more well-known social control theorists would argue, state funded schooling was not a gift that was given easily by dominant groups in society to control the minds of the people. Instead, such schooling was a *result* of concrete struggles among different groups with different social and cultural visions, and of course different resources and power. The form schooling took, the curriculum that was instituted, the way teaching went on, how and by whom it was controlled, all of this was the contradictory outcome of compromises or accords in which government had to respond to those above and below in the social structure.[1]

This is not simply of historical interest. Currently, in a time of what has been called the conservative restoration, new struggles over teaching and curriculum, in essence over what education is *for*, are having a profound impact on the daily lives of educators and students. In this brief essay, I shall focus on what this means for people who self-consciously see themselves as members of the curriculum field, because what these conflicts mean to the tradition of asking curriculum questions in the United States is of no small interest in the politics of what counts as legitimate knowledge.

The Politics of the Conservative Restoration[2]

Spencer was not wrong when he reminded educators that one of the most fundamental questions we should ask about the schooling process is "What knowledge is of most worth?" This is a deceptively simple question, however, because the conflicts over what should be taught have been, and continue to be, sharp and deep. It is not only an educational issue, but one that is inherently ideological and political. Whether we recognize it or not, curriculum and more general educational issues have always been caught up in the history of class, race, gender, and religious relations in the United States.[3]

Because of this, a better way of phrasing the question, a way that highlights the profoundly political nature of educational debate, is "Whose knowledge is of most worth?"[4] That this is not simply an abstract academic question is made strikingly clear in the fact that right-wing attacks on the schools, calls for censorship, and controversies over the values that are being taught and not being taught have made the curriculum of many school districts throughout the country into what can best be described as a political football.

The public debate on education, and on all things social, has shifted profoundly to the right. The effects of this shift can be seen in a number of educational policies and proposals that are now gaining momentum throughout the country: 1) proposals for voucher plans and tax credits to make schools more like the thoroughly idealized free market economy; 2) the movement in state legislatures and state departments of education to "raise standards" and mandate teacher and student "competencies," thereby centralizing even more at a state level the control of teaching and curricula; 3) the often effective assault on the school curriculum for its supposedly antifamily and antifree enterprise bias, its "secular humanism," its lack of patriotism, and its failure to teach the content, values, and character dispositions that have made the "Western tradition" what it is; and 4) the consistent pressure to make the needs of business and industry the primary goals of the educational system.[5]

What has been partly accomplished has been a successful translation of an economic doctrine into the language of experience, moral imperative, and common sense. A free market ethic is being combined with a populist politics. This has meant the blending together of a rich mix of themes that have a long history in the United States—nation, family, duty, authority, standards, and traditionalism—with other thematic elements that have struck a resonant chord during a time of crisis. These latter themes include self-interest, competitive individualism, and antigovernment rhetoric.

The rightist and neoconservative movement has entered into education in part because the social democratic goal of expanding equality of opportunity has lost much of its political potency and its ability to mobilize people. The panic over falling standards and illiteracy, the fears of violence in schools, the concern with the destruction of family values and religiosity all have had an effect. These fears are used by culturally and economically dominant groups to move the arguments about education into their own arena, an arena of standardization, productivity, a romanticized past when all children sat still with their hands folded and learned a common curriculum, and so on. Because so many parents are justifiably concerned about the economic and social future of their children in an economy that is increasingly shaped by lower wages, the threat of unemployment, and cultural and economic insecurity, the neoconservative and rightist positions connect well with the fears of many people.[6]

One of the conservative movement's major successes has been to marginalize a number of voices in education and in the government at most levels. The voices of the economically disadvantaged, of many women, of people of color, and so many others are hard to hear over the din of the attacks on the school for its inefficiency, its lack of connection to an economy, and its failure to teach "real knowledge." Another group of people who have lost even more of their already limited voice is curriculum scholars. Individuals such as E.D. Hirsch Jr. (whose own book, *Cultural Literacy*, owes more of its popularity to the propensity of many educators and the middle-class public to play a more intellectual version of Trivial Pursuit than to the power of its arguments and cultural vision) now provide answers to the Spencerian question.[7]

What some people define as a crisis of loss of voice, others of course see as progress. This is especially evident in a quote from former Secretary of Education William Bennett. In his view, rather than a crisis that is deepening, we are emerging out of one in which "we neglected and denied much of the best in American education." In the process, "we simply stopped doing the right things [and] allowed an assault on intellectual and moral standards." This assault, which the conservatives see as being connected with attacks on the family, traditional values, religiosity, patriotism, and our economic well-being, has led schools to fall away from "the principles of our tradition."[8] It has been led by liberal intellectuals, not by "the people."

Yet, for Bennett, the people have now risen up. "The 1980s gave birth to a grass-roots movement for educational reform that has generated a renewed commitment to excellence, character, and fundamentals." Because of this, "we have reason for optimism."⁹ Why? Because:

> The national debate on education is now focused on truly important matters: mastering the basics—math, history, science, and English; insisting on high standards and expectations; ensuring discipline in the classroom; conveying a grasp of our moral and political principles; and nurturing the character of our young.¹⁰

Part of the solution for Bennett and others is to take authority *away* from many of those professional educators who supposedly have had it. This speaks to a profound mistrust of teachers, administrators, and curriculum scholars at universities. They are decidedly not part of the solution, but part of the problem. It speaks as well to the suspicion of all things public that shapes much of the conservative vision.

As all this has been happening, most people in curriculum have largely stood by, watching from the sidelines as if this was a fascinating game that had to do with politics, not with education. Others may have bemoaned their fate, but fled into increasingly technical procedural questions, thereby again confirming the artificial separation between "how-to" curriculum questions and those involving the real relations of culture and power in the world.

This is not a new phenomenon by any means. Curriculum workers have witnessed a slowly growing but very significant change in the way their work has been defined over the past decades. This change is only visible over the long haul, yet few things have had such an important impact. I am referring here to the transformation of professional curriculum discourse and debate from the issues surrounding *what* we should teach to those problems associated with *how* the curriculum should be organized, built, and, above all, evaluated. The difficult and— as any examination of the reality of schooling would show—contentious ethical and political questions of content, of whose and what knowledge is of most worth, have been pushed into the background in our attempt to define technically oriented methods that will "solve" all of our problems once and for all. For years, professional curriculum debate has been about procedures, not what counts as legitimate knowledge. As a number of social commentators continually remind us, when it comes to real conflict over cultural visions in education, technique consistently wins out over substance.

Although the process did not start in the late 1950s and early 1960s, it was certainly exacerbated during the years that saw a resurgence of discipline-centered curriculum. Government, industry, and scientifically and technically oriented academics formed an alliance that attempted to radically shift curriculum to "real knowledge," that knowledge housed in the discipline-based departments at major universities. Because most teachers and curriculum workers were perceived to not have the capabilities to deal with such "real knowledge," it became clear that this alliance, if it was to be effective, had to select the knowledge and organize it in particular ways. The National Defense Education Act, the massive curriculum development efforts that produced so much teacher-proof material, and the boxes upon boxes of standardized kits that still often line the walls of schools and classrooms stand witness to these attempts.

There are few better examples of the deskilling of a field than this. If curricula are *purchased*—and remember that 80 percent of the cost of most of this new curriculum material was repaid by the federal government—if all curricula come ready made, largely teacher proofed, and already linked to pretests and posttests, why would teachers need the skills of curriculum deliberation?[11] Of what use were those increasingly isolated curriculum scholars, unattached to "real" disciplines and housed primarily in schools of education, when what counts as legitimate knowledge was already largely predetermined by its disciplinary matrix?

The hidden gender relations here need to be mentioned. We need to remember a simple but very telling fact. Most teachers, especially at the elementary school level, are *women*. By, in essence, disempowering them, by centralizing curriculum deliberation, debate, and control in the hands of academics in the disciplines and through government intervention, we undercut the skills of curriculum design and teaching for which women teachers had struggled for years to gain respect.[12] I shall return to the issue of the relative power of teachers in a moment, since it bears directly on the question of who has really made decisions about curriculum in the past.

Yet it was not only teachers who lost power here. A good deal of the scholarly literature in curriculum at this time was filled with questions about the declining power of curriculum "experts" to determine what should be taught.[13] Power was seen to have shifted from those people who were closely attached to a long tradition of curriculum debate to those— like, say, Bruner and his coterie of disciplinary-based experts— who may have had interesting things to say about what should be taught in schools, but whose primary affiliations were to their disciplines rather than to schools and teachers. And although many curriculum scholars raised serious objections to what they believed was an unwise turn toward an overly subject-based and perhaps elitist curriculum, they were by and large ignored outside of the limited professional audiences for whom they wrote. The parallels between then and now are more than a little interesting. Once again, powerful groups and alliances in the larger society, in government, and in the academy had more to do with shaping curricular debate than those individuals whose special purchase on educational reality was supposed to be exactly about that.

This situation was heightened by the curriculum field's own propensities as well, by the increasing dominance of procedural models of curriculum deliberation and design. The model that became, in essence, the paradigm of the field—that articulated by Ralph Tyler in *Basic Principles of Curriculum and Instruction*[14]—even taking into account its avowed purpose of synthesizing nearly all that had gone on before, was by and large a behaviorally oriented procedural model. It provided almost no assistance whatsoever about the difficult issues of *whose* knowledge should be taught and *who* should decide, preferring to focus on the methodological steps one should go through in selecting, organizing, and especially evaluating the curriculum.[15] Although it may not have been intended, one of its ultimate effects was to evacuate political and cultural conflict from the very center of curriculum debate. So successful has that been that the curriculum field now confronts resurgent conservative movements that have thoroughly politicized the curriculum and the entire schooling experience only to be faced with the loss of any substantive ways of justifying *why* x should be taught rather than y.[16] Teachers are not the only ones who have been deskilled here.

Although it may be too harsh of an assessment, curriculum experts, then, increasingly became irrelevant in many ways. Curriculum specialists were often transformed into "experts for hire," people with more limited expertise in the procedures for writing documents based on what other people have decided is important to know, in quantitative or qualitative evaluation, in methods of goal setting and assessment and in techniques of writing behavioral objectives. What they are decidedly not experts in is the immensely difficult and contentious issue of what we should specifically teach. And because of the ahistorical nature of the field and the increasingly technical and specialized quality of graduate education, the knowledge of the traditions of dealing with those issues withers. Many people simply do not have the resources, ones so dependent on a knowledge of past conceptual, educational, and political curricular debate over what is worth knowing, to deal both with the dilemma of what a society's collective memory should be[17] and with the politics of cultural criticism that might enable them to answer these questions.

This has its democratic side, to be sure. By not centralizing curriculum determination in the hands of a few curriculum experts, we are trying to ensure that more power will reside at a local level. This is largely a meritorious goal. Yet, as we know, this is also often a fiction, because, whether we like it or not, we do basically have a national curriculum in the United States. Instead of it now being organized around national curriculum policies specified by academics and the government, however, it is determined by the market in *textbooks* and this market in turn is determined by what is seen as important in the primarily southern and western states of the Sun Belt that have state textbook adoption policies and where conservatives have considerable power to influence what is taught. Curriculum scholars have very limited influence at this level. Here, too, curriculum scholars argue in a vacuum, turning away from the actual processes that determine the most important elements of the curriculum—what I have called "the culture and commerce of the textbook"[18]—and in the process have little to say about the political, economic, and ideological conditions that make the curriculum look the way it does.

Instead of focusing on the social and political realities that stand behind the curriculum and on the way that the curriculum has once again become an arena where different groups fight out their distinct social agendas, we look nostalgically backward to a time when teachers, administrators, parents, business leaders, federal and state government officials, and others all sat up and paid attention to our words of wisdom. In many ways, this is just as mythic a past as that found in the conservatives' romanticization of the perfect school, family, and community where we all shared the same values, and pastoral settings reigned supreme.

I want to focus on this mythic past a bit more since I believe it is very much part of the problem we face. We need to be very cautious about assuming that there was some golden age in which members of the curriculum field had an immense amount of independent power over the content of the curriculum. As I have stressed here and commented at great length elsewhere, controversies over the content and form of the curriculum, over what and whose knowledge should be granted high status, are most often informed by larger conflicts between and within groups who are now in, or want to have, power.[19]

If we were to be true to the historical record, we would acknowledge that the school curriculum has always been the result of past conflicts and compromises that are themselves the product of wider social movements and pressures that extend well beyond the school. More often than not, curriculum people have been carried along by these movements. Rather than leaders, they have quite often been followers. Indeed, as the example of the discipline-based curriculum movement shows, it is difficult to find more than a very few instances in the last thirty years in which scholars *specifically within the curriculum field* had any appreciable impact on debates over the content of the curriculum.

If it was not the community of curriculum scholars who had so much power, what then are some of the major forces that have shaped the curriculum? As I have argued in considerable detail in *Teachers and Texts*, among the least talked about but most significant have been the gendered nature of teaching and the dominance of the standardized textbook. It is not simply an historical accident that the curriculum of, say, the elementary school has been tightly controlled, text- and test-based, and subject to continued rationalization. Women's paid work in a number of fields has historically been dealt with this way. Yet the fact that elementary teaching has been largely women's paid work also points to women teachers as activists as well. Indeed, the growth of the standardized textbook was not only due to rationalizing influences imposed from above, or to textbook publishers who recognized a lucrative market when they saw one, but was due as well to elementary school teachers collectively pressuring from below for help in changing the awful conditions in which many of them worked. Planning for multiage groups, for many subject areas in which they were not given either sufficient time or preparation to teach, in overly crowded classrooms—all this and more caused teachers to argue for texts to help them.[20] The result was a curriculum that was increasingly dominated by standardized and finally grade-level-specific texts, and in which textbook authors and publishers, compromising with local and state regulators, administrators, and teachers, had a significant amount of power to determine the form and content of the curriculum.

Thus, the *major* organizing element of the curriculum—the textbook—was never the result of curriculum scholars, but was the complicated result of social policies and dynamics surrounding gender, the politics of rationalization and bureaucratization in schools and teachers' responses to it, and the economics of profit and loss in the field of publishing. To look for the determining impact of a few specialized curriculum scholars in this is to live in a world divorced from reality.

Among the other external forces were the rise of what has been called a "technocratic" belief system in education and in the larger society, in which the assumption seemed to be that if it moved it should be measured. Of great importance as well was the steady growth of federal and state intervention in the shaping of curriculum policy,[21] a growth that was itself stimulated by Cold War ideologies and the pressures of international economic competition. This later set of pressures has had a very long history; but as the conservative restoration gains increasing power, this process of intervention has become even more visible in the aforementioned pressure both to make economic needs the primary goals of education and to return to an idealized and educationally problematic version of the corpus of "Western culture" as the core knowledge we should teach.[22]

Of course, much more could and needs to be said about the influence of state intervention, of crises in the economy on the national reports, about who has the power to speak and to be listened to on matters educational, and about where money goes in—or away from—education. A similar story needs to be told about how a conservative government has used the media in such a masterful way to control the public debate on education. On a more positive note, the intense pressure from below by social activists in the African American, women's, Latino/a, and other communities have led to major shifts in curricular content and authority and this story too needs to be recovered and brought center stage.

Many other areas could be focused upon. Yet, my point is really a simple one. Almost none of this can be traced to the efforts, no matter how well intentioned, of the curriculum field. The nostalgic gaze into the golden age of the past is largely a misreading of the historical record. It is actually a flight from recognition of where power may often lie and an even more dangerous flight from seeing the real depth of the problem.

Oddly, however, perhaps the feeling that curriculum scholars have lost their voice is the first step in the right direction. Perhaps some members of the curriculum field feel that they have lost their collective voice because they do recognize the objective conditions that surround not only their lives but the lives of so many talented and committed educators. That is, as we are witnessing all around us, curriculum determination at the level of the classroom, in teacher education, and elsewhere is being increasingly politicized, and is being more and more subject to legislative mandates, mandates from state departments of education, and so on. Test-driven curricula, overly rationalized and bureaucratized school experiences and planning models, atomized and reductive curricula—all of this *is* happening. This *has* often resulted in the deskilling of teachers and curriculum workers, a separation of conception from execution as planning is done away from the local level, and has as well led to a severe intensification of educators' work as more and more has to be done with less and less time available to do it.[23] Power over curricula is being centralized, taken out of the hands of the educators who must put it into practice. This is occurring at a much faster rate than are the experiments of local, school-based models.

Yet, why should all this surprise us? Tendencies toward the deskilling and depowering of jobs, toward the removal of reflection and thoughtfulness from one's work, and toward technically oriented and amoral centralized management are unfortunately part and parcel of the kind of society in which we live. So many millions of people in the United States have already experienced the loss of power and control in their own daily lives.[24] Why should we assume that this won't happen to people involved in curriculum and education in general? The real issue is not what is happening, but why it took us so long to realize that we, like most other educators, do not stand above the centralizing and disempowering logics and the political and economic forces that affect so many other individuals in this society. Perhaps the very way people in curriculum are themselves educated, in which education is too often treated as unconnected to economic, political, and ideological conflicts and in which we can supposedly solve our problems easily by looking only internally at the school, bears some of the responsibility for this dilemma.

Do not misunderstand my argument. My argument has not been that members of the curriculum field have been totally powerless, have only been puppets whose strings are pulled by large-scale social forces beyond their control. I am asking that we be realistic, however. If social, political, and economic forces and movements have played such a large role in determining the shape of the curriculum and have provided much of the impetus behind whose knowledge is taught, then individual action by curriculum scholars is not enough. We can and must join together with other groups who need the knowledge of curricular debates and traditions and who wish to make schools more progressive in intent and outcome.

There are collective voices we can join with, that we can contribute something of value to, and, perhaps just as importantly, that we can learn from. There are numerous groups throughout the country who are fighting in very uncertain conditions to build both an education worthy of its name and a curriculum that responds to the knowledge of all of us, not only to those who, because of their power, have sought to shape the curriculum in their own limited political and cultural image. These include the teachers in the Rethinking Schools group in Milwaukee and those involved in Substance in Chicago and Chalkdust in New York. It includes the community-based advocacy groups such as, among others, the Southern Coalition for Educational Equity, Chicago Schoolwatch, Parents United for Full Public School Funding in Washington, D.C., Citizens Education Center in Seattle, and People United for Better Schools in Newark who have been engaged in defending and building upon many of the gains made in the democratization of curriculum and teaching over the past two decades and in making them more responsive.[25] Only by forming coalitions with these groups in the hard and time-consuming political and educational work to restore a democratic vision and practice to education, can we also restore the voice of the curriculum tradition to the public debates over whose knowledge should be taught. If we continue to stand above the fray, perhaps we don't deserve to have our voice restored.

The right has done a good job of showing that decisions about the curriculum, about whose knowledge is to be made "official knowledge," are *inherently* involved in political and cultural conflicts and power. And unless we learn to live in that world and join with others to find the *collective* voice that speaks for the long progressive educational tradition that lives in so many of us, the knowledge our children will be taught will reflect that unequal power. Sidelines may be comfortable places to sit. But they have little to do with the lives of the real children and teachers who are losing today.

Notes

1   Michael W. Apple "Social Crisis and Curriculum Accords," *Educational Theory* 38 (Spring 1988): 191–201.

2   Much of what follows is based on a longer treatment of these issues in Michael W. Apple, "Is There a Curriculum Voice to Reclaim?," *Phi Delta Kappan* (in press).

3   See, for example, William Reese, *Power and the Promise of School Reform* (New York: Routledge and Kegan Paul, 1986).

4   For further discussion of this, see Michael W. Apple, *Ideology and Curriculum*, 2d ed. (New York: Routledge, 1990).

5   Michael W. Apple, *Teachers and Texts* (New York: Routledge and Kegan Paul, 1986).

6   This is treated in considerably more detail in Michael W. Apple, "Redefining Equality," *Teachers College Record* 90 (Winter 1988): 167–84.

7   For interesting criticisms of Hirsch's proposals for "cultural literacy," see Herbert M. Kliebard "Cultural Literacy or the Curate's Egg," *Journal of Curriculum Studies* 21, no. 1 (January/February 1989): 61–70 and Stanley Aronowitz and Henry Giroux, "Schooling, Culture, and Literacy in an age of Broken Dreams," *Harvard Educational Review* 58 (May 1988): 172–94.

8   William J. Bennett, *Our Children and Our Country* (New York: Simon and Schuster, 1988): 9–10.

9   Ibid., 10

10   Ibid.

11   See Michael W. Apple, *Education and Power* (New York: Routledge and Kegan Paul, 1985), especially chapter 5, for further discussion of the deskilling of teachers.

12   Apple, *Teachers and Texts*.

13   See, for example, some of the reflections on the previous decade of curriculum work in Elliot Eisner, ed. *Confronting Curriculum Reform* (Boston: Little, Brown and Co., 1971). See also A. Harry Passow, ed., *Curriculum Crossroads* (New York: Teachers College Press, 1962) and Glenys Unruh and Robert Leeper, eds. *Influence in Curriculum Change* (Washington, DC: Association for Supervision and Curriculum Development, 1968).

14   Ralph Tyler, *Basic Principles of Curriculum and Instruction* (Chicago: University of Chicago Press, 1949).

15 Herbert M. Kliebard, "The Tyler Rationale," *School Review* 78 (February 1970): 259–72.

16 Michael W. Apple, "Curriculum in the Year 2,000: Tensions and Possibilities," *Phi Delta Kappan* 64 (January 1983): 321–26.

17 For further elaboration of these traditions, see Herbert M. Kliebard, *The Struggle for the American Curriculum* (New York, Routledge and Kegan Paul, 1986) and Kenneth Teitelbaum "Contestation and Curriculum: The Efforts of American Socialists, 1900–1920," in *The Curriculum: Problems, Politics, and Possibilities*, ed. Landon E. Beyer and Michael W. Apple (Albany: State University of New York Press, 1988): 32–55.

18 Apple, *Teachers and Texts*. See also Michael W. Apple "Regulating the Text: The Socio/Historical Roots of State Control," *Educational Policy* 3, no. 2, (June 1989): 107–23.

19 See Apple, *Ideology and Curriculum*, Apple, *Teachers and Texts*, and Apple, *Education and Power*.

20 Apple, *Teachers and Texts*.

21 Aronowitz and Giroux, "Schooling, Future, and Literacy."

22 Kliebard, "Cultural Literacy," and Aronowitz and Giroux, "Schooling, Culture, and Literacy."

23 Apple, *Teachers and Texts*.

24 Marcus Raskin, *The Common Good* (New York: Routledge and Kegan Paul, 1986).

25 Ann Bastian, Norm Fruchter, Marilyn Gittell, Colin Greer, and Kenneth Hoskins, *Choosing Equality: The Case for Democratic Schooling* (Philadelphia: Temple University Press, 1986).

Chapter 3

There Is a River: James B. Macdonald and Curricular Tradition

It would not have been possible for us to engage in the kind of curriculum work we do if past members of the field had not struggled mightily to keep alive certain traditions. This may seem to be a relatively trite statement, but its implications are striking. It implies that there can never be the solitary curriculum theorist, pursuing meaningful questions in isolation. Extant curriculum theory is by necessity not only a conversation with oneself and one's peers, but in a very real way a continuing dialogue with one's predecessors. The past is always with us. It shapes our discourse. It gives us our questions—questions that may be answered or rejected, but questions that are there nonetheless.

These points signify something else. Not only are we constantly in conversation with past members of the field, but we stand on their shoulders. I do not mean to slight the work of the many people reading this when I say that we are all footnotes to our curricular mothers and fathers. Just as Western philosophy has been labeled a series of footnotes to Plato, so too are even the most creative political, phenomenological, empirical, or conceptual analyses done by us today merely extensions of the visions of others. We see things more clearly only because we have added our sight to theirs. Without them, we would be nearly blind.

This sense of how reliant we in curriculum are on those who came before is not a sign of personal weakness. It is, on the contrary, a recognition of our strength. The intergenerational movement of firmly held beliefs, of the critical nature of particular questions, of a positive vision of what education can become—the very fact that all these things *are* intergenerational—secures for us a sheltered place, even if only for a moment. We can withstand reactionary tendencies and those who would deny us our collective memories in large part because we know that others have taken a stand in the past.

Although these points are significant for the curriculum field in general, in many ways they carry even more weight for me. Given where I am, it is impossible for me not to recognize the crucial importance of past figures in the field. I write this sitting in a chair in which Virgil Herrick (a professor at the University of Chicago and then at the University of Wisconsin, where I currently teach) sat, at a desk on which Virgil Herrick wrote, illuminated by the lamp that has always been on that desk. Herrick was James Macdonald and Dwayne Huebner's major professor, their mentor,[1] when they did their doctoral work at the University of Wisconsin, a position I now hold but whose shoes I can never totally fill. Thus, Macdonald and Huebner stood on Herrick's shoulders. I stand on the shoulders of Jim and Dwayne.[2]

I want to stress these points about the intergenerational mobility of particular traditions, for they bear in important ways on the issue of what has been called the reconceptualist movement. There has actually been no reconceptualization of the field. Instead, we are the successors of an exceptionally long line of people, from Dewey, Bode, Counts, and Rugg to a larger number of lesser known people, each of whom contributed to keeping alive what Vincent Harding has called in another context that vast river of hope and struggle.[3] And it has been a struggle, as some of you know from personal experience. It was this struggle, kept alive by an enduring recognition of its power and its rootedness in our collective past, that was so evident to anyone who grew up in the field in the mid-1960s with Herrick's progeny.

Macdonald himself understood the issue clearly. He often saw each and every one of his points as having long and valued precedents in the various tributaries of that river. Speaking about the debates over discipline-centered curriculum, for example, he said:

> There is, indeed, nothing in recent curriculum development which alters in any fundamental way the historically available thought in the field of curriculum. Indeed there is much in the present process and direction of change that violates long lasting values and/or developmental procedures that have been hard won from experience over the years.[4]

There are a number of key words here: process, values, experience. These served as organizing concepts for much of Jim's work as I came to know him. It is not to slight him, but to honor the river in which he swam and helped keep on course, to note that these too are aspects of that intergenerational movement that works through all of us. If we briefly turn to Herrick, this will become clearer.

A major priority in Herrick's theoretical work was the struggle to "cut through the shell of specific instances and [reveal] the underlying assumptions" behind all of our curriculum deliberations.[5] What were the value choices and logic that lay behind our practical concerns? What is the relationship between content and process? How do we integrate "emotions and valuing operations" with "intelligence and ideas"? How do classroom interactions work? What are the basic concepts we need in order to think intelligently about curriculum? What are the components of any serious curriculum and how do they relate together in some meaningful way?[6]

As one reads Herrick, one is struck by his insistence on rigorous theoretical work, his sense of the importance of empirical research that is linked as well to a recognition of the restrictions of the "old classical concepts of the scientific method," a mind that was truly synthetic, and the emphasis he placed on both values and the teaching/learning situation when creating curriculum designs. On the same pages, the work of a new generation of descriptive curriculum researchers would be linked to analyses of new forms of child study and inservice education, which in turn would be connected both to evolving currents in social theory and to, say, the theories of Carl Rogers.[7] Although always his own person, it is hard to miss the elements of Herrick in Macdonald. Macdonald's continual search for better theoretical awareness (always grounded in a concern for values), the mind that found important insights in the entire range of people's knowledge, and his commitment to the concrete practices of teachers and students—these too were the marks of the mentor's student.

Of all these concerns, though, there were some that were more marked than others in my own personal experience with Jim. A constitutive concern of his was always personal meaning. At root, his project was always to infuse that issue back into curriculum discourse. At the height of the discipline-centered movement, when so many educators and curriculum developers were standing on the sidelines, so to speak, watching the parade of programs based on the structure of disciplines pass by on their way from the developers to the classroom, Macdonald asked whether that is all there is to knowing. Are the organized disciplines the only symbolic structures worth serious consideration? He wrote:

> Gaining knowledge, then, is not quite the simple matter of mastery of man's statements about reality, no matter how well organized these statements may be for pedagogical purposes and social uses. The very form of man's symbols are creations of the culture in which he lives and predispose him to limit and shape his awareness of the "to be known" in the forms of his symbolic structures. Yet the abstracting of experience through symbolic form does not encompass all of what is to be known with reference to the statements of reality, nor does it preclude the necessity of knowledge being possessed by a living person.[8]

Thus, something was being lost in the anonymization and technicization of curricular language and classroom reality—the self. Human engineering, attempts to rationalize and systematize all human interaction, all in the service of efficiency, were being wedded to a pedagogy and curriculum that excluded all but the recognized disciplines. Our technological society seemed to be leading inexorably to dehumanization and depersonalization. These were the issues confronting educators. Our language, though, had cut us off from past moments in curriculum that had taken these issues seriously. (Once again that river.) Just as important, the search for the objective structure of disciplines and a curriculum based on the results of that search could never, as if by magic, "reduce the threat of nuclear holocaust, bring justice and equality to all people or provide a basis for freedom from poverty for all."[9]

Nowhere is this sense of personal meaning and moral values joined quite as clearly as in his 1966 statement in "The Person in the Curriculum." For Macdonald, unlike the dominant tradition in curriculum, the *person* was not the psychological monad, the individual. Rather, she or he was "a subject (in contrast to an object)," a subject with her or his own unity.[10] Not to recognize this, and he often meant the following phrase literally, was to be immoral. Thus, the dominant value proposed for education "is a moral value and the concept of a person is a moral concept."[11] As he went on to say,

> Education, and more particularly schooling, is thus a moral enterprise because we create a contrived environment, called "curriculum and instruction," and we attempt to influence persons in this environment. We assume the responsibility for the influencing of persons in the directions of our curriculum specifications, and this is essentially a moral act.[12]

In a society that was increasingly losing this sense of the person, in a culture in which technique was constantly winning out over substance and the self was being submerged in anonymity, the major role that schools should play was clear. They must be reorganized around an ethic (and I choose that word deliberately) of humanization. They can and must "[buttress] the person from the massive dehumanization of the broader society" until she or he can "develop a reasonable sense of integrity and self worth, a coherent set of values and personal goals with which survival in our modern age as a human being is at least possible."[13]

Alongside these very evident humanistic and moral concerns, however, is the basis of something that was to become even more evident during my association with Jim throughout the decade of the seventies. This was a clearer sense of oppression. What was wrong with schools was not only dehumanization. It was their almost total use for economic purposes, "as training grounds for the production of [economic] role players" and for "national security."[14] As Jim worked through his own political position on this, so too did those of us who studied with Jim and Dwayne during the 1960s. Yet in many ways, it was the efforts of a small group of Herrick's students and their students who worked together on one project that helped all of us, in different ways, to clarify where we stood on the relationship between curriculum as a theory and practice and the social sources of oppression.

I refer here to one specific project, the joint writing of the 1975 Association for Supervision and Curriculum Development (ASCD) yearbook, *Schools in Search of Meaning*.[15] There were five of us on the committee that produced the volume—Jim Macdonald, Dwayne Huebner, Esther Zaret, Steve Mann, and myself, to be later followed by one of Dwayne's students, Bill Burton.

For more than two years we struggled with the questions and answers that the river provided. Some of its currents were helpful; some were less so. Yet it was not only a struggle in and with what curriculum's past had made available. It was a profoundly personal struggle as well, for it required that each of the participants examine some very closely held values. Jim's struggle was evident, for not only was he intellectually and politically challenged to come to terms with more structural accounts of how our economy and society influenced the schools, but it was in the very question of the central place of values itself that he loved to swim. At times, we all thought we might drown. Yet some inner resources—probably related to the strength of curriculum's past and those broad shoulders that had formed generations of insightful progressively inclined curriculum work even before Herrick—kept us at it.

The political controversy within the committee was intense. In many ways, it was a battle over which set of beliefs should provide the guiding problematic for our work. Should political considerations concerning an oppressive society serve as the theme, with humanistic arguments and values being put in the service of the larger political goals? Or should it be the opposite, should humanism be in the driver's seat with politics added on to help us raise the issue of why this society was not humane? In essence, it was a question of humanized Marxism or a partly Marxified humanism.

Of course, these positions are stereotypical. We all stood on both sides of this debate at one time or another. But there were clear tendencies and the debates continued unabated for nearly two years, sometimes showing convergence on a number of points and at other times signifying some quite important differences in emphasis. Yet, even given some major disagreements, at no time did any one of us lose respect for each other. At no time were arguments not considered at length and in depth. We argued and argued and argued. We sent long letters, and responses to each other's letters, and responses to responses, all in an attempt to create a document that we hoped would create the same sense of urgency in the reader as we felt about the current state of inequality in education and the larger society.

I bring this up for two reasons. First, and not unimportant, we were engaged in a profoundly curricular task. How could we create the conditions in our own joint environment to teach each other something of importance without losing individual autonomy? How could we write a document that provided the same thing for the reader? We were more successful at the former than the latter, for *Schools in Search of Meaning* stands as a very flawed document. Second, and here I want to bring us to the most significant part, we were all reshaped by this process. Much of this is due to Jim's immense patience and his own sensitivity to the inevitable tensions between broad social concerns and a commitment to the individual.

As cochair of the committee with Esther (whose own contributions, along with Dwayne's, must not be slighted in any way), Jim kept us sane. When it seemed that we would forget about schools and the pedagogic, curricular, and evaluative practices that went on inside them and instead focus only on the external systems of economic, political, and ideological power relations, he constantly brought us back. What does this mean for teachers, for students, for curriculum? When the more structural concerns of the Marxist and neoMarxist approaches that, say, Steve and I were apt to bring to bear on our deliberations left the group nearly paralyzed as educators, Jim again would raise the issue of the person. He could not accept that people had little or no autonomy. His constant intuitive prodding actually prefigured the theories of resistance to domination now so popular today. This intuitive prodding by Jim, and by Dwayne and Esther as well, forced us all to clarify what we were about. In a major way, I cannot now engage in my own work today without hearing those same questions.

In a time of rightist reaction, when greed and selfishness are again in vogue, when the public good is transformed into the private gain, and when schools are once again tools of, in the words of the National Commission on Excellence in Education, "rearmament," the act of listening to these questions and remembering these concerns helps us to shape our anger and our commitments in such a way that we will not lose the person in the process.

In the midst of the river, I stand on the shoulders of Jim and others, and I struggle to hear their words every day, to keep them from being muted by the clarion calls of the economically mean and the pedagogically senseless. In the words of Tevye in *Fiddler on the Roof,* "Tradition!" It is a tradition I am proud to call my own. Let us hope that we too are strong enough to let those who come after us continue it, with the compassion and openness that always characterized James B. Macdonald.

Yet, even given my respect for Macdonald (or perhaps because of it), we do not need hagiographic treatises on Jim, although thinking about his influence on us may lead to that. What we need, instead, is to *use* his work, to hone it, but not as an unreconstructed guide to present and future curriculum work. Rather, we need to see it as a major link to our own curricular past that has been in danger of being devalued. This is not the past of the conservative curriculum theories of Bobbitt, Charters, and Snedden, but a vital and living tradition that places ourselves as political and moral actors at the center of curriculum debate. *This* tradition worked through Macdonald and it works through us here. It is what we reconstruct as it constructs us. It helps provide us with a sense of meaning and purpose, of being part of a long line of real people who fought real battles to enable us all to take the positions we wish to avow today. The way to honor James B. Macdonald is to continue to take that tradition as seriously as it demands. Dehumanization, domination, and exploitation are still all around us and the battle against them is even more important today. The river continues.

Notes

I would like to thank Rima D. Apple for her perceptive suggestions on my remarks here.

1   James B. Macdonald, Dan Andersen, and Frank B. May, eds. *Strategies of Curriculum Development: The Work of Virgil E. Herrick* (Columbus, Ohio: Charles E. Merrill, 1965), vi.

2   Dwayne Huebner was my doctoral advisor at Teachers College, Columbia University, during my graduate studies there in the late 1960s. Although the most profound influences upon me during these years of graduate work were Dwayne Huebner's politicized phenomenology and Jonas Soltis's work in analytic philosophy, Jim Macdonald—Huebner's close friend—was always present in spirit and was often at Teachers College to visit Dwayne. I shall focus on him here.

3   Vincent Harding, *There Is a River* (New York: Vintage, 1981).

4   James B. Macdonald, "Language, Meaning and Motivation: An Introduction," in *Language and Meaning*, ed. James B. Macdonald and Robert R. Leeper (Washington, DC: Association for Supervision and Curriculum Development, 1966), 3.

5   Macdonald, Andersen, and May, *Strategies of Curriculum Development*, vi.

6   Virgil Herrick, "Problems of the Curriculum Theorist," in *Strategies of Curriculum Development*, ed. Macdonald, Andersen, and May, 1011.

7   This is especially evident in Herrick, "Problems of the Curriculum Theorist."

8   Macdonald, "Language, Meaning and Motivation," 5.

9   Ibid., 56.

10 James B. Macdonald, "The Person in the Curriculum," in *Precedents and Promise in the Curriculum Field*, ed. Helen F. Robison (New York: Teachers College Press, 1966), 40.

11 Ibid., 39.

12 Ibid.

13 Ibid., 52–53.

14 Ibid., 51.

15 James B. Macdonald and Esther Zaret, eds. *Schools in Search of Meaning* (Washington, DC: Association for Supervision and Curriculum Development, 1975).

Chapter 4

Social Evaluation of Curriculum

(with Landon Beyer)

In this essay, we want to demonstrate some of the inherent limitations of the usual ways educational evaluation is carried on.[1] In particular, we wish both to challenge the dominance of curriculum evaluation based on achievement test results and to suggest a set of questions and strategies that will be more responsive to the actual socioeconomic reality of schools. In so doing, we will propose ways to engage in the social evaluation of curriculum that go beyond the more individualistically and psychologically oriented models in use today. We will argue that because evaluation is a process of *placing value* on a procedure, process, goal, or outcome,[2] alternatives to the current ways we do place value on curricula can only be developed by seeing how values now work through our activity and by expanding the ways we look at these procedures, processes, goals, or outcomes to include the ideological and economic "functions" of our educational system.[3]

Our discussion construes evaluation somewhat differently than it has often been construed in the past. Evaluation is seen by many educators as demonstrating whether a specific program, text, etc.—given the "limitations" of student background and ability—is successful and then giving feedback to participants, administrators, or funding agencies about its degree of success. A comparison between the stated goals of curricular programs and how far the students have gone is not inherently wrong. After all, there may be times when goal directedness and efficiency are important. However, most of the procedures developed to deal with these concerns, although often technically sophisticated, remain relatively unreflective about the interests, values, and ideologies in the curriculum or even embodied in the concerns themselves. Given this, we take one fundamental task of evaluation in education to be that of unpacking what schools and curricula actually do socially.

Technical Concerns and Social Interests

Most evaluations of school curricula rely on measures of the achievement scores of pupils to determine the success of a specific curricular offering. They rest on particular assumptions regarding efficiency, cost effectiveness, ability and mean gain in student achievement. Curricula "work" if they "produce" higher test scores, for less money, in a measurable and relatively uncomplicated way. We break down the knowledge we want to teach into atomistic units of behavior (ignoring in the process the potent practical, conceptual, and political limitations of such a reductive approach), give pretests, determine "ability," teach, then test, and start the whole cycle over again. The focus is on technical questions (Did we get from point A to point B?), rather than on whether point B, or the process of getting there, is ethically or politically defensible.

This emphasis on what has been called process/product thinking has had a rather long history. For the better part of this century educators have searched long and hard for a general set of technical procedures that would guide curriculum planning and evaluation. In large part, this has reduced itself to attempts to create *the most efficient method* of doing curriculum work. This stress on method has not been without its negative consequences. At the same time that process/product rationality grew, the understanding that curriculum planning and evaluation was through and through a political enterprise withered. The questions we asked tended to divorce ourselves and our work from the ways that the unequal economic and cultural apparatus of our society operated. A "neutral" method meant that both we and the knowledge we selected and tested were neutral, or so it seemed.[4] The fact that the methods we used had their roots in industry's attempts to control labor and increase productivity and profit, in the popular eugenics movement, and in maintaining particular class and status group interests became increasingly invisible. At the same time, educators seemed to assume that the development of these supposedly neutral methods would somehow eliminate the need to deal with the difficult issues of whose knowledge should be or already was preserved and transmitted in schools, and what the social impact of this knowledge and our evaluations of it would be. Although a number of alternative traditions continued to try to keep this kind of political question alive, by and large the faith in the inherent neutrality of our institutions, in the knowledge that was taught, and in our planning and evaluation efforts was ideally suited to help legitimate the structural bases of inequality.

The key to this last sentence is the concept of legitimation. Like the late philosopher Ludwig Wittgenstein, we are claiming that the meaning of a good deal of our evaluative methods and theories is in their use. And the use in this case has often been twofold. The traditions that have come to dominate education help to reproduce inequality at the same time that they serve to legitimate both the institutions that recreate inequality and our actions within those institutions. This is not to claim that *individual* children are not often helped by our methods and practices; nor is it to argue that all of our day-to-day actions are misguided. Rather, we want to point to the fact that macroeconomically and macroculturally our efforts may function in ways that bear little resemblance to even our best intentions.

Part of the problem rests on the issue of neutrality. As we shall see, our theories and methods of research and evaluation do not protect us as much as we might like from serving hidden social interests.

All too many evaluators and researchers tend to neglect the fact that their work already serves social interests. These interests and values tend to be constituted by the very questions they often ask. Let us give one example. In the midst of the data–gathering phase of a program to "rehabilitate" juvenile offenders, one of the questions asked was "Why do these people steal?" A logical extension of this is the development of a program to reeducate these people. This sounds quite straightforward and neutral, does it not? However, it is here that one can begin to see values working through one's research and evaluation efforts. Given the evident maldistribution of income in the United States (recent government reports suggest that the gap between rich and poor is increasing at approximately 7 percent per year above the inflation rate), given the massive and almost ignored unemployment and underemployment rate among minority youth, and given the intense psychological manipulation by corporate advertising to consume more and more, one could just as easily ask "Why don't more people steal?" The question of "Who benefits?" looms large here.

Our point is not to claim neutrality for the second question; rather it is to illuminate the second–order nature of our research and evaluation questions. They have their biases in particular tacit conceptions of social justice, conceptions that tie us to social arrangements in important ways.

Redefining Our Unit of Analysis

The foregoing discussion of how the questions we ask are connected to ideological values and outcomes points to the importance of seeing the enterprise of schooling itself as connected to these same ideological values and outcomes. Unfortunately, as we noted earlier, the theoretical framework that most educators have employed has made it difficult to face these connections honestly. Questions of who benefits, questions about what might be called the latent social effects of the curricula and social organization of schools, are not overtly dealt with in our dominant evaluative enterprise.

Let us examine this in somewhat more detail. Theory does not merely determine what we observe. It determines what we cannot observe as well. As Wright has noted, our questions "are always embedded in conceptual structures and if these structures lack certain pivotal elements . . . certain questions cannot or will not be asked." In particular, questions of what constitutes a *proper unit of analysis* are often determined by our unconscious theoretical presuppositions.[5] And it is here that we need to make serious headway if we are to more fully understand curriculum. For just as our questions do not stand alone but are linked to external social relations, so too is the school itself (as an isolated entity) not a proper unit of analysis if we are interested in the social functions of curricula. If our unit of analysis is "only" the school, then the issues surrounding curriculum evaluation can stand alone and present less of a serious challenge to the process/product path evaluation has taken in the past. If, however, the school is interpreted as inextricably connected to powerful institutions and classes "outside" of itself, then our unit of analysis must include these connections. We are arguing, hence, that one commits a serious category error by thinking about the school as if it and its programs and problems existed independently. And such an error can have disastrous consequences for evaluation.

Thus, a first step in going beyond the usual disconnected framework, and toward a more relational analysis of curriculum and evaluation, is to accept one fundamental social fact, one that may be hard to deal with given where many of us are employed, but one that is accurate nonetheless. At one level, this can be stated easily. The way our institutions are organized and controlled is not equal. What this means is rather important. A number of lines of recent social research have devoted themselves to providing us with rather impressive documentation of the extent to which our society remains at heart unequally responsive by class, race, and gender. In brief the evidence suggests the following: that we do not live in a meritocratic order; that as the sociologist of medicine Vicente Navarro has documented, slogans of pluralism aside, in almost every social arena from health care to anti-inflation policy one can see a pattern in which the top 20 percent of the population consistently benefit more than the bottom 80 percent;[6] that although schools may often be avenues for individual mobility (though this is more accidental than we might suppose), there has been little consistent loosening of the ties between origins and attainments through schools over time;[7] and, finally, that schools are not now nor have they ever been immune to social pressures, economic, racial, and gender-specific ideologies, or to patterns of differential benefits.[8]

Now we may not all agree with the social implications of this evidence; however, the accumulated evidence over the past few years has clarified how schools are not socially neutral, meritocratic institutions, tied into a pluralistic and meritocratic social order, an order which by policy and practice is organized to distribute educational and economic goods and services equally. For schools are not isolated entities, divorced from the maintenance of economic and cultural inequality. Exactly the opposite is sometimes the case. Yet this assertion, on its own, is so general as to be less than helpful unless we become more specific about how schools are situated in this wider array of institutions.

Recent research about the social, ideological, and economic role of our educational apparatus has pointed to three activities that schools engage in. We can label these functions as assisting in accumulation, legitimation, and production. First, schools assist in the re-creation of an unequally responsive economy by helping to create the conditions necessary for capital accumulation. They do this in part through their internal sorting and selecting of students by "talent," thus roughly reproducing a hierarchically organized labor force. As students are hierarchically ordered—an ordering often based on the cultural forms of dominant groups[9]—different groups of students are often taught different norms, skills, values, and dispositions by race, class, and sex. These tend to embody those values that are "required" by their projected rung on the labor market ladder. In this way, schools help meet the needs of an economy for a stratified and at least partially socialized body of employees. Clearly, this does not mean that what goes on in schools is mechanistically determined by economic forces.[10] Just as clearly, as anyone who has worked in an inner-city school realizes, many students do not accept the values that the school teaches in this hidden curriculum.[11] It is still essential, though, to realize that there are some very important ties between an economy and the social outcomes of schools.

Second, schools are important agencies of legitimation. That is, they distribute social ideologies and help create the conditions for their acceptance. Thus, schools tend to describe their internal workings as meritocratic (inaccurately, so it seems)[12] and as contributing to wide-spread social justice. In this way, they foster a social belief that the major institutions of our society are equally responsive by race, sex, and class. Unfortunately, as we have noted, the available data suggest that this is less the case than we might like to think.

Finally, the educational apparatus as a whole constitutes an important set of agencies for production. Our economy requires high levels of technical and administrative knowledge for the expansion of markets, the artificial creation of new consumer needs, the control and division of labor, and for technical innovation to increase or hold one's share of a market or increase profit margins. Schools and universities help in the production of such knowledge. This, in part, explains why most school systems and the curricula within them are organized toward the university and why there is so much emphasis on establishing programs for gifted students now. Students who can ultimately contribute to the production of this knowledge are sponsored by the school. Those who cannot are labeled as somehow deviant or are formally or informally tracked in schools.[13]

These three functions—accumulation, legitimation, and production—need to be understood if we are to grapple with what schools do and, especially, with what they are capable of doing. Such understandings are essential if we are to deal with problems in evaluation in a more complete, sophisticated way. One of the important facts about these functions is that they may be contradictory. That is, they may work against each other at times. For instance, education is caught between selecting and sorting an "adequately socialized" work force and at the same time acting as if it were part of an open system. The school's need to legitimate ideologies of social justice (and to make its own operation legitimate to its clientele) may, hence, be objectively at odds with the equally (and given current economic conditions, now more) compelling pressure on it to serve the changing needs of industry. Only by placing our research and evaluation efforts within a more thorough analysis of these social functions, these connections, can we make progress in our understanding of what is happening in schools.

Making our unit of analysis the connections between school curricula and the larger society implies reorienting our methods of inquiry. First, this change in our unit of analysis would involve carefully scrutinizing a program one is evaluating in light of this wider social role, in light of the three socioeconomic functions we just examined. This would mean that our initial task would require that we ask what have come to be called "prior questions." Thus for any evaluative activity in curriculum, the prior question should be, evaluation for what social, economic, and ideological purpose?

Let us give an example of the importance of asking the prior question of "evaluation for what social purpose." Let us assume that we are engaged in the evaluation of a program to keep minority and poor teenagers in high school. We wish to ask whether and on what grounds it is "successful." But, successful according to what? As Jencks, et al., have shown, the economic returns for blacks who complete elementary and secondary schools are still only half what they are for white students.[14] Further, completing secondary school gives relatively few advantages to students from economically disadvantaged backgrounds. As these researchers put it:

> Apparently, high school graduation pays off primarily for men from advantaged backgrounds. Men from disadvantaged backgrounds must attend college to reap large occupational benefits from their education.[15]

In clearer words, getting those minority and poor students to stay in school has few economic rewards associated with it, no matter what our commonsense assumptions would lead us to expect.

This example documents a rather interesting point. In order to take seriously a claim for the retention, elimination, or modification of a curricular program, in order for our evaluation to make sense socially, our unit of analysis must be extended beyond the achievement scores of the pupils. It must include the social connections between the school's role in accumulation that produces students of this type (with their probable economic trajectories) and the tacit legitimation of an ideology of opportunity (if only you would finish high school everything would be all right), when the opportunity structure of the economy may preclude that reward as an actual statistical probability.[16]

Making the unit of analysis the isolated school system, classroom, program, or the achievement scores of students would preclude this kind of investigation. Yet look at what the extended socioeconomic appraisal that we have argued for does. It immediately raises the competing ideological and political claims made upon the school. It forces us to confront the latent ideological and economic outcomes of the institution and asks us to make certain that our programs, curricula, policies, research, and evaluations are not covering things that we may not want to go on. This appraisal would obviously involve a good deal of debate at the level of policymaking and between the school and its varied clientele. Yet the dominant ways we evaluate school programs tend to preclude serious consideration of competing ethical, political, or economic claims in large part because of their technical orientation and their focus on the achievement or IQ scores of the students.[17]

In the example of the evaluation of the drop-out program above, we can see how this occurs. A political and economic issue is transformed into a less powerful one. Here we are left to argue about the relative merits of a specific curricular program—Are the test scores of the students raised? Do they stay in school longer? and so on—as if these issues were separate from the real distribution of power and benefits in our society. In this case, evaluators have taken the problems as defined by both the administrative managers of the institutions and elite groups in society as the major issues. Yet taking, rather than making, our problems can lead to the acceptance of elite values and policies in such a way that, as Murray Edelman reminds us, the material aspects, the benefits, of these programs and policies "are likely to favor dominant groups" while the symbolic aspects of such programs and policies may tend to "falsely reassure mass publics that their interests are being protected" against dominant groups.[18] Closer scrutiny of the evidence of the social effects of such curricular programs might indicate that the problem is *not* dropouts. The problem is not how to get students to stay in school longer. This is how the problem is defined for us. A more searching appraisal, a more intensive examination of how value is placed on it, would place the issue squarely where it belongs, in the unequal economic apparatus of the larger social order. Any curricular evaluation that ignores this misses the reality of the connections between our curricular programs and that larger society. The evaluation of the program that we have proposed—examining it in light of the connections the curriculum has to external socioeconomic structures—makes it much more difficult to miss this reality.

Toward Social Evaluation Inside the School

So far we have looked at curricular programs from the outside, as it were. Although this has been of no small moment, we have not gone inside the school itself to examine the actual content and social relations embodied *within* the curriculum and their relation to the structures of inequality. Yet no social evaluation of curricula can be complete unless it also gets inside the "black box" of the school and investigates what is actually taught and what the concrete experiences of students are within the programs. In the space available here, we can only point to the kinds of issues that need to be raised, though a much more detailed analysis can be found elsewhere.[19] We urge the interested reader to pursue it further there.

Three basic areas of curricula need to be scrutinized to see the connections between curricula and ideological and economic structures. These include: 1) the day-to-day interactions and regularities of school life—what has come to be called the hidden curriculum—that teach important norms and values related to, say, the world of work (paid and unpaid) and to class, race, and gender divisions in our society; 2) the formal corpus of school knowledge—that is, the overt curriculum itself—that is planned and found in the various materials and texts and is filtered through teachers; and, finally, 3) the fundamental perspectives, procedures, and theories—such as social labeling practices that "blame the victim," a vulgar and reductive positivism, industrial models such as systems management, and so on—that educators use to plan, organize, and evaluate what happens in schools. Each of these elements should be examined to see to what extent the day-to-day meanings and practices that are so standard in classrooms—although they are often intended to help individual children—may tend to be less the instruments of help and, unfortunately, more part of a complex process of the reproduction of the unequal class, race, and gender relations in our society.[20] Because the third area, the one about the perspectives, procedures, and theories we usually employ, has already been partially discussed in our treatment of the evaluation of both the drop-out and juvenile rehabilitation programs, let us turn our attention to the overt and hidden curricula.

It has become increasingly clear that a selective tradition operates in school curricula. Out of an entire universe of knowledge in history, science, social studies, language, and so on, only some is selected for teaching in our schools. Because of this, curriculum evaluation needs not only to be guided by a concern for how we might get students to acquire more knowledge (the dominant question in our efficiency–minded field), but by another set of questions as well. *Prior* to measuring whether or not students are "able" to learn or have learned a particular set of facts, skills, or dispositions we should want to know *whose* knowledge it is, *who* selected it, and *why* it was organized and taught in this particular way, to this particular group.[21] This would require us to examine what the institution considers "legitimate" knowledge and teaching and testing strategies to be and to unpack their actual social outcomes. How do curriculum, teaching, and evaluation function in the accumulation, legitimation, and production roles played by the school? Is this what we as parents, community activists, and educators really want to go on? Notice again that these sorts of queries require us to recapture the ethical, political, and economic sensitivity that has been lost over the years in our analysis of curriculum, as well as to take much more seriously data similar to Jencks' and Navarro's findings about the unequal returns from most of our social and cultural institutions.

But what about the hidden, not the overt, curriculum? What questions should guide our investigations in this area? Here it is important to remember that not every group receives the same tacit social messages; nor are the effects of this tacit teaching the same. Thus, the following issues are significant: What ideological norms and values does everyone get? What is differentially taught by race, gender, and class simply by living in the school day after day for most of one's preadult life?

Some simple examples of why we might want to interrogate the formal and informal knowledge found within the institution may be helpful here. For instance, in most schools little labor history is taught.[22] Instead, we teach military history and the history of the presidents. Women, people of color, and other minority and oppositional cultures are still strikingly misportrayed as well. The form, not only the content, of curricula—that is, the way the knowledge is organized—tends more and more to be individualized and prepackaged into standardized sets of material with one standard correct answer. It often denies or cuts short opportunities for cooperation and serious group inquiry. We also find behavior modification techniques (that emphasize doing exactly what someone in authority says for a small reward) more widely in use in black, brown, and poor neighborhoods. In more economically advantaged areas, pedagogical and curriculum strategies are less likely to be dominated by such techniques and are more likely to allow for intellectual curiosity, multiple answers, more flexible behavioral norms, and student–initiated projects.

We may also find that the categories and procedures we use in our curriculum organization and evaluation are also strongly related to unequal socioeconomic relations. Thus, we establish "remedial curricula" for "slow" learners and then find that being slow and being remediated is often related to the history of racial oppression and to poverty. Further, we find that it is not unusual that once a student is placed in a remedial group, the objective chances of doing markedly better are very small. The label of "slow" sticks. For it seems that if we look at the macro level, when we establish "bluebird," "blackbird," and "buzzard" groups, once you are a buzzard you stay a buzzard.[23]

If these various examples are widespread (and they do seem to be) we are learning a good deal about what the overt and hidden curricula and our ways of evaluating students and programs may be doing socially. They may in fact be strongly related to both reproducing particular social and economic divisions in society and providing a "helping" ideology that legitimates these divisions.

Against Mechanistic Social Evaluation

Questions and examples of the type we just discussed are powerful tools for evaluating the school and its programs. However, these kinds of prior questions can lead to a mechanistic style of social evaluation by which we assume that the school always furthers the interests embodied by larger social tendencies that favor production, legitimation, and accumulation. This would be unfortunate. No social institution, no set of ideological forms and practices, is ever totally monolithic. Students, for instance, do not necessarily accept what the school teaches, nor do teachers passively acquiesce to larger pressures and tendencies. Therefore, we cannot take for granted that students are passive receptacles into which the school "pours" ideological content and values;[24] nor should we assume that students do not have some creative responses to the sorting and selecting functions of the school. In fact, recent research points to the critical nature of asking what students reject, because the research documents the ability of many students to reinterpret dominant ideologies in the overt and hidden curricula. The students often act in ways that make a simple conclusion about the social effects of curricula inside the black box difficult to make. In much the same way, teachers often seek to reinterpret, moderate, and reject outright the dictates of others that they know are not in the best interests of their students, or in the interests of social justice.[25]

One thing is certain. If we are to find all of this out—what is accepted and what is rejected—if we are to really see what impact the curricula, social relations, and evaluative practices of the school have on the students themselves, then accepted evaluations based on achievement scores and other various forms of testing are simply inadequate. This means a different style of evaluation, one that is more sensitive to the social role of the school, needs to be sponsored. Process/product evaluation does not enable us to get at the lived experience of students, to show *why* curricula fail, why programs are accepted or rejected, how conceptions of ability and achievement actually cover a much more complicated relationship between what a student experiences and acts on, on the one hand, and dominant ideologies and economic relations on the other. What we need is a greater emphasis on ethnographic analyses that would show the complex interaction among the strengths of the culture the students bring with them to school, the formal and informal curricula, and the unequal society outside the institution.

The crucial importance of not relying on "objective" test or achievement data to evaluate the effects of curricula is demonstrated quite well in a powerful ethnographic study by Paul Willis.[26] Willis focuses on a group of working-class high school students in a heavily industrialized city. He shows how, even in a school that tries to develop curricula to "meet the needs" of its students, its curricular programs fail for many students. Achievement is not raised; the students remain cynical.

Why this occurs and a large part of its actual social effects are exceptionally interesting and would be totally missed by an emphasis on test scores. It has less to do with the students' IQ or "ability" than we might think. Rather, it has an immense amount to do with the vibrant culture of the students themselves and their place in the social and sexual division of labor and the class structure. The students reject *both* the knowledge that the school wants the students to learn and the hidden curriculum of punctuality, individual achievement, and authority relations. What the school considers legitimate knowledge bears little resemblance to the actual world of work, to life "on the street," to the facts of labor that these students experience from their parents, friends, and their own part-time jobs. Willis shows that because of this, the youth reject "book learning" and glorify physical labor and "being cool." They spend a good deal of their time in school creatively finding ways to beat the system and get out of doing school work. By rejecting the "legitimate" culture of the school, by affirming manual work and physicality, they also affirm their own background. At the same time, they act in a way that actually constitutes a realistic assessment that, *as a class*, finishing their schooling or trying hard will not enable them to go much further than they already are.

This is a paradoxical situation, of course. By rejecting the overt curriculum, the students are rejecting "mental labor." They harden and make even more legitimate a distinction that lies at the heart of the social relations of production in our unequal economy, the separation between mental and manual labor. Although they affirm and act on the strengths of their own lived culture, a culture that almost unconsciously recognizes the low statistical probability of high school really paying off in the end, they also close off whatever paths to advancement schools may in fact offer, and reinforce unfortunate ideological distinctions at one and the same time. Yet, by rejecting the authority relations of the hidden curriculum, by learning to control their own time and space and beat the system, they are also learning skills that will give them more informal control at their own workplaces later. The social effects of the hidden and overt curricula are, hence, quite complicated. (Willis largely deals with white, working-class boys. This is a severe limitation. Similar kinds of analyses are absolutely essential to show the intricate connections among race, gender, and class in the approaches of students to schools.)

This ethnographic study does not assume a mechanistic process of domination in the school; yet at the same time it places the connections among the school, the students, the curricula, and the larger socioeconomic framework at the heart of its analysis. It even enables us to more fully answer traditional questions about curricular success or failure by not only focusing on test data but also by illuminating how and why these data are produced. Social evaluations of curricular programs in our inner cities, among poor Latino/a, African American, and Native American populations, in industrialized working class areas, in the rural areas of the south and west, and elsewhere could profitably draw upon similar kinds of analysis.

Beyond the Maintenance of Inequalities

At the heart of the suggestions we have made here is the knowledge of what our society's institutions are like, and how school practices are related to them—in complicated and even contradictory ways. We have claimed that because of this knowledge evaluators are compelled to take more seriously the question of how the social meanings within the curriculum and the social impact of school programs work to support dominant groups in contemporary society in a variety of ways. Only by becoming more aware of those varied functions in which the school is called upon to engage can we go further here. We have also warned against becoming so overly mechanistic, however, that we forget that real people, including many educators, may act against the accumulation, legitimation, and production functions of our educational institutions.

To work toward more socially responsive, democratic evaluation of curricula, several ideas must be taken more seriously than they now are by evaluators. First, the unit of analysis must encompass both the complex nature of school phenomena as illuminated by ethnographic investigations, and the larger social realities that are dynamically connected to classroom practices. This involves a fuller grasp of both educational phenomena and larger patterns of production and consumption in U.S. society, as well as a normative framework with which these activities can be assessed.[27] An increased sensitivity to the shortcomings of an individual unit of analysis must be accompanied by an awareness of other categories of evaluative inquiry—the ethical and political, for example—if evaluation is to promote a more just society.

Second, the very language of evaluation must undergo a similar transformation. The overly psychological discourse we have inherited—discourse that emphasizes "the learner," "behavioral objectives," treatments and outcomes, the measurement of "time on task," and the like—must change as we widen our evaluative horizons. This of course involves an increased familiarity on the part of evaluators with modes of discourse that are not always considered central—especially the languages of politics, ethics, and aesthetics.

Third, the very real, practical concerns of teachers faced with increased pressures toward standardized outcomes, accountability, and deskilling of teaching must be confronted honestly in evaluation studies. If we are to seriously work toward more fair, complete, and comprehensive evaluative practices, we must be prepared to deal with the pressures on teachers, administrators, and students to comply with criteria that have other aims. The key proposal in this regard may be to democratize the process of evaluation itself, so that teachers, students, parents, and other community members are included in the process of "placing value" on educational activities and curricular offerings. In this way the interests of nondominant groups may be represented and respected, and the ideological tendencies of dominant interests may be critiqued as we enlarge the circle of participants. Here, as elsewhere, democratizing educational practices may expose the contentious nature of curricular practices as competing groups argue over decisions based on ethical and political, as well as exclusively psychological, criteria.[28]

Fourth and last, we need to develop in greater detail than is possible here a vision of educational and social practices that foster cooperation, equality, participation and social action to redress political injustices because these values represent key principles of democracy. This would involve curricular and evaluative activities of a number of kinds. For example, curriculum projects could explore and develop precisely those areas now excluded by formally sanctioned school knowledge. The history of women; working-class activists; and alternative conceptions of science, technology, and the arts would become a focus for inquiry. Similarly, we might reorient at least a portion of our evaluative studies to emphasize student- and teacher-initiated inquiry into areas selected out by the standard curriculum, and support efforts to oppose continuing forms of domination and oppression of the nonprivileged. A positive evaluation would in that case mean not the raising of standardized test scores but the raising of the consciousness of students and others.[29]

Certainly these ideas are controversial and will require a good deal of debate to implement. In particular, the concern of parents and teachers that their children and pupils do well on standardized tests is understandable, especially in times of fiscal uncertainty. Yet we must find ways to discuss with these groups how such concerns, although legitimate, do not really guarantee the futures we desire.[30] The concerns of this chapter have centered on who ultimately gains the most from the hidden and overt curricula and the evaluative practices that are found in schools. The effort to alter these so that a more just, democratic, and humane set of educational and social practices can occur will indeed necessitate protracted debate. But at least the debate will be over a substantive and not technical question: the shape of the world that is in the process of being built by all those involved in democratic practice.

Notes

1   These ideas were explored initially in Michael W. Apple and Landon E. Beyer, "Social Evaluation of Curriculum," *Educational Evaluation and Policy Analysis* 5, no. 4 (Winter 1983).

2   Michael W. Apple, "The Process and Ideology of Valuing in Educational Settings," in *Educational Evaluation: Analysis and Responsibility*, ed. Michael W. Apple, Michael Subkoviak, and Henry Lufler Jr. (Berkeley: McCutchan Publishing Corp., 1974), 3–34.

3   Throughout this essay, we shall be using the concept of the social "functions" of education. We do *not* mean to imply either that these functions are all that schools do or that schools always successfully perform the social roles that they are called upon to do. As one of us has argued at length elsewhere, there are serious conceptual and empirical difficulties with a totally functional analysis of education. See Michael W. Apple, *Education and Power* (Boston: Routledge and Kegan Paul, 1982).

4   For a critique of the assumptions embedded in this search for a "neutral method," see Landon E. Beyer, "The Reconstruction of Knowledge and Educational Studies," *Journal of Education* 168, no. 2 (Fall, 1986).

5   Erik Olin Wright, *Class Structure and Income Determination* (New York: Academic Press, 1979), 57–58.

6   Vicente Navarro, *Medicine Under Capitalism* (New York: Neale Watson Academic Publications, 1976), 91. See also Manuel Castells, *The Economic Crisis and American Society* (Princeton: Princeton University Press, 1980).

7   Michael Olneck and James Crouse, "Myths of Meritocracy: Cognitive Skill and Adult Success in the United States." Institute for Research on Poverty Paper # 485–78, University of Wisconsin, Madison, March 1978.

8   See Jerome Karabel and A.H. Halsey, eds. *Power and Ideology in Education* (New York: Oxford University Press, 1977).

9   See Pierre Bourdieu and Jean Claude Passeron, *Reproduction in Education, Society and Culture* (Beverly Hills: Sage Publications, 1977) and John Ogbu, *Minority Education and Caste* (New York: Academic Press, 1978).

10   Apple, *Education and Power*.

11   Ibid., and Paul Willis, *Learning to Labour: How Working Class Kids Get Working Class Jobs* (New York: Columbia University Press, 1981).

12   See James Rosenbaum, *Making Inequality: The Hidden Curriculum of High School Tracking* (New York: John Wiley, 1976). On the school's role in legiti-

mation, see John Meyer, "The Effects of Education as an Institution," *American Journal of Sociology* 83 (January 1977), 55–77.

13   Michael W. Apple, *Ideology and Curriculum* (Boston: Routledge and Kegan Paul, 1979). On the relationship between the control of knowledge and the economy, see Harry Braverman, *Labor and Monopoly Capital* (New York: Monthly Review Press, 1974) and David Noble, *America By Design* (New York: Alfred Knopf, 1977).

14   Christopher Jencks, et al. *Who Gets Ahead?* (New York: Basic Books, 1979), 174–75.

15   Ibid., 175.

16   Wright, *Class Structure and Income Determination.*

17   Apple, *Ideology and Curriculum.*

18   Murray Edelman, *Political Language* (New York: Academic Press, 1977), xxi.

19   Apple, *Ideology and Curriculum*; Landon E. Beyer, "The Parameters of Educational Inquiry," *Curriculum Inquiry* 16, no. 1 (Spring 1986). See also Michael W. Apple, ed. *Cultural and Economic Reproduction in Education: Essays on Class, Ideology, and the State* (Boston: Routledge and Kegan Paul, 1982).

20   Apple, *Ideology and Curriculum*, 14.

21   Ibid., 7.

22   Jean Anyon, "Ideology and United States History Textbooks," *Harvard Educational Review* 49 (1979), 361–86.

23   See Ray Rist, *The Urban School: A Factory for Failure* (Cambridge: MIT Press, 1973) and Jeannie Oakes, *Keeping Track: How Schools Structure Inequality* (New Haven: Yale University Press, 1985).

24   Anyone who has taught in an inner city school knows the intense resistance that goes on. Even more subtle forms of resistance occur in more middle class schools in many areas. See, for example, Linda McNeil, "Economic Dimensions of Social Studies Curriculum: Curriculum as Institutionalized Knowledge" (Ph.D. diss., University of Wisconsin Madison, 1977).

25   See Linda McNeil, *Contradictions of Control: School Structure and School Knowledge* (New York: Routledge and Kegan Paul, 1986).

26   Willis, *Learning to Labour.*

27   Walter Feinberg, *Understanding Education* (New York: Cambridge University Press, 1983) and Landon E. Beyer, "The Parameters of Educational Inquiry."

28   For a very interesting attempt to expand the discourse and methodology of evaluation, see Ernest R. House, *Evaluating with Validity* (Beverly Hills, CA: Sage Publications, 1980).

29   Patti Lather, "Research as Praxis," *Harvard Educational Review* 56, no. 3 (August 1986).

30   See Ann Bastian, Norm Fruchter, Marilyn Gittell, Colin Greer, and Kenneth Haskins, *Choosing Equality: The Case for Democratic Schooling* (Philadelphia: Temple University Press, 1986).

THE CURRICULUM AS
COMPROMISED KNOWLEDGE

Chapter 5

Power and Culture in the
Report of the Committee of Ten

For the past sixty to seventy years, educators have witnessed a slowly growing but significant change in the way they approach their work. This change is only visible over the long haul, yet few things have had such an important impact. I am referring to the transformation of curriculum discourse and debate from those issues surrounding *what* we should teach to those problems associated with *how* the curriculum should be organized, built, and now, above all, evaluated. The difficult ethical and political questions of content, of what knowledge is of most worth, have been pushed to the background in our attempts to define technically oriented methods that will "solve" all of our problems once and for all. Professional curricular debate tends now to be about procedures, not about what counts as legitimate knowledge. As a number of commentators continually remind us, in the cultural sphere in general technique is winning out over substance.[1]

Ample evidence that this was not always the case is provided in the intense controversy involving one of the more important documents in curricular history, the National Education Association's 1894 *Report of the Committee of Ten on Secondary School Studies*.[2] Chaired by Charles W. Eliot, the president of Harvard University, the committee had to consider a range of issues that simply have not, and will not, go away. But most of all they dealt with the questions surrounding what one should teach and to which specific group of students it should be taught. Their primary focus was on the problem of uniformity in the high school curriculum, but the implications for elementary schools were certainly not invisible.

Few official documents have been the center of such heated discussion in their time. For a decade, from 1894 to 1905 and even beyond, "almost every treatment of matters educational was referred to, compared with, or distinguished from the report of the Committee of Ten."[3] In recent years, perhaps only the debates over the positions of Bruner and others about the structure of disciplines exemplified in *The Process of Education* parallel what was happening then in curriculum.

Even in an age when public debates were well known for their stentorian tones and their real sense of theater, the responses to the report were more than representative. Perhaps two quotes will give you a sense of the widely divergent responses. While William Maxwell, the Superintendent of Schools in Brooklyn, New York saw in the report "the cloud by day and the pillar of fire by night that is to lead us into the promised land,"[4] A.E. Winship, editor of the *Journal of Education*, was somewhat less enthusiastic. As he put it, the report produced by the committee "only escaped being a gigantic fraud because it was so well intentioned."[5]

Other kinds of criticisms have been and were levelled against it as well, especially in terms of its membership. Of the ten committee members, all were men, though a large portion of the students and teachers these men "represented" were women. Six were from colleges; five of these were college presidents. Three of the men were secondary school administrators. The last, William Torrey Harris, was United States Commissioner of Education. Clearly questions of representativeness, elitism, college domination, and similar issues could, and did, come to the fore.[6]

Yet those historians who have carefully studied the documents, the meetings, and the correspondence of the committee members suggest that the composition of the committee was done rather casually, without a conscious attempt to limit its membership through any conspiracy, and with little real sense of the possible lasting importance of its work. What bound the committee members together was a shared "desire to promote the development of high schools and to make it possible for more pupils to find a convenient route to the colleges in their high school work."[7]

The *Report of the Committee of Ten* did not spring up out of totally untilled soil. It was an outgrowth of a good deal of earlier work sponsored by the NEA, in particular the National Council of Education's *Report of the Committee on Secondary Education* in 1891. It too was concerned with the question of uniformity. The immense variation in courses required for admission to different colleges *and* the different content within each of the courses themselves often led to confusion at best. The loss of interest in and even outright antipathy toward the classics in many high schools was also leading to a situation in which a number of colleges looked to the nation's secondary schools to maintain the high standards that the classicists believed were being lost. At the same time, adherence to the import of more modern academic subjects was rising. And within the classicist and modernist positions themselves, disagreement was prevalent.

Proponents of Greek argued with supporters of Latin, each group seeking to preserve its own power. Followers of science were at odds with others who saw English, or modern foreign languages, or history, or philosophy as being the rightful heir to the position of most important content. Given the complexity (and the obvious politics) involved in these questions, the Committee on Secondary Education could not hope to solve them. Instead, it emphasized the urgency of further considering uniformity and recommended convening a conference in which a limited number of representatives of colleges and secondary schools could meet and begin the process of linking the curricular requirements of the high schools and colleges together in a more rational manner. Out of this conference, held in the summer of 1892, came the recommendation that an executive committee of ten persons be formed to arrange for further conferences organized according to "departments of instruction" (that is, subject areas) to deal with the problems.[8] Thus, the Committee of Ten began out of political, organizational, and curricular tension. As we saw from the response to its report, the controversy doesn't end with the completion of its assigned charge.

What kind of content could have caused such a response? In order to understand the disputes over the report and the criticisms it was subjected to, we need to place it briefly into the social, intellectual, and educational reality of the time.

We need to remember that in the 1880s and 1890s the high school was a very different institution than it is now. Comparatively few students attended it (though the numbers were growing) and those who did came primarily from cities. Few high schools existed outside urban centers.[9] Furthermore, even in cities only a limited number of school-age youth actually enrolled in high schools. And, of these, only a very small percentage—often between 6 and 10 percent—ever graduated.[10]

On an intellectual level, subtle shifts were occurring in widely held beliefs among educators about mental discipline. The reliance on fac-

ulty psychology, with its concomitant emphasis upon classical languages such as Latin as the training subject par excellence, was gradu-
ally giving way "to a more 'modern' concept of mental discipline, which
was concerned with developing the mind as a whole [and] which took
a broader view of the curriculum."[11]

Although these academic challenges to mental discipline had an
impact, among the most powerful forces that led to changes in these
theories came from outside the school. The growth of industrial capitalism and its need for a different kind of knowledge and a different
kind of student with different interests and expertise undoubtedly played
a major part here.[12] The report occurred at a time of intense conflict
in another way. Class and ethnic antagonisms were very visible in the
society at large. This manifested itself not only in the world of work
but in the academy itself, most crucially over competing definitions of
legitimate culture. This is not unimportant. Controversies over the
content and form of the curriculum, over what and whose knowledge
should be granted high status, are often informed by larger conflicts
between and within groups who are now in, or want to have, power.

Just as the high school itself was originally conceived of as an institution rooted in the cultural norms of the Anglo-Protestant upper–
middle class, and was conceived of in both content and method to
teach the values and culture of an idealized society,[13] so too did similar
concerns about culture and power work their way through here. These
points are perhaps best summarized in Michael F.D. Young's assertion that "those in positions of power will attempt to define what is
taken as knowledge, how accessible to different groups any knowledge
is, and what are the accepted relationships between different knowledge areas and between those who have access to them and make
them available."[14] Shifts in power within and outside the educational
system itself thus played a significant role in the production and reception of the report. In essence, as we shall see, the report that the
Committee of Ten finally brought to print was a political and cultural
compromise between contending groups *within* that section of people
who had controlled academic discourse for a long period in the United
States.

As I noted, when the Committee of Ten was initially formed its
primary task was to deal with the problem of uniform requirements for
college entrance. This was not an inconsequential issue. In the presence of many different colleges with what were sometimes widely dis-
similar entrance standards and curricular expectations, high school

administrators and teachers were faced with a very real dilemma. This was heightened by the fact that larger numbers of parents and students saw the high school as an important avenue for future success and advancement.[15] Of course, greater numbers of students meant different *kinds* of students as well, ones whose economic and educational trajectories might not be the same as each other's.

Because there were internal disagreements among the Committee members, disagreements that often mirrored many of the issues that surfaced in the *Report of the Committee on Secondary Education*, compromise over the place of the classics, over the kinds of subjects to be required for admission to college and for mental discipline, and so on had to be made.

In preparation for the deliberations of the committee, conferences were held in various locations. Each of the conferences was to take up the problem of how to achieve uniformity within the subjects offered in secondary schools. All the desired curricular subjects were grouped into nine categories, categories that illuminated both the residual power of the classics and the emerging power of newer academic subjects. These included: 1) Latin; 2) Greek; 3) English; 4) other modern languages; 5) mathematics; 6) physics, astronomy, and chemistry; 7) natural history, including botany, physiology, and zoology; 8) history, civil government, and political economy; and 9) geography, including geology, meteorology, and physical geography.[16]

Missing, obviously, were manual or vocational training, business, and other "practical" subjects, as well as art and music. Although some members of the committee did not dispute the fact that, in various ways, certain parts of these subjects should be offered, the (mental) disciplinary value of such subjects was less visible. Hence, they were not included. It is evident, however, that the nine areas primarily represented the cultural capital of two particular segments of the dominant group within the academy and within the gentry itself, those whose cultural background, visions of "civilization," and affiliation were with the older classical subjects and those "moderate reformers" who wished to expand the definitions of high-status curricular knowledge somewhat to include a wider array of more "modern" academic subjects.

Given this list of major content areas and the attempt to create uniformity of content within each of them, a problem still remained. How were they to be organized? Four programs were suggested: Classical, Latin-Scientific, Modern Languages, and English. Although each program or course of study had at least some formal study of foreign language, English, science, history, and mathematics, if one went down the list of programs from Classical to English one saw that they did represent a decreasing amount of foreign languages and an increase in the allotment for modern academic subjects.[17] It was Eliot's desire that these programs be *only* suggestions, that they would be modified, rebuilt, etc. Unfortunately, although they are not engraved in stone, suggested programs like these have a tendency to be reified and to be taken on with less reflectiveness than one might like.[18]

With the development of four programs, with the partial fracturing of the power of the classics (a fracturing that had been building for a long period), one other position was being pressed for. This was the establishment of the roots of a system of choice, of electives, for students. This bore the stamp of Eliot. Although it was not the case that Eliot imposed his will on the Committee, his influence is unmistakable here. Eliot had a strong belief in electives, an idea that at the time had few proponents especially among educators involved in elementary and secondary programs. He did not dismiss the notion of mental discipline, but rather gave it a personal and thoughtful reconstruction. Mental discipline was enhanced to the extent that students could work in depth on a relatively limited selection of subjects for which they had both inclination and talent.[19]

Eliot's position on electives was tied to another strongly held belief. Although in favor of disciplined student choice, he was articulate and clear about what he was against—differentiation of the curriculum in terms of where a student might find him or herself in the occupational hierarchy after completing school. To Eliot's liking, it was clearly the sense of the conferences that such curriculum differentiation should not be proposed. Both college and non-college bound students were to be treated the same regarding the curriculum. Though perhaps this was one of its most progressive positions, it is here that one senses some of the contradictions of the report and the social position of its authors. Curriculum differentiation should be put off as long as possible. It is not the place of the school to sort and channel students through different systems of content and instruction that merely ratify a student's background. All students should be uniformly given the opportunity for an education for "life." This surely is an optimistic stance, one of great power and social vision because it assumes that the great majority of secondary school students are capable of disciplined inquiry and doing well. Yet even with this vision and its accompanying (and very realistic) fear that curriculum differentiation would lead to the school helping to recreate inequality, the kind of subject matter that was to be taught and many of the methods of teaching subject matter remained relatively limited to the cultural resources of dominant groups.[20]

As one would expect, given the debates that had led to the formation of the committee in the first place, internal dissension over a number of the positions taken in the report was not totally absent. James Baker, president of the University of Colorado, for example, objected to what he believed was a serious danger in the final written document. The report might be interpreted to imply that each and every subject was equally as good as any other for mental discipline. This was particularly problematic for Baker because he believed that any subject's potential for mental training was dependent not on its disciplinary form but on its specific content.[21] The matter of content continued to be a source of dissatisfaction, in fact. The committee's decision to leave the question of content to the individual conferences and focus the final report primarily on the form of organization of the curriculum led to the charge that the committee by and large ignored the issue of the actual content of the curriculum.

A compromise had been struck, though, one that managed to actually ratify a good deal of existing practice at many secondary schools and one that still preserved some of the previous power of the classics at the same time that it helped legitimate certain principles of curriculum within schools. Newer modern subjects were given a stronger relative position; electives were highlighted, though not necessarily in the form that Eliot would have ideally preferred; and a position against curriculum differentiation was taken—all within the bounds of an expanded version of the relationship between formal secondary education and mental training. Legitimate knowledge for high schools was enlarged, but still mainly defined and defended as that which led to mental discipline. Though partly resolving the problem of uniformity and the disputed place of particular subject areas and though wisely recognizing the place of schools in trying to systematically develop the reasoning power of all students,[22] the report still did so on the terrain of specific definitions of cultural status.

However, even with these compromises, the report's message to school personnel was rather clear. One of the wisest interpreters of the report, Edward Krug, stated the basic position that was made public and Eliot's own desires concerning it. As he put it:

> On the whole, the message of the report ran along these lines: There should be no difference made in the teaching of any subject on the grounds of whether

or not a pupil was going to college. The modern academic subjects should be rescued from their scrappy inferiority; this could be done by following the recommendations of the conferences. With this done, colleges could and should accept these subjects for admission. One could get good mental training and should be admitted to college even though he [or she] had never studied either Latin or Greek. The elective principle was clearly endorsed, although not in the form Eliot would have preferred; still he clung to his hope that the four courses of study were only temporary and would in time be abandoned.[23]

Yet the painstakingly constructed "moderate" compromise between the proponents of the older classical studies and the modern academic subjects soon came under attack from outside, with individuals such as G. Stanley Hall taking the lead of one faction. Against what Raymond Williams and Herbert Kliebard have called the old humanists' conception of legitimate knowledge as that best suited for mental discipline, Hall and others proposed the scientific study of students' minds. Uniform curricula were indefensible; they represented college domination of high school curricula.[24] Other conflicts and reactions abounded, thereby guaranteeing both that the report would be talked about and that its acceptability would be limited.

What was its impact, however? Did it accomplish what it set out to do? In one way it succeeded. As I mentioned earlier, it did give legitimacy to existing school practices and curricular offerings that went beyond the classics. On what may seem to us one of its most important goals—the building of a curricular program that did not reproduce inequalities—the verdict is far less favorable. Again Krug probably offered the most honest assessment:

> It would not be unfair to say that on the matter of treating pupils alike regardless of their educational destinations, the Committee was almost without influence. Not only did the school world of that period continue the traditional distinction, on the basis of the classics, between the curricula of pupils who were preparing for college and those who were not; it also began to look with favor on more refined versions of that distinction, involving the modern academic subjects as well. Over the years the idea of a college-preparatory curriculum became as rigidly fixed from this point of view as it had ever been with reference to Greek.[25]

As Krug concluded, in the final analysis, "It has been much easier to assert that [the *Report of the Committee of Ten*] had great influence than to present evidence for it."[26] There are many reasons for this, not the least of which was the declining cultural power of the old humanists in the face of massive demographic and economic changes that altered the very fabric of society. In practice, its vision of a curriculum that did not differentiate among students in terms of the possible future economic and educational careers would fall prey to the realities of school life. In a period of rapid industrialization, in a period in which an oddly disembodied version of science and technique slowly replaced ethical and political deliberation in the schools and elsewhere, in a period in which enrollments were increasing, and in a time when the social and intellectual goals of the high school were very much in flux, these proponents of an equal education for all students who entered the school fell short. The committee members could not make the necessary connections with popular classes who demanded equality, in part because of their backgrounds and implicit theories of culture and civilization.[27] Nor did they ultimately have the ability either to provide the practical skills necessary to accomplish that meritorious goal (given the reality of the school) or to develop the political skills necessary to withstand the increasing power of emerging groups—including industrialists, the systematic efficiency experts, and educational "scientists"—who made even more powerful claims upon the school.

Why is it then that a document that seemed to have little direct influence on U.S. education continues to arouse our interest? Perhaps one of the reasons is that, for all its compromises and weaknesses, it speaks eloquently to the very real urge for equality in all of us. In the present moment, when so many political and economic inequalities and our current government conspire to attain that belief, to purge it from modern memory, it is no small thing to remember some of the earlier struggles to keep it alive.

Notes

I would like to thank Rima D. Apple and Herbert Kliebard for their help in refining the conceptual framework used in this article.

1   I have argued this in more detail in Michael W. Apple, *Ideology and Curriculum* (Boston: Routledge and Kegan Paul, 1979) and more recently Michael W. Apple, *Education and Power* (Boston: Routledge and Kegan Paul, 1982).

2   National Education Association, *Report of the Committee of Ten on Secondary School Studies* (New York: American Book Co., 1894).

3   Edward A. Krug, *The Shaping of the American High School, 1880–1920* (Madison: University of Wisconsin Press, 1964), 66.

4   William Maxwell, cited in Ibid., 73.

5   A.E. Winship, cited in Ibid., 72.

6   Ibid., 39.

7   Ibid., 43. This does *not* mean that significant ideological commitments about class, gender, and race were absent in the selection of the committee or in its own deliberations. Rather, these commitments were not an overt element and probably would have worked at the level of common sense. For a further discussion of this issue, see Goran Therborn, *The Ideology of Power and the Power of Ideology* (London: New Left Books, 1980).

8   Ibid., 32–37.

9   Ibid., 11. Krug notes that more girls attended and graduated from public high schools than boys. In private secondary schools both were about equal. Patriarchal social relations would still be markedly dominant in the home, the paid workplace and elsewhere, of course. It would be important to know who the girls were who attended high school, what their actual experiences were, and where they went after completing secondary schools.

10   Ibid., 13–14. See also Randall Collins, *The Credential Society* (New York: Academic Press, 1979), 109–18.

11   Walter Kolesnik, *Mental Discipline in Modern Education* (Madison: University of Wisconsin Press, 1958), 23.

12   Herbert Kliebard, "Education at the Turn of the Century: A Crucible for Curriculum Change," *Educational Researcher* 11 (January 1982): 16–17.

13   Collins, *The Credential Society*, 110–11.

14   Michael F.D. Young, "An Approach to the Study of Curricula as Socially Organized Knowledge," in *Knowledge and Control*, ed. Michael F.D. Young (London: Collier-Macmillan, 1971), 32.

15   Kliebard, "Education at the Turn of the Century," 17.

16   Krug, *The Shaping of the American High School*, 52.

17   Ibid., 61.

18   That this problem has had a long history is documented in Alice Miel's impor-
     tant but unfortunately nearly forgotten volume, *Changing the Curriculum*
     (New York: D. Appleton-Century Co., 1946).

19   Krug, *The Shaping of the American High School*, 21.

20   In essence there is something of a paradox here. Although the committee was
     elite in its makeup, the report at least partly argues for equality by rejecting
     programs of curriculum differentiation. This does point out the possibility
     that elite groups are capable of democratic behavior. In his interesting and
     informative analysis of the Committee of Ten, however, Sizer contends that a
     commitment to the doctrine of mental discipline often entailed a commitment
     to teaching all children the same curriculum. Differential content was less
     important than mental training, and mental training was "something that all
     persons needed whether they were to become mechanics or classics schol-
     ars." See Theodore R. Sizer, *Secondary Schools at the Turn of the Century*
     (New Haven: Yale University Press, 1964), 115. Elements of both kinds of
     explanations may be required here.

21   Ibid., 57.

22   Kliebard, "Education at the Turn of the Century," 17.

23   Krug, *The Shaping of the American High School*, 65.

24   Kliebard, "Education at the Turn of the Century," 18. See also Raymond
     Williams, *The Long Revolution* (London: Chatto and Windus, 1961).

25   Krug, *The Shaping of the American High School*, 89.

26   Ibid., 88.

27   Eliot himself played a rather involved role here, especially in the twentieth
     century. For an interesting documentation of Eliot's relationship with the
     emerging power of capital, see Daniel T. Rogers, *The Work Ethic in Indus-
     trial America, 1850–1920* (Chicago: University of Chicago Press, 1978).

Chapter 6

Do the *Standards* Go Far Enough? Power, Policy, and Practice in Mathematics Education

Introduction

Education does not exist in isolation from the larger society. Its means and ends and the daily events of curriculum, teaching, and evaluation in schools all are connected to patterns of differential economic, political, and cultural power. In order to understand this, one must engage in *relational* analysis.[1] That is, one must see both inside and outside the school at the same time. And one must have an adequate picture of the ways in which these patterns of differential power operate. In a society riven by social tensions and by increasingly larger inequalities,[2] schools will not be immune from—and in fact may participate in recreating—these inequalities.[3]

If this is true of education in general, it is equally true of attempts to reform it. Efforts to reform teaching and curricula—especially in areas such as mathematics that have always been sources of social stratification,[4] as well as possible paths to mobility—are also situated within larger relations. Success or failure will be dependent on these relations and on our ability to deal with them seriously. My discussion of the major documents underpinning this reform, *Curriculum and Evaluation Standards for School Mathematics* (1989) and *Professional Standards for Teaching Mathematics* (1991), will situate both the documents and their possibilities within this larger social reality.[5]

At the outset, it is important that I state that there is much that I support in the documents. The attempt to create a nonelitist curriculum in which the focus is not a mathematics whose only goal is to identify "talent" but on a curriculum for all students is a powerful vision. The stress on teaching mathematics through the use of real-world problems is wise as well, because it can reduce the alienation so many students now feel about the subject. In the process, the volumes recognize that the entire current curriculum excludes many children not only in mathematics but in so much else as well.[6] An emphasis on multiple forms of assessment—assessment that focuses not simply on evaluating student achievement, but on the pedagogy and curriculum provided by the school and on the differential hidden curriculum that may be taught—is refreshing. This responds to some of the major criticisms of our reliance on sets of evaluative procedures that usually act to label children without providing sufficient understanding of the problems surrounding financial and material resources, poor teaching and curriculum, poverty, and so on that may cause low achievement in the first place.[7] Given the movement toward standardized national testing, the position taken in the *Standards* volume becomes even more significant.

With this said, however, I shall not spend a good deal of time documenting the many real strengths of the volumes. Indeed, discussions among mathematics educators have been quite suggestive here. Instead, I want to highlight areas that require further thought, areas that may not usually surface in discussions within the mathematics education community. It is because I support a number of the initiatives articulated in the *Standards* that I offer these questions and criticisms. Only by taking them seriously can the project succeed in other than rhetorical ways in its major goals.

No article of this size can deal with all of the issues that require examination, nor can it analyze them in sufficient detail to reveal their total complexity. Because of this, this essay should be seen not as a final statement, but as an effort to raise questions, especially social questions. Further analyses can be found in my references and notes, where I point to more detailed investigations of the range of issues I raise.

Among the issues I shall deal with are the depth of the financial crisis in education and its economic and ideological genesis and results, the nature of inequality in schools, the role of mathematical knowledge in our economy in maintaining such inequalities, the possibilities and limitations of a mathematics curriculum that is more grounded in the experiences and problems of students, and the complicated realities of the lives of teachers.

The Standards as a Slogan System

The *Standards* volumes come close to being a kind of educational literature that is called a *slogan system*.[8] By calling them by this name, I do not mean to denigrate them. After all, some of the most powerful literature in curriculum, from Ralph Tyler's classic little text, *Basic Principles of Curriculum and Instruction,* to Jerome Bruner's almost poetic arguments for discipline-centered education, *The Process of Education,* have been of the same genre.[9] Rather, what I want to do is direct our attention to some of these specific characteristics, since slogan systems have peculiar properties and perform a variety of functions.

Slogan systems need to have three attributes if they are to be effective. First, they must have a penumbra of vagueness so that powerful groups or individuals who would otherwise disagree can fit under the umbrella. Again, the example of Bruner can illuminate what I mean here. *The Process of Education*, by speaking to the importance of discipline-centered curricula, was able to integrate the interests of a Cold War–oriented community of industry, government, and academics. At the same time, by calling for teaching the disciplines by discovery, it also enabled child-centered educators (who were losing power anyway) to find something responsive in it for them.[10] Thus, coalitions to support a movement for curricula change could be built.

Yet successful slogan systems cannot be too vague, and here we find their second characteristic. They need to be specific enough to offer something to practitioners here and now. The large amount of money spent by the government on the development of "teacher-proof" curriculum materials in the 1960s in, say, science and mathematics, that were based on the academic disciplines nearly guaranteed that a discipline–centered approach would at least get into classrooms. (Whether it was actually taught in the manner in which its developers wanted is another issue, of course.)[11]

Finally, and this is most difficult to specify, a slogan system seems to need the ability to charm. Put simply, its style must be such that it "grabs us." It must offer us a sense of imaginative possibility and in doing so generates a call to and a claim for action. It can do this through a positive vision, as in the *Standards*, or it can accomplish this by playing on the fears of its readers as in, say, E.D. Hirsch's cleverly written but inherently problematic proposal in *Cultural Literacy.*[12]

The *Standards* bring together a variety of people with different positions. Among them are: economic modernizers and conservatives who want to transform mathematics into economically useful knowledge and want a technically prepared and flexible workforce; process-oriented and constructivist educators and researchers who want more dynamic and interactive styles of curriculum and teaching; democratically inclined educators who seek to make mathematics somewhat more based on community needs and who question the patterns of differential achievement that now exist; mathematicians who are concerned about the state of mathematics as a field; advocates of a national common culture and common curriculum (most, though not all, of whom are cultural conservatives worried about the decline of standards and the loss of a vision of the "Western tradition"); and, finally, many teachers who are laboring under difficult and uncertain conditions in schools.

The formation of this umbrella, under which groups with often decidedly different ideological and educational agendas may come together, is complemented by the volumes' strategy of giving sample lessons, problems, and vignettes. Finally, the authors have been careful and creative in their style. Indeed, I know of no current curriculum documents of this type that are as nicely crafted in a way that pulls the reader in.

In all these ways, the *Standards* volumes are a success as a slogan system. Yet, *because* of these elements, because of ideological and educational tensions within the coalition and within schools and the larger society, there will be problems—not only solutions—generated out of this success.

Perhaps one of the most important questions to raise here is this: As a slogan system builds this coalition for "reform," which of the diverse tendencies under its umbrella will exert the most power? Which will provide leadership, even if tacitly? This is crucial here, for the *Standards* do not exist in an ideological vacuum and no matter what the meritorious goals of the authors, the full range of proposals will not be accepted or put into practice. Rather, a selective process will occur in which those groups that already exert the most powerful leadership for school reform will choose from the documents those elements that cohere with the general framework and tendencies already in motion.[13]

Facing the Crisis

Because they are slogan systems, all public educational documents of this type are compromises. They are compromises about what should count as legitimate knowledge, what is appropriate pedagogy and evaluation, and ultimately about what norms and values should guide the schooling process itself. The *Standards* are part of a larger reform movement; most of its elements are at the more humane end of that movement. But we must ask whose vision is currently leading the overall reform efforts. By and large, the major trends and agendas of this more general set of educational reform initiatives have been integrated within the conservative project.[14]

We have entered a period of reaction in education. Our educational institutions are seen as failures. High drop-out rates, a decline in "functional literacy," a loss of standards and discipline, the failure to teach "real knowledge," poor scores on standardized tests, and more—are all charges leveled at schools.[15] And all of these, we are told, have led to a decline in economic productivity, a loss of international competitiveness, unemployment, poverty, and so on. Return to a common culture, make schools more efficient, more competitive, and more open to private initiative; this will solve our problems.[16]

As I have claimed elsewhere, placing most of the blame on the school for the crisis in the economy and in culture and authority relations is largely wrong. It allows dominant groups to export the crisis from their own past decisions. It also has a misplaced sense of cause and effect.[17] In large part, behind this is an attack on egalitarian norms and values. Although hidden in the rhetorical flourishes of the critics, in essence "too much democracy"—culturally and politically—is seen as one of the major causes of "our" declining economy and culture.[18]

The conservative restoration is not only occurring in the United States. In Britain, Australia, and many other nations similar tendencies are quite visible. The extent of the reaction is captured by the former British Secretary of Education and Science in the Thatcher government, Kenneth Baker, who evaluated nearly a decade of rightist governmental efforts by saying in 1988 that "the age of egalitarianism is over."[19] He was speaking positively, not negatively.

The threat to egalitarian ideas that this ideological trend represents is never made explicit since it is always couched in the discourse of improving standards and quality in an educational system that is seen as in decline if not in crisis.[20]

One of the effects of this conservative reaction has been to transform our collective sense of the roles schools are to play in this society. This has meant that equalizing the opportunities and outcomes of schooling has been seen increasingly not as a public right but as a tax drain. Public schooling—unless it is defined to meet the more conservative goals now in ascendancy—is too expensive economically and ideologically.[21] The *Standards* often stand in direct contrast to this movement. But can they prevail against the economic and ideological needs articulated by some of the most powerful parts of the coalition—economic and cultural conservatives who see schools as large holes into which money is poured?

Among the major effects of this changing perception of schooling is that a large number of states have had to make Draconian cuts in education because of sharply diminished tax revenues and a loss of public support for schools. This has created a situation in which federal and state aid to local school districts—never totally sufficient in many poor school districts—has been less and less able to keep up with mandated programs such as classes for children with special needs or for those who speak languages other than English. It has meant that for many schools it will be nearly impossible for them to comply with, say, health and desegregation programs mandated by the state and federal governments, to say nothing of other needs.[22]

Part of the situation has been caused by the intensely competitive economic conditions faced by business and industry. Their own perceived imperative to cut costs and reduce budgets (often no matter what the social consequences) has led many companies to exert considerable pressure on states and local communities to give them sizable tax breaks, thereby "cutting off money needed to finance public education."[23]

For many chronically poor school districts, the fiscal crisis is so severe that textbooks are used until they literally fall apart. Basements, closets, gymnasiums, and any available space are used for instruction. Teachers are being laid off, as are counselors and support staff, including school nurses. Art and foreign language programs are being dropped. Extracurricular activities—from athletics to activities more socially and academically oriented—are being severely cut back. In some towns and cities, the economic problems are such that it will be impossible for schools to remain open for the full academic year.[24]

The implications of all this—what has been called the fiscal crisis of the state—are profound.[25] The economic crisis faced by local school districts, and especially those districts whose schools are already in advanced states of decay as the cycle of poverty worsens measurably, may make it nearly impossible for the more democratic vision articulated in the *Standards* to be put into practice in a serious way.

For example, *Curriculum and Evaluation Standards* calls for a markedly expanded presence of computers and a wide array of physical materials and supplies in classrooms. In many ways I agree, though as I have documented elsewhere the role of the new technology in schools may not be an unalloyed blessing. The "technology-rich class-room" called for by the *Standards* can *increase*, not decrease, the wide disparities that now exist in class, gender, and race in educa-tion.[26] Further, the effects of technology on teaching can be the deskilling of teachers and the intensification of their labor. That is, rather than leading to the development of new skills and dispositions, unless it is done with an immense amount of care and a clearer under-standing of the economic and social realities of schools, the large-scale introduction of computers into classrooms can increase the work load of teachers immensely and can cause teachers to increase their use of commercially prepared material that often has little educational benefit. The *Standards* criticism of the dominance of the standard-ized mathematics textbook is correct. But if such a textbook is simply be replaced by an electronic version of it, the result can be the disempowering, not the empowering of students and teachers.[27]

The possible deskilling and intensifying effects of technology on teachers is an important question and I shall return to it, but this is not my major point concerning the call of the volumes for more comput-ers and other physical resources. Although I do not want to be cyni-cal, I am concerned that there is a danger that we will read these documents in a social and economic vacuum. The *Standards* do not sufficiently recognize the immensity of the economic crisis that is cur-rently besetting so many of our school systems, especially urban sys-tems. They naively assume that more money will be somehow forth-coming (from business? government?) to compensate for this.

As I noted above, it is not at all likely that further resources will be given to schools to create the rich environment the volumes envision, especially to inner-city schools populated by children of color. Much more consideration needs to be given to this reality that goes well beyond the very brief call in the "Next Steps" section for efforts to be made to secure funding. Unless this situation is thought through now in terms of the *competing* interests that exist under the umbrella of the *Standards*, inequality in resources and outcomes will again be the results.[28] The call for more resources at exactly the same time as most of the business community is consciously and aggressively seeking to reduce their contributions to the common good fails to understand the role that economically dominant groups have played and now play in creating the crisis and the ensuing condition of insufficient and un-equal resources in the first place.[29]

A number of questions must be asked by mathematics educators in this regard. Does their vision depend on a massive infusion of funds for a technology-rich environment? If it does, is the entire package of reforms utopian? Can we expect federal, state, and local governments and economically dominant groups to provide extensive amounts of additional funding (except for the isolated gifts of, say, computers) when these same governments and groups cannot or will not now even provide sufficient funds to maintain buildings, books, and teachers? What is *essential* to the *Standards* that does not depend on such funding? Are the more democratically oriented members of the coalition that is incorporated under the umbrella of the *Standards* willing to entertain the fact that some of the most powerful members of that supposed coalition may be unwilling to alter economic and human priorities to give the most important parts of its proposals a real chance to succeed?

The suggestions of the *Standards* for taking the "next steps" are weakened considerably by the authors' lack of a more structural appraisal of the logic of our kind of economic organization and by a rather too romanticized proposal for finding the resources and power to support the more democratic parts of their agenda that seek more egalitarian social and educational norms.[30]

Class, Race, and Gender in the Classroom

It is important to stress, however, that even with their relatively naive assessment of the ways in which this society is organized to *produce* inequalities, the volumes do not ignore some of the crucial inequalities in schools.[31] In fact, the *Standards* explicitly point to how schools may now operate to produce them. For example, cautions are built in so that teachers will think about the possible race–, gender– and class–stratifying effects of their practices, even those practices suggested in the *Standards*.

This in itself is quite welcome. However, little is said about how one might prepare our future teachers to do this. Thinking critically is not necessarily a natural occurrence. It doesn't automatically arise simply because one is told to look for problems. Rather, such an awareness is built through concentrated efforts at a relational understanding of how gender, class, and race power actually work together in our daily practices and in the institutional structures we now inhabit.

The mere process of thinking about something is only the beginning; *how* we think about something makes a difference. Let me restate the example from Chapter One. We are now quite used to seeing pictures of disasters in which thousands of people lose their lives due to storms, drought, and so forth. We are told to think of these as "natural disasters." But is this the appropriate way of understanding the situation or is it really a form of category error?

Take the massive mudslides that occurred in parts of South America in which large numbers of people were killed as torrential rains washed their houses down the mountainsides. A closer examination of this case reveals nothing natural about this at all. Every year there are rains and every year some people die. This particular year an entire side of a mountain gave way. "Only" the thousands of people living on it lost their lives. No one in the valleys—the safe and fertile land—died. Poor families are forced to live on the dangerous hillsides. This is the only land they can find in which to eke out an existence that is barely survivable. They crowd onto this land not because they want to, but both because of poverty and because of the land ownership patterns that are historically and grossly unequal.

Hence, the problem is not the yearly rains—a natural occurrence—but the economic structures that allow only a small minority of individuals to control the lives of the majority of the people of that region. Notice that this altered understanding of the problem would require a different practice. Not only would we send immediate aid to help the victims of the rains, we would also engage in a large–scale program of land redistribution to make the social structure much more equal.

In a more educational context, we can see similar kinds of uses of the term "natural." For example, we are quite accustomed to a discourse that pervades schooling concerning the "natural ability" of students in school achievement. Students are talented and gifted, average, or below average, as measured by our usual methods of determining achievement levels. These differences then guide us in choosing curriculum, pedagogy, and classroom organization. Yet, these supposedly naturally occurring differences are again less natural than we might expect. They too are often profoundly social, deeply rooted in the relationship between poverty and school achievement and in the ways gender, class, and race are interconnected in our dominant institutions. The affixing of labels by the school to signify "natural" ability here often serves to ratify differences based on economic and cultural capital.[32] Thus, once again how we think about our daily activity is a fundamental determinant of what would count as an appropriate response. Like the example of the necessity of land redistribution, absent a more vigorous national commitment to eliminate poverty, we may be focusing on symptoms rather than causes.

These examples are quite important to my argument. One can be a truly caring person and worry about the negative effects of everyday events on people—in the case of the recommendations of the *Standards,* about the differential effects of teaching and curricula. But there is a major difference, both in theory and in one's response, in how one interprets these events. Yes, we should applaud the recognition of the possibility of differential processes and outcomes in the *Standards.* But such recognition if it is to be meaningful needs to be taken considerably further.

How will teachers be taught to interpret these differential processes? What intellectual resources will they need to do it? Just as in the case of the failure of the *Standards* to sufficiently analyze, in a relational and structural manner, the pressures on and needs of business—a failure that may cause mathematics educators to call for resources from economic sectors whose major current interests are often *opposed* to such resources—so too may the *Standards* have an insufficient understanding of the ways in which class, race, and gender divisions are structurally part of the schooling process.[33]

Of course, I want to be cautious about being too critical here. After all, in placing such inequalities on the official curriculum agenda in mathematics education, the documents have clearly done all of us a public service. However, stating a problem and understanding its roots, complexities, and what is necessary to act on it are not always logically entailed. As Secada has argued, much of the way we have construed gender, race, and class issues has been centered around enlightened self-interest, not equity.[34] This construction of the problem can be disempowering for those most affected. When courses and experiences in critically appraising the ends and means of our institutions and in ethical deliberation are seen as equally (or perhaps more) important as additional work in mathematics and statistics for our teachers and researchers, then perhaps some headway will be evident.

It is not only in the treatment of race, gender, and class differences in school experiences that we must be cognizant of inequalities. This awareness needs to be extended to some of the predominant uses of mathematical knowledge itself. Mathematical and scientific knowledge are forms of high-status knowledge in this society. An understanding of what this means and why it is the case is crucial if we are to go further in recognizing the relationship between differential power and mathematics education.

On the Question of High-Status Knowledge

Any analysis of high-status knowledge must begin with the question of "for what purpose is the knowledge used?" Although we must be very careful not to be overly reductive here, it is clear when we think macroeconomically that mathematical knowledge has particular uses in this kind of economy.

Like all forms of knowing, mathematical knowing is of course partly aesthetic. Yet, in industrialized nations, it gains its high status because of its socioeconomic utility as a form of what I have called *technical/administrative knowledge*.[35] The accumulation and control of technical/administrative knowledge by a limited group of people is essential to our science-based industries and for the production of material and weapons systems for the Defense Department.[36] In the calculus of values we use to sort out "important knowledge" from "less important knowledge," business and industry—and the government—place a high value on knowledge that is convertible ultimately into profits and control. The possession of such knowledge through patents, hiring practices, funding research institutes, and so on is crucial in the highly competitive economic system we live in.

But by possession here I do *not* mean that you and I should have such knowledge or that it be widely distributed. Rather, I mean that those with economic, political, and cultural power can employ it in ways they see fit.

In order to understand this, we again need a more structural appraisal of what schools do. We have, for instance, assumed that the role of education is primarily the *distribution* of knowledge to students in a manner that makes it accessible to them. Although the counterarguments are too complex to fully detail them here, this may not be an adequate account. Our educational systems are also organized to ultimately *produce*, not distribute, particular kinds of knowledge that are needed by business and industry and the defense establishment.[37]

In calling this "technical/administrative knowledge", I mean to signify the scientific and mathematical knowledge upon which the expansion and control of markets and products, cultural and economic control, and basic and applied research to support this are dependent.[38] Schools are then organized as well to sponsor those students who may ultimately produce this knowledge.

Thus, schools are caught in a contradictory situation. To preserve democratic deliberation, to enhance the possibility of a more knowledgeable population, and to produce a more technically knowledge-able and flexible workforce, specific knowledge will be distributed (usually but not always the knowledge of groups with economic, political, and cultural power).[39] Yet, an overemphasis on distribution of knowledge may detract from the equally powerful demands placed on the educational system, and especially on universities, to produce technically oriented knowledge that can be controlled and utilized in the economy.

This may seem too abstract, but its import is considerable. It implies that proposals for, say, the democratization of mathematical knowledge embodied in plans to teach everyone well—and which, as I noted earlier, will be quite expensive—may be blocked by the imperatives of an economic need to produce a limited number of highly qualified students whose ultimate role is to produce economically useful knowledge. After all, in our kind of economy, the important thing is that technical/administrative knowledge is *available for use*, not necessarily that large numbers of people have it, especially if distributing it more widely through reformed curricula and teaching is more expensive as in the case of the *Standards*.[40] Although it may be in capital's interest to have an oversupply of trained workers,[41] and to have a paid workforce that is more technically competent, powerful economic groups often give rhetorical support to this while at the same time they do not see the cost as justified. The fact that the kinds of paid jobs that are largely being created in our more service-oriented economy are very often increasingly deskilled and have less need for autonomy and high levels of technical knowledge is of considerable import here as well.[42]

Effective efforts that seek basic reforms of our policies and practices in curriculum, teaching, and evaluation are only as strong as their understanding of the relations between schools and the larger society. Mathematical and scientific knowledge is not just any knowledge. It performs specific functions currently—functions that are tied to the kind of economy that we have, the unequal pattern of benefits generated by this economy, and the distribution of social and economic power that supports this structure. Technical/administrative knowledge and the importance of its production, accumulation, control, and use may contradict a proposal for widespread distribution of such knowledge. The return on investments of capital in education may not be worth the cost in the eyes of the business community. Thus, in the absence of a recognition of the larger social functions of the knowledge itself, any call for a curriculum that is based on a wider distribution of mathematical knowledge that involves expensive changes in resources and time (and that may interfere with more elitist uses of the knowledge) is vulnerable unless it participates in much larger efforts to transform the use and control of knowledge in more democratic directions.[43]

Of course, much more could and should be said here about the relationship between mathematical and scientific knowing as they are currently practiced and other forms of power relations—in particular, the connection between our definitions of rationality and gender relations.[44] My basic point, though, is to have us think much more rigorously about the ways that particular forms of knowledge act in schooling and the wider society. In our kind of economy, knowledge is also a commodity, a form of what Pierre Bourdieu calls *cultural capital*.[45] Who has it, what social purposes it serves, what socially structured patterns of benefits result from it all make a difference in determining how reforms work or indeed whether they are fully enacted in the first place.[46]

Whose Knowledge, Whose Problems?

The recognition that mathematical knowledge is often produced, accumulated, and used in ways that may not be completely democratic requires us to think carefully about the definitions of mathematical literacy with which we now work and which are embedded in the *Standards* volumes.

Educators have allowed the kinds of questions that are asked about the schooling process to be reduced largely to procedural questions. We are quite adept at answering "how-to" questions, less adept at asking and answering "why?" Thus, before we can select and organize curricular knowledge, teach it, and test it, we must take seriously Spencer's query "What knowledge is of most worth?" In doing so, we may quickly realize that behind this most difficult question lies another, even more contentious issue, "*Whose* knowledge is of most worth?"

My arguments in this article are based on a recognition that there is a complex relationship between what comes to be called official knowledge in schools and the unequal relations of power in the larger society.[47] Part of our task as educators is to enable our students in mathematics and in all of our subjects to be able to critically assess the nature of truth claims and the uses and abuses of the knowledge they are being asked to learn. I have claimed that one of the primary reasons mathematical knowledge is given high status in current reform efforts is not because of its beauty, internal characteristics, or status as a constitutive form of human knowing, but because of its socioeconomic utility for those who already possess economic capital. In order for our students to see this and to employ mathematics for purposes other than the ways that now largely dominate this society, a particular kind of mathematical literacy may be required. This draws on, but clearly extends, part of the idea of an expanded mathematical literacy called for in the *Standards*. Once again, it involves a sense of relational analysis both at the level of educational policy and in what we choose to do with students in classrooms.

Whose definition of mathematical literacy is embedded in the *Standards*? Literacy is a slippery term. Its meaning is varied because it is used by different groups with different agendas. Take the concept of "functional literacy." Functional for what? For whom? With what social effects?[48] Competing definitions of literacy are really a form of *cultural politics*.[49] They involve the very nature of the connections between cultural visions and differential power over schooling.

An example is provided by the definition of literacy as the "simple" act of learning to read and write. Books—and one's ability to read them—have themselves always been caught up in cultural politics. Take the case of Voltaire, that leader of the Enlightenment who so wanted to become a member of the nobility. For him, the Enlightenment should begin with the "grands." Only when it had captured the hearts and minds of society's commanding heights could it concern itself with "the masses" below. To Voltaire and many of his followers, one caution needed be taken very seriously, and that was to ensure that "the masses" did not learn to read.

Yet for others, teaching the masses to read had a more "beneficial" effect. It enabled a "civilizing" process, in which less powerful groups could be made more moral, more obedient, more effective and efficient as workers, and more influenced by "real culture." And for still others, literacy brought social transformation in its wake. It led to a "critical literacy," one that was part of larger social movements for a more democratic culture, economy, and polity.[50]

Thus, activities that we ask students to engage in every day, activities as "simple" and basic as reading, writing, and computing (or becoming mathematically literate) can at one and the same time be forms of regulation and social control and potential modes of social criticism and transformation. Here, one is reminded of Caliban's cry, "You taught me language; and my profit on it is, I know how to curse."[51]

My point here is that the concept of mathematical literacy is a sliding signifier. It can be used to cover a multitude of social goals. Even with the articulation of a range of goals in the *Standards* these remain largely rhetorical.[52] The goal of literacy as *critical literacy* remains muted both in the stipulation of the goals themselves and in the many examples of mathematics teaching and curricula throughout the volume.[53]

Perhaps this point can be made clearer if we focus on one of the more interesting claims of the *Standards*—that mathematics curricula and teaching should be more closely connected to the real world of student experience. A mathematics curriculum and pedagogy that is largely problem-centered and more focused on integrating mathematics into the daily lives of students is pedagogically wise. Yet, the question of *whose problems* still remains to be answered. Take as one historical instance the curricular models of the early behaviorally oriented curriculum theorists Bobbitt and Charters that influenced nearly all subsequent models of "rational" curriculum planning. They too urged all subjects to focus on, say, social problems. But their construction of these problems and their methods of generating them were strikingly conservative.[54] Their emphasis was on preserving society as it was; a more efficient society perhaps, but with the social problems chosen in such a way that there would be education for "leadership" and education for "followership." Their proposals for choosing real–world problems around which the curriculum was to be organized were based on an ideological vision that was less than democratic.[55]

The *Standards* include hints of a wider range of problems—a range that would include somewhat more socially critical material such as the proposal to organize a mathematics unit around the causes and effects of traffic congestion[56]—but such examples are relatively rarer than is necessary to overcome the conservative tendencies that already exist in schools. Thus, examples based on job loss, on the lowering of wages and benefits, on the cutbacks in welfare payments that conservative governments are forcing on already poor parents—each example and problem perhaps centered on how mathematics can help us understand what the effects of all this mean for health care (or the lack of it), nutrition, the family's finances, and even on the budget and resources of the schools the students attend—*these* kinds of problems would have been powerful ways to link mathematics to the real world of those students who are least likely to succeed in school.[57]

This question of "whose knowledge, whose problems?" is heightened when one examines the often meritorious volume on the *Profes-*

sional Standards for Teaching Mathematics. It too is articulate and organized in a style that can grab the imagination of teachers, especially in its use of a vignette format. Its focus on discourse and environment and on *how* students learn rather than merely *what* they learn, is clearly an advance. Yet, in volumes such as this, what is missing is often just as important as what is present.

One searches in vain among the specifics of what teachers should know for a substantive sense of social criticism and for a more detailed understanding of the complex and contradictory roles that mathematical knowledge may play in an unequal society. This is not an unimportant point, given my arguments about the issue of a curriculum based on real world problems. Although the experiences of girls in mathematics classes are highlighted, teachers get little help in thinking through and choosing social problems on which to focus their mathematics instruction. In a context of increasing conservatism in schools, unless teachers are prepared to deal with this as a serious issue, the positive vision of a mathematics curriculum more closely connected to the social needs and experiences of students may be transformed once again into a curriculum based on social efficiency and on definitions of "appropriate" problems of a very limited portion of the public. This may be exacerbated by the fact that the focus on the reform of mathematics education for "everyone" may marginalize or ignore the specific problems and situations of students from groups who are in the most oppressed conditions.[58]

As I noted earlier, the groups in leadership in the larger efforts to reform education are centered around the conservative agenda. In order to make its umbrella wide enough, the *Standards* gave a prime place to these groups as well. If history is any indication, such groups will selectively respond to a limited number of the reforms proposed in the documents and will sponsor those reforms publicly.[59] They will take the idea of a problem-centered curriculum and attempt to limit the range of problems that are considered to be legitimate and important. Critical literacy is decidedly not part of their agenda.

The Intensification of the Work of Teachers

The questions I have raised here about differential outcomes and how we are to think about them, about the complex roles mathematical knowledge plays in our economy, and about the redefinition of mathematical literacy and its connection with social problems obviously imply a much more active and socially aware teacher. The *Standards* do recognize this and here again they are ahead of many aspects of the conservative agenda that wishes to tighten control of curricula and teaching, a process that will ultimately deskill entire segments of the teaching profession.[60] Yet even given my positive response to the *Standards* in this regard, it is possible that the volumes do not go far enough in recognizing the depth of what is happening to the work of teachers.

One of the major groups in the coalition that the *Standards* volumes wish to include is teachers. Teaching is seen correctly as a highly complex professional activity, one that is not reducible to sets of stipulations and behavioral rules laid down from on high. This is a distinct shift from the strategies of teacher-proofing curricula that were used in earlier generations of educational reform in mathematics. In a time of increasing centralization of control and standardization of curriculum and teaching, this perspective on teaching should be applauded. However, we need always remember the reality of many teachers' lives.

Let me take as an instance, the correct recognition of the *Standards* that teaching is decision-making and its call for much greater influence by teachers in the entire range of decisions they must put into practice. I want to place this in one of the more negative changes that is occurring in the worklife of teachers, that of *intensification.*[61]

Intensification is one of the most tangible ways in which the working conditions of teachers have eroded. It has many symptoms, from the trivial to the more complex—ranging from having no time at all to even go the bathroom, have a cup of coffee, or relax, to having a total absence of time to keep up with one's field. We can see it most visibly in the chronic sense of work overload that has escalated over time. This has led to a multitude of results.

Intensification leads people to cut corners so that what is essential to the task *immediately* at hand is accomplished. It forces people to rely on "experts" to tell them what to do and to begin to mistrust the expertise they may have developed over the years. In the process, quality is sacrificed for quantity. Getting work done is substituted for work well done. And as time itself becomes a scarce commodity, isolation grows, thereby reducing the possibility of interaction and discussion among teachers to jointly share, critique, and rebuild their practices. Often the primary task is, to quote one teacher, to "find a way to get through the day." And, finally, pride itself is jeopardized as the work becomes dominated by someone else's conception of what should be done.

Because of the growth over the last decade of interventionist styles of management and a focus on reductive accountability schemes in many states, more and more curricula and the act of teaching itself are dominated by prespecified sequential lists of behaviorally defined competencies and objectives, pretests, and posttests to measure "readiness" and "skill levels," and standardized and rationalized text and worksheet material. The amount of paperwork necessary for evaluation and record keeping is often phenomenal under these conditions. These increasingly common situations often require teachers to be busy with such tasks before and after school and during their lunch hour. Teachers often come in very early and leave very late, only to be faced with two more hours of work at home every night.[62]

This is exacerbated by the fact that, given the criticisms of schools and the tendency to blame the educational system for nearly all of the social ills currently besetting the larger society, what has actually happened is that not only are curricula and teaching more tightly controlled but more, not less, has to be accomplished. Nothing has been removed from the curriculum. Instead, a considerable amount of new elements and responsibilities has been added on, not only in our elementary and secondary schools, but in our teacher education programs as well. New curriculum mandates often seem endless.

It is in this context that a call for more decision making on the part of teachers must be seen. I bring this up not to criticize the *Standards* for its articulation of what teachers need to do if its vision is to be met. Rather, it is to comment on the dangers of romanticizing the situation. Calling for a more complex perspective on teaching and arguing for more power for them in decision making is necessary, but relatively easy. The challenge is to recognize the economic, political, and ideological reasons behind the ways schools function and behind the ways teachers are currently treated and then organize to change it.[63] The inclusion in the *Standards* of teaching about such strategies for organizing and the addition of more material about the institutional realities of schools would have strengthened the *Professional Standards for Teaching Mathematics* quite a bit. As it now stands, their vision of, say, peer evaluation and peer assistance in schools and of reformed teacher education programs can too easily founder on the rocks of the daily life of teachers who already hardly have any time to complete what is now required.

To take but one example, although it is not the only dynamic at work here, one of the major underlying causes of the conditions of the work of teachers is the history of gender relations in schools and the larger society.[64] The movement by state legislatures, departments of education, educational managers, and accountability and efficiency experts to rationalize and standardize the process and products of teaching, to define all teaching as a collection of measurable competencies, to mandate very specific content and teaching, and so on, is related to a longer history of attempts to control the labor of occupations that have historically been seen as women's paid work.[65] That is, it is not possible to understand why teachers are subject to greater control and to greater governmental intervention, and what the effects of such mandates are, unless we step back and ask a particular kind of question. *Who* is doing the teaching?

Although the answer varies from field to field, in general, teaching has been constructed as women's paid work. In most Western industrialized nations, approximately two-thirds of teachers are women, a figure that is much higher the lower one goes in the educational system. Administrators are overwhelmingly male, a trend that increases significantly the higher one goes in the educational system. Thus, both statistically and in terms of its long-term effects, it would be a mistake of considerable proportions to ignore the gendered composition of teaching in general when we discuss either the underlying causes or the struggle to alter the rationalizing and intensifying conditions teachers now face.

In a document that does recognize the differential ways that girls and women are treated in mathematics and urges steps to alter that dynamic, it is equally essential that the larger gender structures that partly underpin the reasons so many teachers daily face difficult circumstances be given more recognition as well. For to change these circumstances—as the *Standards* so clearly wish to do—requires a deeper understanding of the processes of state intervention into teaching and curricula and the longer history of state intervention into the work of a female-dominated labor force.[66] A similar kind of analysis would need to be done for the issue of race and its own history and dynamics for both teachers and students.[67]

Once again, the very real insights that are incorporated into the *Standards* are limited by their lack of a more structural appraisal of the history and current functioning of schooling in general. Although a sense of some of the historical roots of why the work of teachers looks the way it does will not guarantee that we can change it, it remains very difficult to get at the underlying causes of teachers' lack of respect and power over important aspects of their lives without it.[68]

Conclusion

Murphy's well-known law, "If anything can go wrong it will," contains an important insight. Aside from the pessimism embodied in its humor, it does tacitly recognize that institutions are not organized "in ways that permit [them] passively to conform to our needs or good ideas." Given the fact that we often seem to have an infinite capacity to oversimplify, it is clear that ends and means are not always as closely linked as we often suppose. This, of course, explains the need for Sullivan's Law: "Murphy's Law is a gross underestimation."[69]

As most of us are all too well aware, the educational landscape has been littered with the remains of past efforts to reform educational that bear stark witness to Mr. Murphy and Mr. Sullivan. Because of this, and because the immense efforts of many talented educators have produced in the *Standards* a set of principles and practices that need to be taken very seriously, I have pushed the boundaries that have been defined in these documents. We must not oversimplify reality and what it will take to change it.

In this article, I have chosen to focus on a number of the areas of the *Standards* volumes that need further thought both educationally and socioeconomically. Let me reiterate, however, that this should not be taken as a negative assessment of the efforts as a whole.

At root, my claim has been that the very real elements of democratic potential within the *Standards* can be washed away in a context of rightist reaction. An understanding of this context is an essential precondition for transforming mathematics education.

I have claimed that, without giving much further thought to the realities of differential power, the economic crisis, and the social construction of what counts as mathematical literacy and of the problems it should focus on, it will be all too easy for leadership to be exerted by the most conservative elements in the ideological coalition that is organized under the umbrella of the *Standards*. Its lasting impact may be to give support to the formation of a national curriculum, guided by a national test, largely organized around rightist ideological and educational policies.[70] Its more progressive tendencies may then become rhetorics of justification, but in the long run will not be put into practice.

Yet, there are very important elements in the volumes that could help us counter parts of the conservative agenda. A broadened definition of mathematical literacy, one that is used in *critical* ways to support open and honest questioning of our society's means and ends, is clearly better than a definition that stresses workplace skills and values that largely benefit those who have power. A vision of assessment that is more humane and is guided by broader goals is clearly miles away from those proposals that would impose industrial models of artificial, and reductive, evaluation standards and procedures. A nation is not a firm and schools are not factories. We do damage to the human drama of education by even thinking of them in this way.[71]

A pedagogy of mathematics that strives to connect with the experiences of students—when these lived problems include a serious effort to use mathematical knowledge as part of a process of social criticism and renewal—is an advance over highly classified and framed curricula and teaching in which knowledge is insulated from the problems of the real world and from the lives of students.[72]

This vision is important and it does require "next steps," as the *Standards* recognize. Their listing of these steps needs considerable expansion, however. What, then, should be the next steps? These steps are both intellectual and practical. Many of the issues I have noted here have their genesis in a kind of analysis that has not had as large an impact on the community of mathematics educators as it has in other areas. Mathematics educators have begun to more clearly understand that the solution to the problems of curriculum and teaching requires a clearer focus not only on subject matter but on the institutional environment and on the structure of inequal resources in schools. But these institutions and resources, and the people who must cope with them, are themselves situated in a larger set of structural relationships that involve economic, political, and cultural power.[73] In the absence of a more thorough grasp of the connections between schooling and these larger power relations, mathematics educators may not have the intellectual resources necessary to make the changes they so clearly urge on us.

Yet such intellectual resources need to be complemented by more practical resources. There are organizations and groups of practicing educators who are now engaged in the difficult and time-consuming efforts to build considerably more progressive and community-based approaches to curriculum, teaching, and evaluation in schools throughout this country. What they do, how they deal with the crisis in resources and time, how they build a different kind of coalition that seeks progressive ends can teach mathematics educators—and all of us—what might succeed in a time of conservative reaction.[74] After all, mathematics education exists as part of a larger curriculum and needs to be thought about and integrated into the larger picture of policies and practices of transformations in the entire school itself.

Only by participating with this coalition rather than by observing it can we extend the insights found in the *Standards* into the reality of reform. In the process, we can develop resources that can counter the negative forces I have portrayed in this article. Too much work has gone into the *Standards*, and the lives and futures of too many children and teachers are at stake, for us not to take action.

Notes

1   M.W. Apple, *Ideology and Curriculum*. 2d ed. (New York: Routledge, 1990).

2   M.W. Apple, "American Realities: Poverty, Economy, and Education," in *Dropouts From Schools,* ed. L. Weis, E. Farrar, and H. Petrie (Albany: State University of New York Press, 1989), 205–23.

3   Apple, *Ideology and Curriculum;* M.W. Apple, *Education and Power* (New York: Routledge, 1985).

4   W. Secada, "Agenda Setting, Enlightened Self-Interest, and Equity in Mathematics Education," *Peabody Journal of Education* 66 (Winter 1989): 22–56.

5   Apple, "American Realities," 6; M.W. Apple, "Conservative Agendas and Progressive Possibilities," *Education and Urban Society* 23 (May 1991): 279–91.

6   M.W. Apple and L. Weis, *Ideology and Practice in Schooling* (Philadelphia: Temple University Press, 1983).

7   M.W. Apple and L.E. Beyer, "Social Evaluation of Curriculum," in *The Curriculum: Problems, Politics, and Possibilities,* ed. L.E. Beyer and M.W. Apple (Albany: State University of New York Press, 1988), 334–49.

8   B.P. Komisar and J.E. McClellan, "The Logic of Slogans," in *Language and Concepts in Education,* ed B.O. Smith and R.H. Ennis (Chicago: Rand-McNally, 1961), 195–214.

9   R. Tyler, *Basic Principles of Curriculum and Instruction* (Chicago: University of Chicago Press, 1949); J. Bruner, *The Process of Education* (New York: Vintage Books, 1960).

10   H. Kliebard, "Cultural Literacy or the Curate's Egg," *Journal of Curriculum Studies* 21 (January/February 1986): 61–70.

11   S. Sarason, *The Culture of the School and the Problem of Change* (Boston: Allyn and Bacon, 1982).

12   E.D. Hirsch Jr., *Cultural Literacy* (New York: Houghton Mifflin, 1986); Kliebard, "Cultural Literacy"; S. Aronowitz and H. Giroux, "Textual Authority, Culture, and the Politics of Literacy," in *The Politics of the Textbook*, ed. M.W. Apple and L. Christian-Smith (New York: Routledge, 1991), 213–41.

13   M.W. Apple, *Teachers and Texts* (New York: Routledge, 1988). I do not want to imply that this is always necessarily the case. Sometimes compromises are made that result in partial victories for progressive reforms. See, for example, W. Reese, *Power and the Promise of School Reform* (New York: Routledge, 1986).

14   M.W. Apple, "Redefining Equality," *Teachers College Record* 90 (Winter 1988): 167–84; Apple, *Teachers and Texts.*

15   C. Kaestle, H. Damon-Moore, L. Stedman, K. Tinsley, and W.V. Trollinger Jr., *Literacy in the United States* (New Haven: Yale University Press, 1991). The educational and political meaning of the term "functional literacy" are varied and are defined by different social agendas. *Literacy in the United States* has an interesting discussion of whether there has indeed been a sharp decline in functional literacy in the United States. I shall return to the issue of competing definitions of literacy later in this chapter.

16   Apple and Christian-Smith, *The Politics of the Textbook.*

17   Apple, *Education and Power*; Apple, "American Realities."

18   Apple, *Education and Power.*

19   M. Arnot, "Schooling for Justice" (paper presented at the 12th National Conference of the New Zealand Association for Research in Education, Auckland, New Zealand, 1990), 2.

20   Ibid., 3.

21   Apple, "Redefining Equality."

22   W. Celis, "School Districts Reeling in Weakened Economy," *The New York Times,* 5 June 1991, B10.

23   W. Celis, "Schools Lose Money in Business Tax Breaks," *The New York Times,* 22 May 1991, A1.

24   Celis, "School Districts Reeling," B10.

25   Apple, *Education and Power.*

26   Apple, *Teachers and Texts.*

27   Apple, *Teachers and Texts*; M.W. Apple and S. Jungck, "You Don't Have to Be a Teacher to Teach This Unit," *American Educational Research Journal* 27 (Summer 1990): 227–51. Although space considerations preclude my going into depth here, the issue of the new technology is a problem in its relationship to the creation of a double-peaked economy and its effects on teaching. I have discussed this in much more detail in Apple, *Education and Power;* Apple, *Teachers and Texts;* and Apple and Jungck, "You Don't Have to Be a Teacher." Before we commit ourselves to spending huge sums of money on the computerization of education, we need to understand what the paid labor market will actually look like. In many ways, economically powerful groups are not presenting a full and accurate picture to the American public. See Apple, *Teachers and Texts;* Apple, "American Realities."

28   Secada, "Equity in Mathematics Education."

29   M. Raskin, *The Common Good* (New York: Routledge, 1986).

30   See M. Levine, C. MacLennan, J. Kushma, and M. Raskin, *The State and Democracy* (New York: Routledge, 1988) and F. Green and B. Sutcliffe, *The Profit System* (New York: Penguin Books, 1987) for criticisms of and alternatives to this form of economic and political organization. Of course, the *Standards* themselves are not always sufficiently concerned with the extension of a positive structure of democracy that would focus on the most oppressed people in the United States. See Secada, "Equity in Mathematics Education" for further discussion of the contradictory tendencies at work here.

31   Apple, *Education and Power.*

32   Apple, *Ideology and Curriculum*; see also R.W. Connell, D. Ashenden, S. Kessler, and G. Dowsett, *Making the Difference* (Boston: George Allen and Unwin, 1982).

33   Apple, *Education and Power*; Apple, *Teachers and Texts*; Apple, *Ideology and Curriculum.*

34   Secada, "Equity in Mathematics Education."

35   Apple, *Education and Power.*

36   As an example, we need to remember that the largest proportion of our nation's computer operators are financed through the Defense Department or through its ancillary structures. See J. Weizenbaum, "The Computer in Your Future," *The New York Review of Books* (October 27, 1983), 30, 58–62.

37   Apple, *Education and Power.*

38   Apple, *Education and Power.*

39   Apple, *Ideology and Curriculum.*

40   Apple, *Education and Power.*

41   Secada, "Equity in Mathematics Education," 48–49.

42   See Apple, *Teachers and Texts*; Apple, "American Realities."

43   It is important to emphasize that there are and can be democratic ways of producing, controlling, and using such knowledge. The roles played by Tecnika in Nicaragua and Tec Africa in South Africa are very interesting in this regard. Currently, Tec Africa is working with the African National Congress in South Africa to provide technical assistance as the nation moves toward a true democracy. Information is available at Tec Africa, 1230 Market Street, Suite 230, San Francisco, CA 94102.

44   N. Tuana ed., *Feminism and Science* (Bloomington: Indiana University Press, 1989); D. Haraway, *Primate Visions* (New York: Routledge, 1989). For a useful description of women's contributions to mathematics and science, see G. Kass-Simon and P. Farnes, ed., *Women of Science* (Bloomington: Indiana University Press, 1990).

45   P. Bourdieu, *Distinction* (Cambridge: Harvard University Press, 1984).

46   Apple, *Education and Power.*

47   Apple, *Education and Power*; Apple, *Teachers and Texts*; Apple, *Ideology and Curriculum.*

48   Kaestle, et al., *Literacy in the United States.*

49   Apple and Christian-Smith, *The Politics of the Textbook.*

50   C. Lankshear and M. Lawler, *Literacy, Schooling and Revolution* (Philadelphia: Falmer Press, 1987).

51   J. Batsleer, T. Davies, R. O'Rourke, and C. Weedon, *Rewriting English* (New York: Methuen, 1985), 5.

52   *Standards*, 3–5.

53   A practice of mathematics education based on a more critical approach to mathematical literacy can be found in the work of Marilyn Frankenstein. See, for example, M. Frankenstein, "Critical Mathematics Education," in *Friere in the Classroom: A Sourcebook for Liberatory Teaching* (Portsmouth, NH: Boynton/Cook, Heinemann, 1987), 180–210; M. Frankenstein, *Relearning Mathematics* (London: Free Association Books, 1989).

54   H. Kliebard, *The Struggle for the American Curriculum* (New York: Routledge, 1986).

55   Apple, *Ideology and Curriculum.*

56   *Standards*, 77.

57   One could usefully compare this to Frankenstein, "Critical Mathematics Education"; Frankenstein, *Relearning Mathematics;* or to the more general emphasis in R. Simon, D. Dippo, and A. Schenke, *Learning Work* (New York: Bergin and Garvey, 1991) and I. Shor, *Critical Teaching and Everyday Life* (Chicago: University of Chicago Press, 1987).

58   See Secada, "Equity in Mathematics Education," 25.

59   Apple, "Redefining Equality"; Apple, *Teachers and Texts.*

60   Apple, *Education and Power*; Apple, *Teachers and Texts*; Apple and Jungck, "You Don't Have to Be a Teacher."

61   Apple, *Teachers and Texts.*

62   Apple, *Teachers and Texts*; A. Gitlin, "School Structure and Teachers' Work," in *Ideology and Practice in Schooling* (Philadelphia: Temple University Press, 1983), 193–212.

63   See D. Liston and K. Zeichner, *Teacher Education and the Social Conditions of Schooling* (New York: Routledge, 1991).

64 Apple, *Teachers and Texts*.

65 As I argue at greater length elsewhere, the emphasis on "teacher-proof" material in mathematics and science curricula in the 1960s and early 1970s is a prime example of this phenomenon. See Apple, *Teachers and Texts*.

66 Apple, *Teachers and Texts*; S. Franzway, D. Court, and R.W. Connell, *Staking a Claim: Feminism, Bureaucracy and the State* (Boston: Allen and Unwin, 1989).

67 M. Omi and H. Winant, *Racial Formation in the United States* (New York: Routledge, 1986); D. Warren, ed., *American Teachers: Histories of a Profession at Work* (New York: Macmillan, 1989).

68 See Warren, ed., *American Teachers*.

69 S. Sarason, *The Predictable Failure of School Reform* (San Francisco: Jossey-Bass, 1990).

70 Apple, *Teachers and Texts*.

71 Apple and Christian-Smith, *The Politics of the Textbook*.

72 B. Bernstein, *Class, Codes, and Control*, vol. III, 2d ed. (London: Routledge and Kegan Paul, 1977).

73 See Apple, *Education and Power*; Apple, *Teachers and Texts*; Apple, *Ideology and Curriculum*.

74 See Apple, "Conservative Agendas and Progressive Possibilities."

Chapter 7

How the Conservative Restoration Is Justified

In a series of recent volumes, I have critically examined the increasingly conservative turn taken by educational policy in recent years. In the process, I have analyzed the major transformations that have occurred in what education is for, in how it is to be carried out, and in who ultimately benefits the most from these transformations.[1] Although these policies have complex and sometimes even contradictory histories and impulses, it is becoming ever more clear that—although they are couched in democratic rhetoric—the ultimate effect of these "reforms" will be to exacerbate existing inequalities.[2]

In this essay, I want to ask a seemingly simple question. How are these inequalities justified publicly? What "common sense" is used to explain and legitimize policies that seem to result in more inequalities? I want to offer a suggestive analysis of one of the strands of such logics of justification. In the United States and in many other nations, a major strand that surfaces time and again involves the use of moral and biological logics to "explain" widespread inequalities. Although my analysis will be wide-ranging, a good deal of my focus will be on one case in point: the social uses of such arguments about race, gender, and intelligence as were crystallized in Richard Herrnstein and Charles Murray's *The Bell Curve* to support rightist policies in education and in the larger society.[3]

There have been scores of critical reviews of *The Bell Curve*.[4] It is not difficult to demonstrate that its claims about genetics and about the nature of intelligence—that people of color (and women in a number of important areas) are on average less intelligent than "white" men—are at best shaky and at worst simply untenable. I do not wish to recapitulate these criticisms in this essay, although I very much agree with them. Rather, I want to situate *The Bell Curve* as a phenomenon within the social and educational upheavals experienced by this society currently and in the past.

This is a time when conservative groups have recognized that in order to win in the state you must win in civil society. Thus, there now exists a complicated politics of common sense through which dominant groups are attempting to redefine what we actually mean by democracy, equality, and the common good.[5] In order to understand the reasons behind the broad circulation of ideas such as those embodied in *The Bell Curve*, we need to understand as well the larger processes involved in the reconstruction of common sense. This shall be my agenda for this essay.

In a piece of this limited size, I can but point to the historical and current tendencies and dynamics involved. But an outline of what is going on should be readily visible. In order to accomplish this, I shall need to move back and forth in time. I shall need as well to move back and forth among educational and other institutions and between cultural and economic dynamics, detailing the broader conservative restorational politics in education and other parts of society. In the story I wish to detail—class, gender, and especially racial dynamics will play a large part.

Between Neoliberalism and Neoconservatism

Many of the rightist policies now taking center stage in education and nearly everything else embody a tension between an emphasis on "market values" on the one hand and a neoconservative attachment to "traditional values" on the other.[6] From the former perspective, the state must be minimized, preferably by setting private enterprise loose; from the latter perspective, the state needs to play a strong role in teaching *correct* knowledge, norms, and values. From both perspectives, this society is falling apart, in part because schools don't do either of these tasks. Schools are too controlled by the state and they don't mandate the teaching of what they are "supposed" to teach. It's a bit contradictory, but as I have demonstrated elsewhere the rightist agenda has ways of dealing with such contradictions and has managed to creatively stitch together an alliance that unites (sometimes rather tensely) its various movements.[7]

This new hegemonic alliance has a wide umbrella. It combines four major groups: a) dominant neoliberal economic and political elites intent on "modernizing" the economy and the institutions connected to it; b) economic and cultural neoconservatives who want a return to "high standards," discipline, and Social Darwinist competition; c) largely white working-class and middle-class groups who mistrust the state and are concerned with security, the family, and traditional and especially religious knowledge and values and who form an increasingly active segment of what might be called authoritarian populists; and d) a fraction of the new middle class who may not totally agree with these other groups, but whose own professional interests and advancement depend on the expanded use of accountability, efficiency, and management procedures that are their own cultural capital.[8]

The sphere of education is one in which the Right has been ascendant. The social democratic goal of expanding equality of opportunity (itself a rather limited reform) has lost much of its political potency and its ability to mobilize people. The "panic" over falling standards, dropouts, and illiteracy; the fear of violence in schools; and the concern over the destruction of family values and religiosity have all had an effect. These fears are exacerbated, and used, by dominant groups in politics and the economy who have been able to shift the debate about education (and all things social) onto their own terrain—the terrain of traditionalism, standardization, productivity, marketization, and industrial needs. Because so many parents *are* justifiably concerned about the economic and cultural futures of their children—in an economy that is increasingly conditioned by lower wages, capital flight, and insecurity—rightist discourse connects with the experiences of many working-class and middle-class people.[9]

Behind much of the conservative restoration is a clear sense of loss of control over a number of things: economic and personal security, the knowledge and values that should be passed on to children, what counts as sacred texts and authority, and relations of gender and age in the family. The binary opposition of we/they becomes important here. "We" are law abiding, "hard working, decent, virtuous, and homogeneous." The "theys" are very different. They are "lazy, immoral, permissive, and heterogeneous."[10] These binary oppositions distance most people of color, women (especially "feminists"), gays, lesbians, and bisexuals, and others from the community of worthy individuals. The subjects of discrimination are now no longer those groups who have been historically oppressed, but are instead the "real citizens" who embody the idealized virtues of a romanticized past. In the ideology of the conservative restoration, the "theys" are undeserving. They are getting something for nothing. Policies that support "them" are "sapping our way of life," draining most of our economic resources, and creating government control of our lives.[11]

As with much of the ideological agenda behind such criticisms, the issues in education are the removal of schools from state and bureaucratic control, the enhancement of privatization and marketization, and the reconstruction of a people's character based largely on individual entrepreneurial values or on fundamentalist interpretations of "Christian" morality.

Though my tone may be negative when discussing these seemingly unremitting attacks on the state, on schools, on the public sphere in general, and on the "other," this should not be interpreted as an assumption that everything that the government does "in the public interest" in education or anything else is always wise. Indeed, it is possible to argue that because of ideological conflicts, insufficient resources, and their own interests and internal structures, governments are often organized to generate failure.

In fact, some analysts have provocatively argued that, paradoxically, one of the conditions of government expansion (a very sore point with conservatives, as you know) is that it must fail to reach its goals. Although he overstates his case, Ian Hunter puts it this way: "Government thereby programs its own failure and it does so as a condition of its ongoing and truly remarkable inventiveness."[12] Governments often have ever-expanding horizons, goals, and spheres of interest (for example, equity, equality of opportunity, and so on) that under the current distribution of power and resources simply cannot be met. Yet, in order to maintain its own legitimacy and the continued need for all of its offices, programs, and personnel, the state must be seen to be striving to meet these goals and must continually measure itself against them. Thus, "demonstrating its own failure in this way is the means by which government opens up new tracts of social life to bureaucratic knowledge and intervention."[13] It should not be a surprise, then, that not all of these forms of knowledge and intervention necessarily meet the long-term interests of those who are the subjects of them. And here some of the intuitions of conservatives seem to have an element of insight.

This is *not* to say, however, as the New Right does, that what is public is bad and what is private is good, that the very idea of government regulation is a threat to freedom. Rather, it is to remind us of the connections among resources, power, institutional interests, failure, and hence, continued bureaucratization and expansion. It is clear that this very sense of bureaucratization, inefficiency, and expansion underpins many of the attacks on schools and the state.

Consider the current calls for educational reform that surround the ties between education and (paid) work. A large portion of current reform initiatives are partly justified by a desire to enhance the connections between education and the wider project of "meeting the needs of the economy." This increasingly powerful economic critique of the educational system is grounded in a number of challenges. The system is basically antientrepreneurial. It is horribly wasteful. And, at a time of severe international competition, schools are failing to produce a labor force that is sufficiently skilled, adaptable, and flexible.[14] Attached to this sense of schools as producers of "human capital" is an equally crucial cultural agenda concerning the sets of social logics that should guide our daily conduct.

For neoliberals and neoconservatives alike, the educational task here is "not only [to] encourage members of a market economy to think of themselves as individuals in order to maximize their own interests." This is a crucial goal, but it goes considerably further. People also need to be encouraged to accept that it is entirely "appropriate for there to be winners and losers in the system."[15] Genetic explanations—most of which cannot be evaluated by the general public—assist this acceptance in powerful ways. It is also assisted by claiming that a process such as this is "wealth creating."

Part of this position on the distribution of wealth—that inequality is a good thing and that more inequality is an even better thing—can be found in a quote from Keith Joseph, a former minister of education for Margaret Thatcher.

> The relief of poverty has not in the past been thought to require an equal society and it is difficult to find any necessary connection between them today. On the contrary, everything in the experience of this country since the last war has combined to demonstrate that you cannot make the poor richer by making the rich poorer. You can only make the poor richer by making everyone richer including the rich.[16]

Friedrich Hayek, one of the economic theorists relied upon by many conservatives, states the case even more bluntly:

> If today in the United States or Western Europe the relatively poor can have a car or a refrigerator, an airplane trip or a radio, at the cost of a reasonable part of their income, this was made possible because in the past others with

larger incomes were able to spend on what was then a luxury. The path of advance is greatly eased by the fact that it has been trodden before. It is because scouts have found the goal that the road can be built for the less lucky and less energetic. . . . Even the poorest today owe their relative material well-being to the results of past inequality.[17]

Of course, these empirical claims are subject to evidence. We must indeed ask, in the United States and Britain of the New Right, as the rich got richer did the poor get less poor? The answer to this would be nearly laughable were it not for the disastrous consequences of such redistribution upwards, for that is indeed what has happened as the lives of so many people have become increasingly insecure and even desperate.[18]

Like the neoliberal position with its romantic vision of the market, the neoconservative agenda also has its interesting contradictions. Although it may seem clear that such conservatism lends its support to that which is "traditional" in society, it should be just as clear that its allegiance is more than a little selective. It does not support *all* that is traditional in society.[19]

One of the distinguishing features of the neoconservative position is its vision of character. There is a clear preference for incentive systems rather than the encouragement of social altruism, although the latter is sometimes mentioned in its "bag of virtues" approach to moral education.[20] Yet the tradition of altruism has just as deep roots in our nations and its expression should be expanded, not contracted. Selfishness is simply another form of the possessive individualism that has been one of the more destructive parts of social policies institutionalized in our nations over the past two decades.[21]

When they criticize the educational system, commentators of the neoconservative persuasion are often so very concerned about the supposed lack of values found among, say, inner city children. Yet, perhaps this is not the primary place we should focus. Rather, we need to ask critical questions about the values of those groups of people—groups with considerably more power and money—who made the political and economic decisions that segregated these communities economically and racially. In essence, rather than studying the poor, we might justifiably study the nearly "pathological detachment" of the affluent and of their allies in government and in neoconservative intellectual and policy circles.[22]

Even with these variations of emphasis in some of the multiple but overlapping tendencies within the conservative movement, there seems to be agreement on one thing among many of these tendencies. It is an agreement whose class, race, and gender history is certainly not innocent. It is an agreement that enables us to better understand the circulation of material such as *The Bell Curve*.

Creating a Golden Age

In nearly all English-speaking countries, though certainly not limited to them, the various factions of the Right have forced the relationship between the market and the common good onto the political stage. Among the most influential of these ideas have been the following: that the welfare state, and the social contract that stands behind it, has not been a "good thing" for the economy because "we" simply cannot afford it; that it has limited the exercise of free democratic choice because of entrenched, mainly professional, interests; and, that it is destructive to the character of the poor because it makes "them" dependent.[23]

Nearly all of the literature supporting this position invokes an earlier "golden age" before the welfare state, when policies were becoming economically and morally sound, when normative and institutional structures were stable, and when class, gender, and racial harmony prevailed as we moved toward "progress." The state was not needed for the common good. The debate over government's role in both creating and maintaining the common good in education and elsewhere is as old as government itself. Behind the conflict over, say, workfare and learnfare in the United States[24] and the demand that "unworthy" people should not get "something for nothing" is a very long history. This is rooted in the "workhouse test" that played such a significant part in how the United States, England, and other nations have often dealt with the poverty caused by economic dislocations. Earlier relief systems were often based on a conscious attempt to separate the "deserving" poor from the "undeserving" poor. They were also usually characterized by a distinct lack of shyness in blaming the poor for their fate.

In Jane Lewis's words:

> The nineteenth century poor law, which operated in England and parts of the United States, Canada and Australia, aimed firmly to distinguish between the poor and the pauper. Claimants were offered the "workhouse test" to determine whether or not they were truly destitute, the idea being the conditions within the workhouse would be less favorable than those of the lowest paid

laborer. If a claimant were prepared to accept relief on such terms, then s/he might be reckoned to be truly destitute. . . . The principle was clear enough. What the nineteenth century system of welfare provision aimed to do was effectively to segregate the pauper from the market, incarcerating him or her in a workhouse where men were deprived of the vote (if indeed they qualified for one under the limited franchise) and where such work as was offered ([of-ten] stone crushing for men and oakum picking for women) would not inter-fere with the local labor market.[25]

In essence, the poor were a "race apart."[26] They could be incarcer-ated, deprived of basic rights of citizenship, and treated as not worthy of personhood. The relationship of these ideas to class dynamics is clear. Yet there has always been a connection between these policies and race and gender as well; biological and moral explanations usually lie just beneath the surface.

Take the Victorian ideals of gender and the family, for example, as they were institutionalized at the turn of the century in a number of nations. For Victorians, like many of today's conservatives, social prob-lems disappeared when the family was strong and effective. Such a family—husbands who were reliable breadwinners and wives who were efficient managers in the home—cared for the old and infirm and so-cialized children into "the habits of labor and obedience."[27] Women's paid work was frowned upon because it might damage male work incentives. Yet, the Victorians were of two minds when it came to poor women, especially those who were alone. Although they wished to encourage and/or enforce male labor market participation and were attached to the (biologically rooted) idea that the "proper" role of women was in the home, applying the same standard to the increasingly large numbers of, say, widowed, deserted, or unmarried mothers presented them with a dilemma.[28] And here an intricate moral hierarchy entered to complement the effects of the even earlier losses of poor people's personhood, respect, and citizenship rights.

Government officials had a decision to make. Were these women to be treated as mothers or as workers? On the whole, they chose the latter. Here the moral hierarchy entered in new forms. Widows were counted as "more deserving." They were usually allowed to keep as many children as they could support through their paid labor, usually one or two. The rest were taken to the workhouse or to orphanages. "Deserted wives" who had the courage (and it did take immense cour-age) to seek help and to officially declare that they indeed were desti-tute were much more harshly treated. Government authorities were deeply suspicious of collusion between spouses. Working-class men might be living off of "their women's" benefits. "Unmarried mothers" were seen as morally reprehensible. Often the only relief available to them was to enter the workhouse.[29]

All too much of this is redolent of current rightist discourse around the poor and especially poor women (and men). This constructs an image of, for example, the poor African American or Afro-Caribbean man who lives off "his woman's" welfare check; of morally uncontrollable poor women; of poor unmarried women who drop out of school and have baby after baby simply to get more money. This distressingly biased and empirically problematic image of the poor is what stands behind many of the social and educational policies of the conservative restoration today.[30] For the rightist coalition, the answer is to revivify their image of the traditional family, to force a form of slavery or indentured servitude on poor people of color and the poor in general, and to create a vision of the poor once again as totally the cause of their own conditions.[31] Volumes such as *The Bell Curve* provide pseudo-scientific legitimacy for such positions. Back to the future?

The *image* of the family—not the reality, which is and has been very varied throughout the history of the United States and elsewhere— plays a central part in this ideological drama.[32] Just as in earlier times, the discourse of the family can be used for many social purposes. In this case, as before, its use is more than a little retrogressive.

For example, members of the neoconservative and authoritarian populist Right believe that it is the family's role—a role defined by genetic, moralistic, and religious "givens"—to act as a "guardian of social stability within an aggressively competitive economy." How are we to minimize the state? Part of the answer is to maximize the family. In Arnot's words, "By rehabilitating the family, [we] could break down the 'scrounger state' and through a 'moral crusade' counter the effects of permissiveness and arguably feminism."[33]

It is evident from this discussion that there clearly are patriarchal elements and intentions within the conservative restoration; but an anti-feminist stance is not all that is behind a good many of its policies. We need always to remember that the guiding set of principles for a significant portion of this agenda is to increase profits by raising productivity, cutting costs, weakening the collective organizations of paid workers, and disciplining workers through a fear of unemployment. Given the need of capital for the paid labor of women, the Right could not only pursue a policy of returning women to the family and domestic labor. It had to aggressively integrate women into the paid labor market. Yet, the process through which this integration occurred was carried out under the "worst possible terms" for these women. [34] Protection was reduced; unemployment rates remained high; child care was not provided by the state; domestic burdens were actually increased as the state withdrew its support of social services and programs and then threw its responsibilities onto a private sector that never totally compensated for the loss. For working-class women and women of color, the cumulative effect of these policies was devastating. Their opportunities were severely restricted and the kinds of work available to them did indeed represent "the worst possible conditions." An understanding of gender, *and* race, *and* class is essential then to understand both the contradictory intentions and effects of the conservative restoration.

These intentions and effects at times appear contradictory; for example, the proper role for women is at once to be recruited into the paid workforce for economic reasons, *and* to stay at home in order to reproduce the "traditional family." But, overall, the rightist alliance has effectively created the conditions that give it increasing hegemonic power over policies and over even how we talk about what is right and wrong in the economy, social welfare, politics, and, as many of you know all too well from personal experience, education. The discourse of the alliance combines two kinds of language: of children as "future workers," of privatization and market choice for "consumers," of business needs and of tighter accountability and control on the one hand; and of "Christian" values, the Western tradition, the traditional family, and back to the "basics" on the other. These two languages, spoken simultaneously, have created such a din that it is hard to hear anything else. Putting these two kinds of language together, as the rightist coalition does, gives it immense power. It threatens to become truly hegemonic. In the process, it both creates and marginalizes those "others" who do not fit inside either its aggressively competitive and individuating market or its limited yet universalizing moral universe.

Constructing Dependency

So far, I have focused largely on a number of the crucial historic and current social dynamics such as gender that have constructed the terrain upon which the conservative restoration operates. As I noted, behind these dynamics is an attempt to create biological and moral explanations—rather than structural ones—for those populations who remain "uncompetitive." This is part of a larger process in which dominant groups export the blame for the consequences of their own decisions away from themselves and onto those groups who suffer the most from these decisions.[35] A key element in these explanations is how the issue of dependency is construed. And, once again, many nations have powerful historical legacies that make it easier for arguments such as those found in *The Bell Curve* to find a ready audience. Race is the constitutive starting point here. Indeed, I do not think it is possible to understand the conservative restoration at all without placing race in the forefront of our analyses. I shall focus on the United States here, first because the dynamics are clear there and second because I am more personally and politically grounded in these debates in the United States.

As Cornel West reminds us, the enslavement of Africans—over 20 percent of the population of the American nation at the time—"served as the linchpin of American democracy." Thus, it is not an overstatement to suggest that "the much-heralded stability and continuity of American democracy was predicated upon black oppression and degradation."[36] Slavery as a legally sanctioned act may be over, but the racial structuring of the country is worsening every day.[37]

Of course, much the same must be said about the ways in which colonial and neocolonial forms underpinned the economic and ideological power of Britain. A similar point is made eloquently in Homi Bhabha's discussion. As he says, "The Western metropole must confront its postcolonial history, told by its influx of postwar migrants and refugees as an indigenous or native narrative *internal to its national identity*." Bhabha goes on. Paraphrasing the words of a character in a Salmon Rushdie novel, he reminds us that "The problem with the English is that their history happened overseas, so they don't know what it means."[38]

For decades in the United States, new patterns of segregation have become clear and intensified, as European Americans have moved to the suburbs and abandoned the inner cities. One result of this is that urban areas, in essence, have become "reservations," with majority African American and Latino/Latina populations and declining or disintegrating tax bases. Local governments in these urban areas are less and less able to meet even the basic needs of their citizens. The nation as a whole, in concert with these trends, is steadily moving toward a politics centered on the suburban vote. The growth of suburbanization enables white middle-class voters to "fulfill communitarian impulses by taxing themselves for direct services (for example, schools, libraries, police), while ignoring urban decay and remaining fiscally conservative about federal spending."[39] This is an ideal situation for suburbanites since it allows them to shield their tax dollars from going into educational and social programs that benefit the poor and racial minorities.[40] And as conditions in these inner cities worsen significantly, the structural relations that concretely tie suburban benefits to urban disintegration—in a manner so reminiscent of the history of stable democracy and economic progress that was bought at the cost of black slavery and exploitation—lead us to blame the poor for being too "dependent." This is not a new phenomenon for the United States in any way and complements my earlier discussion of gender and the workhouse test.

Historically, the United States has been especially hospitable to the development of the belief that dependency is "a defect of individual character." Given the fact that the country lacked a strong legacy of feudalism and aristocracy, the widespread popular sense of reciprocal relations between lord and "man" was underdeveloped. The older preindustrial meanings of dependency as an *ordinary, majority condition* that were widespread in Europe were very weak here, where pejorative meanings were much stronger. Thus, whereas in the colonial period dependency was seen largely as a voluntary condition (except for the slave) as in being an indentured servant, the American Revolution "so valorized independence that it stripped dependency of its voluntarism, emphasized its powerlessness and imbued it with stigma."[41]

In their investigation of the very idea of dependency and its social uses in the United States, Nancy Fraser and Linda Gordon suggest the following.

> The American love affair with independence was politically double-edged. On the one hand, it helped nurture powerful labor and women's movements. On the other hand, the absence of a hierarchical social tradition in which subordination was understood to be structured, not characterological, facilitated hostility to public support for the poor. Also influential was the very nature of the American state, weak and decentralized in comparison to European states throughout the nineteenth century. All told, the United States proved fertile soil for the moral/psychological discourse of dependency.[42]

In current conditions, there is now increasing stigmatization of any dependency. "All dependency is suspect, and independence is enjoined on everyone."[43] Yet it is wage labor that is the identifacatory sign of independence. In essence, "the worker"—one who is "self-support-ing"—becomes the universal subject. Any adult who is not perceived to be a worker carries an immense burden of self-justification. After all, we all "know" that this economy and this nation have removed the barriers to work for anyone who really wants it. Yet this is not a neu-tral description of reality. It smuggles in a considerable number of normative claims, not the least of which is in its assumption that the worker has access to a job paying a living wage and is also not a primary parent.[44]

There are two major results of this. The first is to increase the already strong negative connotations associated with dependency. The second is to increase even more its individualization. Both are ideally suited to an articulation of the connections between race and gender and dependency that have played such a strong role in constructing dominant discourses in the nation's history. As I noted, seeing depen-dency as a character trait was already beginning to be widespread in the early years of the nation. This sense is given more power currently now that the legal barriers (for example, formal and legally recognized overt segregation in schools and elsewhere) have supposedly ended. With the changes in coverture (the legal status of women in marriage) and Jim Crow (discriminatory laws that in essence legalized apartheid in the Southern states of the United States) brought about by the successful struggles by women and African Americans, it has now become possible for some groups to argue that equality of opportu-nity really exists; that it is individual merit, nothing else, that deter-mines outcomes.[45] Fraser and Gordon put it in the following way:

> The groundwork for that view was laid by industrial usage, which defined dependency so as to exclude capitalist relations of subordination. With capi-talist economic dependency already abolished by definition, and with legal and political dependency now abolished by law, postindustrial society appears to some conservatives and liberals to have eliminated every social structural basis of dependency. Whatever dependency that remains, therefore, can be interpreted as the fault of individuals. That interpretation does not go uncon-tested, to be sure, but the burden of argument has shifted. Now those who deny that the fault lies in themselves must swim upstream against the prevail-ing semantic currents. Postindustrial dependency is increasingly individualized.[46]

In this scenario, the poor get poor the old fashioned way; they earn it. They are dependent and therefore are "the other," either by reason of their individual character traits or by reason of their collective genetic endowment, as *The Bell Curve* would have it. Either way, as in the case of suburbia, it's not "our" problem.

We now face a situation in which "economic dependency" has become a synonym for the immense *creation* of poverty by the economic apparatus of this society. It is as if something of a new personality disorder called moral/psychological dependency is in the air. Those who are poor are talked about as morally and genetically inferior once again. Talk of dependency as a fully *social relation of subordination* has become all too rare.[47] In the process, power and domination become invisible (except of course to those people who experience how such relations are painfully present every day).

The Politics of Whiteness

This lack is very visible in public discussions of educational policy and of social policy in general. Yet it is at the level of common sense, especially in the increasingly common understandings of race that are now circulating in many nations, that some of the most dangerous effects are now taking shape.

Underpinning much of the neoliberal and neoconservative discourse about education—the supposed decline in standards, the call for a return to the "Western tradition," the reassertion of toughness and discipline, the insistent calls for privatization and marketization—lies a vision of "the Other." It symbolizes an immense set of anxieties that are used not only to build a new hegemonic alliance around conservative policies, but also to structure our understanding of daily experience. Let me take the issue of "whiteness" as a way to pry loose how this works.

The growing acceptance of genetic and moral arguments about race and of conservative restorational politics in general can only be understood if we focus on how race is constructed and used as a social category. For many people, "white racial hegemony has rendered whiteness invisible or transparent."[48] Thus, whiteness has become the unarticulated normative structure. It has become so naturalized that people do not even have to think about "being white." It has become an absent presence, the "there that is not there." As Roman puts it, race has become a "reified synonym" that is applied only to racially subordinated groups."[49] The racial "other" always "wants more." "We", on the other hand, do not.

Yet such invisibility is now increasingly articulated with a growing sense of white racial identity that underpins many of the attacks on the gains people of color have slowly made through decades of hard work and struggle. Racial identities among many whites—formed partly out of a politics of common sense during a period of conservative restructuring—are becoming increasingly powerful and volatile. For example, as Gallagher has documented, for many white working-class and middle-class students in schools there is now a belief that there is a social cost to being white. Whites are the "new losers" in a playing field that they believe has been leveled now that the United States is a supposedly "egalitarian, colorblind society."[50] These students have constructed identities that avow a "legitimate, positive narrative of one's own whiteness . . . that negated white oppressor charges and framed whiteness as a liability."[51] Because "times were rough for everybody," but policies such as affirmative action in education and the economy unfairly supported "nonwhites," these students now claimed the status of victims.[52] As Gallagher puts it:

> A fundamental transformation of how [many] young whites define and understand themselves racially is taking place. [They] have generally embraced the belief that the US class system is fair and equitable. [They] argue that individuals who delay gratification, work hard, and follow the rules will succeed regardless of color. . . . For many whites the levelled playing field argument has rendered affirmative action policies a form of reverse discrimination and a source of resentment. White students who believe social equality has been achieved are able to assert a racial identity without regarding themselves as racists.[53]

These arguments point to something of considerable moment in the politics of education in a number of nations. As it is being shaped by the political Right, whiteness as an explicit cultural product is taking on a life of its own. In the arguments of the conservative discourses now so powerfully circulating—arguments that are the absent presence behind the claims about many of the "reform" initiatives such as national curricula, national testing, and privatized choice plans in a number of nations—the barriers to social equality and equal opportunity in education and the economy have been removed. Whites, hence, have no privilege. Any inequalities that occur are "personal"— the result of laziness, immorality, defects of character, or, increasingly, of biological inferiority. *The Bell Curve* becomes "sensible" here. The implications of all these beliefs are not inconsequential in the debates about urban schools, differential educational and economic achievement, educational finance, and over how schools should be "reformed" to deal with these issues.

Conclusion

In this essay, I have suggested that one of the best ways to understand *The Bell Curve* is to place it back into the larger context of transformations of educational, political, and economic institutions. I have argued that the politics of its reception are strongly related to historical dynamics that have played a large part in the past of many nations and in current treatments of gender, class, and especially race—and of the poor in general.

Changing this requires a thoroughgoing reconstruction of our understanding of how this society operates. One of the keys here is at the level of our common sense. We need to stop thinking—as the Right does—of the poor as "others," and instead need to substitute a vision of "us." This change needs to be accompanied by a restriction of market models of human activity to their appropriate, and very limited, boundaries. We should reassert the significance of positive freedom based on human dignity, community, and the realization of democracy not just in education but in all of our institutions.[54]

All of this requires a rejection of arguments such as those found in *The Bell Curve*. Instead, it necessitates the reconstruction of our discourse about poverty and welfare, a reconstruction that seeks to regain our sense of ethics and community. Michael Katz argues that such a reconstitution needs to be based on five general tenets: 1) reawakening our sense of moral outrage at the deadly persistence of homelessness, hunger, absent or inadequate health care, and other forms of deprivation rather than pursuing a pseudoscientific search for genetic explanations; 2) defending and enlarging the principles of human dignity, community, and the realization of democracy in concrete events in our daily lives, rather than the increasing emphasis on social Darwinist policies in the public arena; 3) reinventing ways of talking about poor persons not as "them" but as "us"; 4) restricting market models to very limited spheres so that social justice—not profit and loss—provides the dominant lens through which we examine social and educational policies; and 5) strategically connecting these progressive points to other widely shared values, such as liberty, by showing how poverty undermines families (of many kinds), community, the economy, and so on.[55] It also demands that we look *directly* at the racial dynamics that underlie our national and international histories and present.

Although each of these points requires the development of detailed policies and sources of revenue, they also require creative resources (something in abundance among *all* parts of the United States and British population) and political will. The *fundamental* questions, however, are about "the basis of community, the conditions of citizenship, and the achievement of human dignity." In even starker terms, these questions are simply and profoundly about our definition of personhood, just how much we are willing to do to realize it, who is the "we" in the first place, and who shall be engaged at all levels in deciding this.[56]

The spread of a rightist common sense will no doubt make this difficult. Yet, it is not naturally preordained that the populist sentiments shared by many people must be organized around conservative social movements. The urge to have power over one's life, to actually be listened to by the state, to care deeply about one's cultural roots and traditions, can provide the basis for a less authoritarian and more socially just formation as well.[57] Thus, studying the Right, as I have done here, may be more important than we may realize. They have recognized how important it is to build social movements that connect the local with the global. They have been more than a little successful in reorganizing common sense by engaging in a truly widespread educational project in *all* spheres of society—in the economy, in politics, and in the media and cultural apparatus. There are lessons to be learned here. The Right has proven that long-term engagement in cultural politics can be effective. Those of us who decry the authoritarian tendencies in their message could do worse than to study the ways in which such messages seem to successfully connect with the hopes, fears, dreams, and despair of many people. Taken together, the commissioning, writing, publishing, and massive publicity campaign accorded to *The Bell Curve* provides a case study of how this is done.

I am not asking us to copy some aspects of the Right, in their cynical, well-financed, and often manipulative politics.[58] Rather, I am saying that something important has gone on here, something that is, in essence, one of the largest "educational" projects we have seen this century. Transformations of common sense take time and organization and commitment; but they also must make connections with people's daily lives if they are to be widely successful. These are not inconsequential points. They speak to the need to engage in the long-term project of building such connections in more progressive terms in education and in all other spheres of society, much like the work of the educational activists who reject the moralizing and biological arguments of the Right and work so closely with their communities as described in *Democratic Schools*[59] (Apple and Beane, 1995). Needless to say, there is work to be done. Otherwise, the arguments crystallized in *The Bell Curve* will mark the success of rightist common sense again. We cannot afford to allow this to happen once more.

Notes

This article was given as the Carfax Lecture at the British Educational Research Association annual meeting in Lancaster, 13 September 1996. I wish to thank Geoff Whitty and Sally Powers for their comments on it. A briefer version appears in Joe Kincheloe and Shirley Steinberg, eds. *Measured Lies.*

1   M.W. Apple, *Official Knowledge* (New York: Routledge, 1993); M.W. Apple, *Education and Power,* 2d edition (New York: Routledge, 1995); M.W. Apple, *Cultural Politics and Education* (London: Open University Press, 1996).

2   G. Whitty, "Creating Quasi-Markets in Education," in *Review of Research in Education,* vol. 21, ed. M.W. Apple (Washington, DC: American Educational Research Association, 1997); Apple, *Cultural Politics and Education.*

3   R. Herrnstein and C. Murray, *The Bell Curve* (New York: The Free Press, 1994).

4   See, for example, J. Kincheloe and S. Steinberg, ed., *Measured Lies* (New York: St. Martin's Press, 1996).

5   Apple, *Official Knowledge;* Apple, *Cultural Politics and Education.*

6   G. Whitty, T. Edwards, and S. Gewirtz, *Specialisation and Choice in Urban Education* (London: Routledge, 1993), 48–49.

7   Apple, *Cultural Politics and Education.*

8   For more about this alliance or coalition, see my *Official Knowledge* and *Cultural Politics and Education.* On the new middle class and its own ideological tendencies and tensions, see B. Bernstein, *The Structuring of Pedagogic Discourse* (New York: Routledge, 1990).

9   See Apple, *Cultural Politics and Education,* 42–67.

10   I. Hunter, *Rethinking the School* (St. Leonards, Australia: Allen and Unwin, 1987), 23.

11   I. Hunter, "The Politics of Resentment and the Construction of Middle America" (unpublished paper, University of Madison-Wisconsin, Department of Sociology), 30.

12   Hunter, *Rethinking the School,* 134. I do not necessarily agree with a number of the arguments in Hunter's book, but in this case he is very insightful.

13   Hunter, *Rethinking the School,* 12.

14   Whitty, Edwards, and Gewirtz, *Specialisation and Choice,* 6–7. This is one of the best empirical studies of the genesis and effects of rightist reforms.

15   Ibid., 11.

16   T. Honderich, *Conservatism* (Boulder, CO: Westview, 1990), 196.

17   Quoted in Honderich, *Conservatism,* 197.

18   See A. Sherman, *Wasting America's Future* (Boston: Beacon Press, 1994); Apple, *Cultural Politics and Education.*

19   Honderich, *Conservatism,* 160.

20   Ibid., 105.

21   M.W. Apple, *Ideology and Curriculum,* 2d ed. (New York: Routledge, 1990).

22   J. Kozol, *Savage Inequalities* (New York: Crown, 1991), 193–94.

23   J. Lewis, "Back to the Future: A Comment on American New Right Ideas About Welfare and Citizenship in the 1980s," *Gender and History* 3 (Autumn 1991): 326.

24   Learnfare and workfare are the "reforms" of the welfare system in the United States that have different characteristics depending on the specific state in which a person lives. In general, Learnfare denies or reduces welfare benefits to any parent whose school-age child is not regularly attending school. Workfare denies or limits benefits to those parents who are not engaged in paid work, including, say, mothers of young children. This is the case even though child care is often not provided and/or insufficient jobs are available.

25   Lewis, "Back to the Future," 329.

26   Ibid.

27   Ibid., 331.

28   Ibid., 332.

29   Ibid.

30   P. Burdell, "Teen Mothers in High Schools," in *Review of Research in Education,* vol. 21, ed. M.W. Apple (Washington, DC: American Educational Research Association, 1996).

31   Lewis, "Back to the Future," 332–33. For an impressive analysis of this process, see N. Fraser and L. Gordon, "A Genealogy of Dependency," *Signs* 19 (Summer 1994): 309–36.

32   S. Coontz, *The Social Origins of Private Life* (New York: Verso, 1988); S. Coontz, *The Way We Never Were* (New York: Basic Books, 1992).

33   M. Arnot, "Feminism, Education, and the New Right." (Paper presented at the 1991 Annual Meeting of the American Educational Research Association, Chicago, Illinois, 1991), 15–16.

34   Ibid., 25–26.

35   Apple, *Education and Power.*

36   C. West, *Race Matters* (New York: Vintage Books, 1993), 156.

37   Ibid.; see also M. Omi and H. Winant, *Racial Formation in the United States*. 2d ed. (New York: Routledge, 1994).

38   H. Bhabha, *The Location of Culture* (New York: Routledge, 1994), 6.

39   Omi and Winant, *Racial Formation in the United States*, 150.

40   Ibid.

41   Fraser and Gordon, "A Genealogy of Dependency," 320.

42   Ibid.

43   Ibid., 324.

44   Ibid.

45   Ibid., 324–25.

46   Ibid., 325.

47   Ibid., 331.

48   G. Gallagher, "White Reconstruction at the University," *Socialist Review* 94 (1994): 167.

49   L. Roman, "White Is a Color!" in *Race, Identity, and Representation in Education*, ed. C. McCarthy and W. Crichlow (New York: Routledge, 1994), 72.

50   Gallagher, "White Reconstruction," 175–76.

51   Ibid., 177.

52   Ibid., 182.

53   Ibid., 182–83.

54   M. Katz, *The Undeserving Poor* (New York: Pantheon Books, 1989), 239. I realize that democracy as a concept is a sliding signifier, and in fact have argued such a case in *Official Knowledge,* where I show how it is constructed and used by different groups with very different agendas. However, theoretical elegance can sometimes get in the way of our ordinary insights about things that might bind us together to contest rightist reconstructions. That is my point here.

55   Katz, *The Undeserving Poor,* 239.

56   Ibid.

57   Apple, *Cultural Politics and Education.*

58   For example, *The Bell Curve* received significant financial support from a number of right-wing foundations, including the ultraconservative Bradley Foundation.

59   M.W. Apple and J.A. Beane, ed., *Democratic Schools* (Washington, DC: Association for Supervision and Curriculum Development, 1995).

DOING CRITICAL THEORY

Chapter 8

Education, Culture, and Class Power: Basil Bernstein and the Neo-Marxist Sociology of Education

Beyond the Automaticity Thesis

In *The German Ideology*, Marx articulated one of his most famous claims. Paraphrased, it essentially says that "The ruling class will give its ideas the form of universality and represent them as the only rational universally valid ones."[1] Although some interpreters of this point who have chosen to see this process as a conscious conspiracy, for Marx it was considerably more complicated. For him, out of the constitutive power relations, conflicts, and contradictions of capitalism there were certain specific tendencies that were generated. Among these tendencies was the "natural" production of principles, ideas, and categories that support the unequal class relations of that social formation.[2] These ideas were under constant threat, however. They needed constant attention because hegemonic control was not guaranteed. Because of the class conflicts also generated out of, and causing, changes in that mode of production, there always exists the possibility of different ideological tendencies that could subvert the dominant ones.

In some accounts, this subversion followed naturally. It simply came about in much the same way as the laws of history determined (in the strong sense of that term) the linear progression of development from capitalism to socialism to communism.[3] Culture and ideology are as predictable as the stages of economic organization.

All of this rests on what we might call the "automaticity thesis" within traditional Marxist theory that assumes that somehow—automatically—as conditions worsen within capitalist economies the working class will rise. Because they have no vested interests in society as it currently exists, members of the working class will see through the veneer of ruling class ideologies and develop a "true understanding" of the exploitative relations in which they are caught. The automaticity thesis leads to the conclusion that revolution is inevitable, especially in industrialized nations with large proletarian populations such as Germany, England, Italy, etc.

Yet these predicted revolutions didn't occur or at least did not occur how and where they were supposed to. Among the major explanations for these nonevents are those that see that capitalism is not only an economic system but a cultural system as well. It "penetrates" to the heart of a people's common sense, so that they see the existing world as the world "tout court", as the only world. Capitalism becomes hegemonic. It creates what Williams, following Gramsci's lead, calls an "effective dominant culture."[4] As Gramsci himself recognized in his arguments against economic Marxism, winning popular consent requires dominant groups to attain leadership on a variety of fronts in a social formation. Cultural struggles and conflicts are not epiphenomenal, but are real and crucial in the battle for hegemony.[5]

The questioning of the automaticity thesis has been profound. It has led to a search for alternative explanations. Whereas before nearly everything was explained by the natural working out of the conflicts and contradictions at the economic level, now *cultural and ideological* explanations became essential.[6] In this context, in order to understand the realities of capitalism's continuing power it was essential not to focus only on how economic relations were reproduced. Cultural, ideological, and political relations took center stage as well.

What institutions play an important role here? As Marx himself recognized, the family, the state, cultural institutions surrounding the press and other mass media, and even the arts and literature needed to be examined. The Marxist legacy may often have been relatively reductive in its analyses of these institutions,[7] but it is clear that one had to take relations and resources *outside* the economy seriously if one was to understand how dominance worked.

Over the past three decades, some of the most creative research on "how dominance works" has developed about one of institution—the school. The curriculum (overt and hidden), the pedagogy, and the forms of evaluation have all been interrogated to see how they represent the relations of domination and exploitation in the larger society. Few people have contributed as much to the debate about these relations as Basil Bernstein. As someone who has himself now toiled for over twenty years to understand, and act on, these issues, I am happy to acknowledge Bernstein's influence on my own thinking about how "official knowledge," as both content and form, was implicated in the reproduction and subversion of power relations.

I shall be raising a number of questions about Bernstein's position. But, lest this project be misunderstood, I must preface it with a clear and public statement that my analysis of some of the strengths and silences in Bernstein's corpus could not have been done without standing on his shoulders. A precondition for any critical reflection of the kind I engage in here is the fact that only those whose arguments have been of such substance and such an influence on oneself are worth interrogating in the first place.

Some of my elaboration and analysis of Bernstein's corpus will have parallels with the arguments advanced by postmodernist and poststructuralist work. This is to be expected; the neo-Gramscian and radical democratic position from which I write contains some of the same intuitions that have led to these other approaches as well. I prefer to ground my own discussion within the neo-Gramscian position because I wish to provide an *internal* historical and critical analysis of Bernstein and because of my feelings of discomfort with certain aspects of postmodernism as it has been incorporated into the theoretical discourse in education.

The growth of the multiple positions associated with postmodernism and poststructuralism is indicative of the transformation of our discourse and our understandings of the relationship between culture and power. The rejection of the comforting illusion that there can (and must) be one grand narrative under which all relations of domination can be subsumed; the focus on the microlevel as a site of the political; the illumination of the utter complexity of the power/knowledge nexus; the extension of our political concerns well beyond the "holy trinity" of class, gender, and race; the idea of the decentered subject whose identity is both unfixed and a site of political struggle, the focus on the politics and practices of consumption, as well as production have all been important. But these ideas have not been completely problem-free, to say the least.[8]

With the growth of postmodern literature in critical educational studies, however, we have tended to move too quickly away from traditions that continue to be filled with vitality and provide essential insights into the nature of the curriculum and pedagogy that dominate schools. Bernstein's work actually provides a case in point. From the late 1960s until today, he has worked through much of the complexity surrounding class relations at the microlevel of educational policy and practice and how they may set limits on what is possible in schooling. In his later work, he pointed to the crucial nature of discourse and the construction of identity well before the latest surge in popularity of postmodern and poststructural work. Furthermore, his recent focus on power relations at the cultural level and in the state that are *specific* to education itself and not reducible to simple reflections of "external determinations" comes very close to Foucault at his best. Finally, Bernstein's project—one that I share—is the integration of a number of traditions that complement (and sometimes even creatively act in tension with) each other so that we can better understand and act on the relations of domination and subordination in schools today.

Bernstein started out, as I will here, by thinking about the nature of the relationship between culture and power. For him, this concerned the connections among schools, the economy, and class cultures and their signifying practices. This beginning point is important.

The mere fact that class does not explain all can be used as an excuse to ignore its power. This would be a serious error. Class is of course an analytic construct as well as a set of relations that exist outside our minds. Thus, we must be very careful about when and how it is used. Even given this, however, it would be wrong to assume that because many people do not identify with or act on what we might expect from theories that link, say, identity and ideology with one's class position, class has gone away. Capitalism still exists as a massive structuring force. People may not think and act in ways predicted by essentialist theories of class, but this does *not* mean that their "objective" position in the racial, sexual, and class divisions of labor has been radically altered. It also does not mean that relations of production (both economic *and* cultural, because how we think about these two may be different) can be ignored if we do it in nonessentializing ways.

I say all this because of a number of very real dangers that now exist in critical educational studies. One is our loss of collective memory. Although there is currently great and necessary vitality at the level of theory, critical educational research has often been faddish. It moves from theory to theory rapidly, often seeming to assume that the harder something is to understand or the more it rests on European cultural theory (preferably French) the better it is. The rapidity of its movement has had the effect of denying gains that have been already made in other traditions or of restating these gains in new language. In doing this, and this is my second point, we cut ourselves off from some of the most creative work that continues to have crucial things to tell us, especially if we are interested in what happens in schools not only in the production of elegant metatheories (some of which *are* necessary, of course).

This is decidedly the case with Basil Bernstein. The fact that he continues to stimulate a new generation of empirical and historical studies on the nature of and transformations in curriculum and pedagogy in many nations makes this clear.

I begin historically and partly autobiographically, from within the development of the neo-Marxist position in the United States. As you will notice, my discussion of Bernstein will actually involve an immanent critique of considerable parts of this tradition from the inside. Bernstein himself has had a complex relationship with this tradition, since he has been both inside and outside of it at the very same time. This is one of the reasons his work continues to stimulate considerable debate.

Cultural Reproduction and Education

During the years I was writing *Ideology and Curriculum*,[9] I faced a number of difficult conceptual problems. Among the most pressing was how to think through the relationship between differential power and what counted as legitimate knowledge in *specific* rather than general terms. That is, once one recognized that there is a connection between what is taught in schools and "the larger society," the task was to know what these determinate connections were and how they actually operated in day-to-day school life.[10]

It had become clear to me that the focus on the hidden curriculum of social relations in schools captured only a part of what schools accomplished ideologically. Perhaps because I was trained as a curriculum worker, not only as a sociologist, I was sensitive to another problematic, that concerning the formal corpus of school knowledge.

Reading *Class, Codes and Control, Volume III*[11] was of great importance to me. Certainly I had a number of reservations about both its general structural approach and its overly Durkheimian tendencies, some of which appeared in print in a critical essay that I wrote with

Philip Wexler.[12] Yet just as certainly, I was struck by many of the provocative and insightful claims Bernstein made in the volume. It was
clear to many of us that it represented one of the most disciplined and
serious attempts to specify the terrain on which cultural reproduction
occurred.

Members of the critical educational community in the United States
responded positively to something else that has characterized
Bernstein's work. Bernstein is not in a church, so he is not worried
about heresy. Orthodoxy was part of the problem, not part of the
solution.

Thus, like Pierre Bourdieu, Basil Bernstein worked through his constantly evolving analysis by creatively engaging with a number of tendencies in classical sociology. He has woven a complex fabric with
threads from a Durkheimian concern with the social origins and functions of symbolic forms, classifications, and representations and a partly
Marxian concern for the ways in which power reproduces itself through
class relations.[13] These, of course, are not the only influences. Bernstein
is a master at integrating various perspectives. Yet it is clear that these
two—one representing the world of symbol and meaning, the other
the world of differential class power—play important roles in the drama
Bernstein portrays.

What is Bernstein's problematic? Looking backwards, it is clear
that there is a coherence that may be missed if his entire corpus is not
focused upon. Both the sociolinguistic work and the social analysis of
curricula, pedagogy, and evaluation are part of what was clearly an
ambitious project.

> The project could be said to be a continuous attempt to understand some-
> thing about the rules, practices, and agencies regulating the legitimate cre-
> ation, distribution, reproduction, and change of consciousness by principles
> of communication through which a given distribution of power and dominant
> cultural categories are legitimated and reproduced. In short, an attempt to
> understand the nature of symbolic control.[14]

Thus, the task was to elaborate a middle-range theory that would integrate macro and micro. To say the least, this was both an exciting and
risky endeavor.

One need not agree with all of the specific claims he makes—as I
noted, I for one have disagreements about specific aspects of both
strands of his work—to appreciate the persistence and power he brings
to what are among the most crucial questions we must ask about the
schooling process.

Given the extent of his corpus and the range of topics he has worked on, I shall have to choose only a limited set of issues that bear on the organizing questions dealt with within the Marxist and neo-Marxist *traditions*. I say traditions, plural, here because the heterogeneity of these movements is important to recognize. I can speak to only a few of the multiple interpretations of what the core content of Marxist and neo-Marxist work actually is. Therefore, this paper can be but a selective reading of selective aspects of Bernstein employing the selective lens of part of a larger set of traditions.

In order to understand his specific contributions, it is important that we focus on the context of the debate in which they were taken up. I shall focus largely on the United States and shall use as my point of departure Bowles and Gintis's provocative but seriously flawed volume *Schooling in Capitalist America*.[15]

Bowles and Gintis's problematic was in essence twofold: to understand the role of the school in reproducing the social division of labor and to explain how it is that people *accept* such sorting and selecting. The former question is related to questions of economic reproduction; the latter question concerns issues of cultural reproduction. The former wants to see how people fill the "empty spaces" in the class structure; the latter is an attempt to understand how social consciousness is formed. These questions led to answers that stressed reproduction by correspondence. They were based on a theory of homologous structures, in which the norms and values of one set of institutions (schools) mirrored—in a relatively straightforward and uncontradictory way—those "required" in another institution (the paid labor market). In this theory, only the hidden curriculum was important in one's explanation. The formal corpus of school knowledge was inconsequential.

This position has been challenged repeatedly almost from its very inception, as many of you know.[16] Some of the reasons lie in what Bernstein himself recognized, the necessity for a more complex theory of culture, a more elaborated set of class actors, and a recognition of the relative autonomy of different spheres in society.

For Bernstein, even before Bowles and Gintis's work became widely known, a focus only on the content of the differential social relations that went on in schools radically simplified the processes by which the cultural reproduction of class relations occurred. Without an understanding of the organization of the formal corpus of school knowledge, without an understanding of the regulatory principles underlying the pedagogy, without a more thorough appreciation of how the symbolic actually worked in schools, we could not comprehend the fundamental ways that class operated in educational contexts.

Of course, class was not as evident in his early work on, say, rituals and the instrumental and expressive orders of the school, though it played a key role in his often criticized sociolinguistic research.[17] Given the increasing significance of class relations under capitalism as his work progressed, however, I shall spend a considerable portion of my discussion on this issue.

Class and Culture

For Bernstein, the issue of the relationship between class and culture concerns the distribution of power and how this is reflected in the principles of control between social groups. These principles are themselves "realized in the creation, distribution, reproduction, and legitimation of physical and symbolic values that have their source in the social division of labour."[18] In efforts to understand the processes by which classes reproduce themselves culturally, the task is to show "how class regulation of the distribution of power and the principles of control generates, distributes, reproduces, and legitimates dominant and dominated principles regulating the relationship within and between social groups and so forms of consciousness."[19]

In essence, in more traditional terms the issues are these: What is ideology? How does it function? What does it do to people? In words that echo an Althusserian influence as well as that of the emergence of semiotic and poststructuralist work, Bernstein answers these questions in the following way.

> What we are asking here is how the distribution of power and principles of control are transformed, at the level of the subject, into different, invidiously related, organizing principles, in such a way as both to position subjects and to create the possibility of change in such positioning. The broad answer given by this thesis is that class relations generate, distribute, reproduce, and legitimate different forms of communication, which transmit dominant and dominated codes, and that subjects are differentially positioned by these codes in the process of acquiring them. "Positioning" is used here to refer to the establishing of a specific relation to other subjects and to the creating of specific relations within subjects. In general, from this point of view, codes are culturally determined positioning devices. More specifically, class-regulated codes position subjects with respect to dominant and dominated forms of communication and to the relationships between them. Ideology is constituted through and in such positioning. . . . [Ideology] inheres in and regulates *modes of relation*. Ideology is not so much content as a mode of relation for the realizing of contexts.[20]

On the one hand, as is clear in the above quote, Bernstein has been seen as devoting much of his energy to the sociolinguistic dynamics of class-based forms of communication; much of his energy has focused specifically on working-class linguistic forms.[21] Yet, on the other hand, a considerable portion of his work and the portion that has been most influential on, say, Marxist-influenced sociology of education pays much less attention to the working class. Rather, the emphasis has been on the crucial role other class actors play in the cultural reproduction of class relations in schooling and in the larger society.

Bernstein's primary focus in what has come to be called the sociology of curriculum[22] is less on those classes that have been part of the binary opposition that makes up most traditional class analyses—labor and capital. Rather, he is more interested in much of this work in the middle class. Here he is aligning himself with a considerable number of investigators who have critically examined the assumptions and empirical power of some of the more mechanistic paradigms of class analysis and found them wanting. One of his lasting contributions has been to suggest that we look at a wider range of class actors if we are to specify how cultural reproduction occurs.

It is no longer generally accepted that a two-class, polarized model is anywhere near sufficient to grasp the complexity of class structure within capitalism.[23] In particular, such binary models (working class/ruling class) neglect the crucial role played by the middle strata in a social formation that is increasingly organized around information-based industries and the influence of what I have elsewhere called technical/administrative knowledge.[24]

Yet, although the middle strata—whether we call it the professional middle class, the new petty bourgeoisie, those in contradictory class locations, or, more generally, simply the middle class[25]—has an important place in the economy, the state, and cultural institutions, it would be all too reductive to see it as homogeneous. It is this very sense of difference *within* the middle class that gives Bernstein's work some of its analytic cogency. He rightly recognizes that knowledge and symbols—as commodities and as involved in a set of social practices that are organized around the economic and cultural capital and patterns of mobility of identifiable class actors—are crucial.[26]

In Bernstein's words, his later work on the middle class created a form of analysis:

which distinguished between class fractions who controlled highly specialized principles of communication which were applied directly to the means, contexts and possibilities of physical resources, and class fractions who controlled highly specialized principles of communication which were applied directly to the means, contexts, and possibilities of discursive resources. This distinction gave rise to a concept of the social division of labour of symbolic control, of its specialized agencies and agents. Dominant agents of symbolic control, as dominant agents of production, could function in the field of symbolic control, the cultural field, or the economic field. It was hypothesized that ideological orientation, interests, and modes of cultural reproduction would be related to functions of the agents (symbolic control or production), field location, and hierarchical position.[27]

A focus on a middle class divided by its varied positions in the social division of labor, each fraction of which carries its own core ideological orientations that structure its educational visions, is more than a little useful here. Struggles over the school curriculum and its pedagogy are really struggles between two fractions of the middle class, one that supports "visible" pedagogy (in essence, subject-centered and tightly controlled) and one that supports "invisible" pedagogy (in essence, child-centered and more loosely controlled). One essential insight is that dominant classes in the economic apparatus *need not be the same as* those that dominate some of the cultural apparatus of society. When this insight is added to the recognition that the ideological and discursive relations and resources of these class fractions may differ in significant ways depending on their position in the wider division of labor, it provides a more subtle approach to how cultural reproduction acts in schools.

In this way, Bernstein enables us to see class as a cultural as well as an economic category. In the process, he presents us with a picture of class fractions acting within not only the economy but within political and cultural institutions as well. These actions are *not* easily reducible to the needs and interests of capital nor are they mechanically determined by the economy. This has implications both positive and negative for Marxist theories of class.

Like Szelenyi, Gouldner, and Ehrenreich, Bernstein locates the middle classes not in their relation to exploitation—a key element in most Marxist explanations—but in terms of their relationship to cultural production and reproduction.[28] I do not want to imply that this is necessarily wrong. Indeed, even individuals such as Erik Olin Wright, a major figure in the attempt to base class analysis expressly on relations of exploitation rather than on authority relations, recognizes that a reconstruction, based on cultural production, of the Marxist concept of class may be necessary for certain classes.[29] Rather, my point is to have us recognize that Bernstein is combining a number of approaches in his analysis of class structure. For his determination of "top and bottom," he bases his claims on their relationship to *material* production. In his analysis of the "middle," his theoretical apparatus is now more grounded in *cultural* reproduction.

A more complex reading is possible here, however, one that may make Bernstein's approach seem more coherent. We must remember that his primary focus is consistently cultural (re)production. For him, "Class relations constitute inequalities in the distribution of power between social groups, which are realized in the creation, organization, distribution, legitimation and reproduction of material and symbolic values arising out of the social division of labor."[30] The central category of analysis is *power* and the major concern is how social relations constitute power relations. This analysis is clearly not limited to the traditional Marxist understanding.

James Ladwig, for example, argues that for Bernstein the distinction between material and symbolic "things" is partly only an analytic convenience. All social relations—when viewed, as Bernstein wants them to be viewed, as *cultural*—are connected to both symbolic and material things. "What differs between classes is the 'object' of control or the 'basis' of relations of power."[31]

As Ladwig states:

> In capitalist contexts (which in this view are historically contingent), Bernstein finds that "the top and bottom" are defined by their control over "material" things. Here the object of their control is seen as material—but the status given to material things, its primacy if you will, is simply a historically contingent cultural fact. Hence, there is nothing magical about the "primacy" of relationships to material production (material capital is not somehow inherently more important than any other capital). . . . Recognize here that . . . Bernstein was most likely accepting Durkheim's explicit rejection of Marx's split between material and ideological forces. Here the social division of labor is understood as culturally based. Again there is no magically higher status given to "material" things. [The division between material and symbolic does] not represent ontological, metaphysical, or epistemological distinctions. . . . [Rather] the distinctions being drawn are distinctions describing different social practices.[32]

I have some sympathy with this interpretation, since it points to Bernstein's interest in mapping the class nature of both the field of production and the field of symbolic control as parallel areas of social life that have some degree of mutual indeterminacy.[33] This is one of the most complex areas of Bernstein's analysis, one that has proven to be difficult to unpack. Whether this is indicative of a necessary flexibility or a theoretical incoherence can be determined only by a more rigorous specification of how class relations are to be determined in his account. I personally remain optimistic that his analysis provides some important insights into how we can think about class structure culturally.

Class Formation

These possible gains in our ability to think through the functions and sites of a wider range of class actors are accompanied by a number of risks, however. For all its insights, in much of Bernstein's work, class itself has actually remained relatively opaque. How classes were formed, how class capacities actually were enacted, how class relations changed over time, and as David Hogan reminds us, how class consciousness was partly *created* in struggles over schooling,[34] all of this was not totally clear in his analysis. This latter point is rather telling because classes don't simply exist. They are *formed*. Using older terminology we can say that they become classes "for" themselves, not only "in" themselves, through conflicts over economic, political, and cultural relations and institutions. Let me say more about this.

Because of his structural tendencies, Bernstein was able to think through class largely as a set of *positions* in the economy, the state, or in cultural institutions. This idea has its major benefits. However, it is less able to help us think through class as a *project*, as a creative cultural and political expression.[35]

This can best be understood by pointing to what appears to be a simple distinction between class structure and class formation. Class structure refers to the organization of social relations into which people enter that at the highest level of generality, "determine" their class interests.[36] Unlike class structure, class formation is not a structure of empty places. It refers to the "organized collectives" within this structure. It is not determined by the class structure, but is historically variable and contingent. "Class based collectivities may be organized, disorganized or reorganized within a given class structure."[37] The formation of these groups, their interactions and internal coherence and power, is related to labor market segmentation; unionization; party formation; legal and governmental practices; the development of social movements; the historical relationship among class, race, and gender antagonisms, alliances, and struggles, and so forth.[38]

These are significant points since they challenge a number of the presuppositions that lie behind some structuralist approaches in the sociology of education. Once one rejects the notion that once one understands the nature of class structure one can automatically deduce how class formation operates, a more subtle view is argued for. This is based on the realization that "the process of class formation is decisively shaped by a variety of institutional mechanisms that are themselves 'relatively autonomous' from the class structure and which determine the ways in which class structures are translated into collective actions with specific ideologies and strategies." This is a decidedly less reductive approach, one that highlights how classes form, change, shape, and are shaped by a multitude of social forces. Classes and class formation do not "automatically" appear with particular cultural and ideological attributes simply because they are thrown up by a mode of production as it changes over time.[39] Class formation is not simply a "natural" result of changes in the social division of labor. In the absence of a more coherent theory of institutional forces that provide the possibilities for collective action and for discursive and material transformations, we are left again with a version of something like the automaticity thesis.

Bernstein's position I believe may be able to account for some aspects of class formation with its integrating of concepts such as collective and oppositional voice in later work,[40] but by and large this remains a conceptual possibility rather than a fully fleshed out account. It remains partly essentialist in crucial places.

This has an impact on the limitation of his sense of the creativity that lies at the center of cultural forms and processes. Cultural inversions, what Bakhtin calls "carnival,"[41] the constant playfulness of culture, tends to be deemphasized in Bernstein's work. The *reproduction* of meanings and organizing relationships remains the key focus. This may be a strength rather than a weakness, because Bernstein takes a thoroughly unromantic position on the issue of class power and control. Yet, for all its insight, something seems to be missing.

As Paul Willis, like Basil Bernstein, reminds us, making meaning is not only an individual act, but a profoundly social act as well, one that is structured by location and situation. However, locations and situations are not to be understood only as determinations. They are also, and profoundly, "relations and resources to be discovered, explored, and experienced." As Willis goes on to say, race, class, gender, age, and regional memberships are not simply learned. They are lived and experimented with. This is so even if only by pushing up against the oppressive limits of established order and power.[42]

This very sense of "living and experimenting with" is partly truncated in Bernstein. Collective social movements, as well, are largely missing. Although the possibility of such organized (and perhaps disorganized) activity is built in to his conceptual apparatus, here too it is there only as a conceptual possibility. I shall return shortly to the issues of social movements, and their power in rearticulating class ideologies in different ways.

Although the issues surrounding class formation that I have discussed in this section are important, they actually do not exhaust the questions one might raise here. As I hinted earlier, class itself—its meaning, how one specifies "it", etc.—is actually relatively unspecified in Bernstein's work. Key concepts such as how one determines class location are left rather opaque. There are provocative suggestions concerning where people work and what they work with—especially for fractions of the middle class. But these remain suggestive. This is a crucial lack, since much of Bernstein's work, in particular his immensely interesting arguments about different modalities of control and different processes of the cultural reproduction of class relations, *rise or fall on how one thinks about class itself*. At the least, the reader who wished to test out his theory would have to immerse her or himself in the most current literature on how class is constituted.[43] This is not a trivial point. One needs a coherent theory of class relations—how they come about and change, what the lines of class divisions actually look like, how classes differ from occupational and status groups—to see if one is accurately talking about classes in the first place.[44]

As it stands, however, combining both Durkheimian and Marxist traditions, in most of Bernstein's work the engine of class history is by and large a "black box"[45] called the social division of labor (though what is included and excluded in this sphere aside from where one works and some necessity to control knowledge production is unclear, as is its status as a possible metaphor for the entire economy). For him, as transformations occur in a mode of production, this process "automatically" generates new classes and class fractions with identifiable cultures that are linked directly to their experiences of *paid* work. The gender specificities of dealing only with paid work can be very telling here.[46] I hasten to add, however, that Bernstein's work was very significant in the development of a specifically feminist sociology of education in a number of nations,[47] and gender—as a social construction and as a site of contested subjectivity—did play a larger role as his later work evolved. How this relates to the economic sphere and its transformations remained unclear in his work, though.

Yet, gender issues aside for the moment, nothing is automatic about the social division of labor. It is not simply a "natural" outgrowth of the economy, but is the result of serious conflicts that constantly shape and reshape the environment in which it takes place. Nor is there anything automatic about class cultures, especially in those nations such as the United States in which class itself has been constituted around racial and ethnic (to say nothing of gender) traditions and relations as well.[48] They too are interactively formed out of the conflicts and the hegemonic and counterhegemonic relations of body and meaning that organize and disorganize our daily lives.[49]

Class conflicts are not absent in Bernstein by any means. Yet, the most crucial conflict for him in this work is the conflict between fractions of the middle class, the old and the new. Even here, however, these classes are curiously disembodied. They are shadows, phantoms, who are never seen acting. Only their effects are evident in the transformation of the curriculum from, say, strongly classified and strongly framed (visible) to one that is weakly classified and weakly framed (invisible).[50] *How* these transformations are effected, through the use of what resources and what relations of power within the state and civil society, is curiously cloudy.

Lest I am seen as being overly critical here, however, let me restate what I see as Bernstein's contribution to a theory of class relations in education—a contribution I take as being crucial—and my proposal for strengthening it. Bernstein does present us with the initial and important intellectual resources to begin to suggest how one might think through a theory of class location based on cultural control, codes, modalities, and power. Considerably more work needs to be done, however, to see if it is possible to build a more elaborated theory of what class actually means in these terms. The key concept in all his work and in much of the work of those who, like myself, have been strongly influenced by it, is class. Unless we become more rigorous and critical in our use of it, our work simply remains at the level of suggestion.

It may be, for instance, that—given Bernstein's and our culturalist problematic—rather than a positional concept of class, we need a trajectory-based one.[51] We need to understand how class locations, for example, have particular time horizons. Thus, for instance, how class operates is different for a lower middle-class person who "knows" that his or her probability of upward mobility is higher than for a person who understands that in a crisis-ridden industrial economy there is a high probability of downward mobility.

This may not influence the *basic* core of class cultural codes that Bernstein has delimited. These codes may be relatively immune to altered senses of temporality. At the very least, though, this must remain an open question since it points to the utter importance of lasting economic changes on some of the assumptions that organize our lives. Whether this change relates only to the content of our common sense (in which Bernstein is less interested) or the form or principles of organizing it (in which Bernstein is decidedly interested) remains to be seen.

Reconsidering Middle Class Ideologies

Given these points about the importance of being cautious of class essentialist arguments and of seeing class as an active and formative process, let us return to the middle class and the way these fractions of the middle class reproduce themselves culturally through schooling.

As Bernstein reminds us, the fact that there is an unequal distribution of power does not mean that it is reproduced at the level of the classroom in only one way. As he puts it:

> The fundamental proposition is that the same distribution of power may be reproduced by apparently opposing modalities of control. There is not a one-to-one relation between a given distribution of power and the modality of control through which it is realized. . . . [Pedagogic] practices are cultural relays of the distribution of power. Although visible and invisible pedagogies are apparently opposing types . . . both carry social class assumptions. However, these social class assumptions vary with the pedagogic type. The class assumptions of visible pedagogies are different from the class assumptions of invisible pedagogies. These class assumptions carry consequences for those children who are able to exploit the possibilities of the pedagogic practices.[52]

It is at the level of these differing pedagogies, ones that embody differing modalities of symbolic and bodily control, that Bernstein's analysis of the split within the middle class enters.

> The assumptions of a visible pedagogy are more likely to be met by that fraction of the middle class whose employment has a direct relation to the

economic field (production, distribution, and the circulation of capital). Whereas the assumptions of an invisible pedagogy are more likely to be met by that fraction of the middle class who have a direct relation not to the economic field but to the field of symbolic control and who work in specialized agencies of symbolic control usually located in the public sector. . . . For both these fractions education is a crucial means of cultural and economic reproduction, although perhaps less so for that fraction directly related to the economic field.[53]

Bernstein's position here raises an important point in thinking through the complicated issue of the "class belongingness" of forms of cultural reproduction. These forms may *not* be stable, and in fact may be considerably less stable than he allowed. Because the economy is deindustrializing at a rapid rate in many advanced capitalist nations, the meaning of what it means to be in a particular fraction of the middle class may be radically altered. Invisible pedagogies may be seen as threatening to attempts to preserve class location and more visible ones may be substituted because of the fear of downward mobility or job loss, even by that fraction of the middle class that has expressly advocated invisible pedagogies in the past.[54] We need to think conjuncturally here.

This is heightened by the fact that a particular alliance has been formed that is increasingly articulating many members of the middle class to a rightist ideological coalition and is radically changing much of the commonsense ways we think about education, what it is for, and how it should be carried on.[55]

This is the case because the effects of class structure are mediated by politics and cultural dynamics. We cannot, as I stated, read off the process of class formation and class consciousness automatically from the class structure.[56] Thus, as a number of people have recognized, the Right in the United States, Britain, and elsewhere has recognized the crucial political significance of ideological struggle. To win in the state you must win in civil society.[57] Movements toward a very different *basic* orientation toward schooling—one that is strongly classified and strongly framed—are now considerably more widespread among all middle-class groups. Social movements and general ideological shifts have major effects that cut across class lines.

Thus, even though, as Bernstein argues, the fraction of the middle class who are "professional agents of symbolic control functioning in specialized agencies of symbolic control" are more likely to support invisible pedagogy than that fraction of the middle class that has "a direct relation to the production, distribution and circulation of capital,"[58] this tendency may be more historically contingent than we might suppose. (Bernstein himself points to the crucial importance of such historical specificity. In fact, he is one of the few to suggest this.) The intersections of class and race may be important here since the Right has very cleverly used in employing a tacitly racial discourse about standards—"the Western tradition," and so on—to play off of the cultural and economic fears of many middle-class groups and to pry them loose from earlier hegemonic accords and social democratic coalitions that supported invisible pedagogies.[59]

Bernstein recognizes some of this in his insightful discussion of "market-oriented" visible pedagogies in which educational policy is centered on programs of school choice. This, he correctly believes, is but a "thin cover" for a restratification of schools, students, and curricula.[60] What this means for his analysis of different forms of cultural reproduction that are rooted in fractions of the middle class needs much greater thought, however.

The issue of restratification also points to the crucial role the *state* plays as a sponsor of such market-oriented programs and as a site of class conflict. Although Bernstein's theory does allow for such conflict, its relatively taxonomic approach is not as able to deal with how educational policies and practices are less the result of the influence of pure class categories, modalities, and codes than they are inherently filtered through the state, which has its own relatively autonomous needs for legitimacy and control.

That is, like other aspects of social life, policies for curriculum, pedagogy, and evaluation are themselves not easily understood through class essentialist arguments. Such policies, especially if they have been articulated by the state, are the results of conflicts and their attendant compromises or accords within various levels of the state and between the state and a *wide array* of social movements and forces in the wider society.[61]

His lack of a theory of the state and social movements, then, prevents Bernstein from pursuing his productive insights into a more concrete analysis of how power and control operate. That said, however, it must be noted that in his latest work on the ways power works in multiple sites, on pedagogic discourse and on "recontextualizing agents" he begins to integrate the question of the role of the state as a crucial mediator of the practice of cultural reproduction through what he calls the "pedagogic device."[62] Yet, as in some of his other work this too is in danger of becoming a "black box" which some-how—through some unknown political process—transforms or "recontextualizes" the forces of power and control. Like his sugges-tive analysis of class, here too one would need to go considerably further into the literature on the state to test his insights.

Whither Class?

Yet even without a more elaborate consideration of the role of the state in cultural reproduction there is another reason we must be cau-tious of class essentialist arguments. Just as I have suggested here that there may not *necessarily* be a class belongingness to particular mod-els of pedagogic and curricular relations, so too—because class itself is reconfigured partly along other nonclass lines—this may have an im-portant impact on what counts as cultural reproduction.

For example, class itself is increasingly becoming gendered and raced. (Of course, in many ways it always was. I mean to say that we must reconstruct our assumptions about what class means.) For example, women occupy 60 percent of working-class jobs. African American men and women combined occupy two-thirds of the working-class positions in this country. *Thus, nearly 70 percent of working-class positions in the United States are held by women and people of color.*[63] What this means for cultural reproduction is of great impor-tance. We cannot marginalize race and gender as truly constitutive categories in any cultural analysis. If there are indeed basic cultural forms and orientations that are specifically gendered and raced that have their own *partly* autonomous histories, then we would need to integrate theories of patriarchal and racial forms into the very core of any attempt to comprehend what is being reproduced and changed. At the very least, a theory that allows for the *contradictions* within and among these dynamics would be essential.[64] Of course, this is one of the many areas where neo-Gramscian and some poststructuralist positions that have not become cynically depoliticized intersect.

Bernstein does explicitly recognize the existence of other unequal relations between social groups. "There are today, under conditions of advanced capitalism, many different sites of unequal relations be-tween social groups—gender, ethnicity, religion, region—each having its own particular context of reproduction."[65] Yet class is regarded as a (the?) basic classification. As he puts it, "Whether gender, ethnic, or religious categories (or any combination) are considered, it is held that these, today, speak through class-regulated modes."[66] Obviously, it is the cultural reproduction of these class-regulated modes that concerns him the most. Here Bernstein is in decided agreement with some of the more recent analysts of class. Erik Wright, for example, also argues that although class alone is not "determinate," other mechanisms such as race, ethnicity, and gender operate within the limits established by class structure.[67]

Given the complexity of this issue and given space limitations, I will not take a position on this here, though elsewhere I have argued for a less class-determinate position than that suggested by Wright or Bernstein.[68] My basic point is to have us recognize that if—as many prominent scholars and theorists of racial formation and identity politics would argue—the question of the privileging of class relations over other relations remains open,[69] then so too must our appraisal of Bernstein's position remain open. If the class belongingness of core cultural/ideological orientations is weaker because of the raced and gendered nature of class categories themselves, then we need to reconstruct a good deal of the class nature of the project itself. Let me add, however, that this need not vitiate Bernstein's approach. Rather, it simply makes it more contingent and historical.

Conclusion

In this essay, I have chosen to focus on certain specific issues raised by Basil Bernstein's provocative corpus of work. Issues of class formation, class essentialism, the changing nature of class itself, have been my major objects of scrutiny. I have often chosen to be critical here. Yet so much more could be said positively, especially about the many areas he has opened up for further investigation, about the theoretical resources he has given us, or about the insights we might derive by applying his analyses to the current conservative restoration now underway in education in many countries.[70]

Certain things stand out when one looks back over Bernstein's corpus, themes that continue to suggest new ways of approaching the relationships between culture and power in schooling. These continue to offer both support and challenge to not only the neo-Marxist oriented sociology of education but to all critical educational studies in important ways.

He has given us a striking portrayal of the "relative autonomy"[71] of the symbolic field and of differences within the symbolic field itself.

This is best seen in his discussion of the differences—in terms of inter-est, organization, and discursive practices—between middle-class agents of symbolic control that work in the economic field and those that work directly in the cultural field itself. It is also evident in his sugges-tion that the nature of the dominant pedagogic discourse is "unchang-ing," even when economic forms change markedly. It is here, in his latest discussion of the *pedagogic device* and its distributive, recontextualizing, and evaluative rules, that Bernstein provides us with one of the building blocks to continue our analysis of how cultural reproduction and production occurs.[72]

Yet, even here as with all of his work, there are both opportunities and possible costs in pursuing the road he has taken if we are not very careful.

Let me be specific. Once one begins to understand what is *differ-ent* about the ways symbolic control works in class relations—and Bernstein has been among the most perceptive analysts of this—it is logical to ask, as he now does, just as compelling a question. *What remains the same?* It is here that Bernstein moves away from class categories. What accounts for the remarkable uniformity of basic edu-cational principles and practices across dominant ideologies in a num-ber of countries?[73] By asking the comparative question, we, along with Bernstein, are asking about the relative autonomy of the cultural in a way that can lead us toward many paths. One is to the micropolitical analyses of, say, Foucault, where "pedagogical devices" and discur-sive relations have their own power relations partly independent of macrostructural relations and discourses. *If this remains sufficiently political*, it can lead to a salutary focus on how power works in every-day life without having to reduce it always to the workings of larger economic forces.[74] I take this as a gain, if we do not use it to ignore the economic and the structural.

Another path is to become even more refined in our analyses of class, gender, and race relations (and of the contradictions among and within them). To take but one simple example, we could ask if impor-tant fractions of the middle class control the process of cultural repro-duction independent of competing political/economic systems. This too would be a major gain in our understanding both conceptually and politically and would suggest a very different way of looking at class power. It might mean, for example, that in most educational systems—either capitalist or socialist—the "new class" that depends on cultural capital and forms of symbolic and bureaucratic control may win.[75]

Finally, however, there is a very real danger. By asking what remains the same—in a time when the Right is so resurgent and when exploitative class (to say nothing of race and gender) relations are worsening in so many places throughout the world—we can tacitly evacuate questions of class and its accompanying relations of exploitation and domination from the place they have had to struggle so hard to win in the sociology of education.[76]

As I have argued throughout this essay, even when they are more elegantly treated, class relations may not tell all. But to push them once more to the sidelines would be a tragedy of immense proportions, not only to the vitality of the community of researchers in education, but to the millions of children for whom exploitation and domination are facts of life. Basil Bernstein would undoubtedly agree. And the ways in which he agrees will undoubtedly continue to teach us in the future.

Notes

I would like to thank the members of the Friday Seminar for their criticisms and suggestions on this chapter. Also helpful were Alan Sadovnik and especially Sue Middleton, James Ladwig, and Bruce King. An earlier version of this chapter appeared in *Educational Theory* 42 (Spring 1992).

1 For a discussion of the complicated meanings Marx associated with this position that are often less reductive than some interpreters have claimed, see Jorge Larrain, *Marxism and Ideology* (Atlantic Highlands, NJ: Humanities Press, 1983).

2 Michael W. Apple, *Ideology and Curriculum*, 2d ed. (New York: Routledge, 1990).

3 For criticism of this developmental model, see Erik Olin Wright, "Capitalism's Futures," *Socialist Review* 13(March/April 1983): 77–126.

4 See Raymond Williams, *Marxism and Literature* (New York: Oxford University Press, 1977); and Dennis Dworkin and Leslie Roman, ed. *Views Beyond the Border Country: Raymond Williams and Cultural Politics* (New York: Routledge, 1993).

5 A clear description of Gramsci's position can be found in Tony Bennett, "Introduction: Popular Culture and 'the Turn to Gramsci'," in *Popular Culture and Social Relations*, ed. Tony Bennett, Colin Mercer and Janet Woollacott (Philadelphia: Open University Press, 1986), xi–xix, and Stuart Hall, "The Toad in the Garden: Thatcherism Among the Theorists," in *Marxism and the Interpretation of Culture*, ed. Cary Nelson and Lawrence Grossberg (Urbana: University of Illinois Press, 1988), 35–37.

6 See Goran Therborn, *The Power of Ideology and the Ideology of Power* (London: Verso, 1980).

7 Raymond Williams, *Marxism and Literature*.

8 One of the clearest and most provocative discussions of the problems associated with some of the sometimes overstated claims of postmodernism can be found in John Clarke, *New Times and Old Enemies: Essays on Cultural Studies and America* (London: Harper Collins, 1991), 2041. See also Steven Best and Douglas Kellner, *Postmodern Theory* (London: Macmillan, 1991), although it marginalizes feminist contributions too much. Also helpful here are Nancy Fraser, *Unruly Practices* (Minneapolis: University of Minnesota Press, 1989); Bryan Palmer, *Descent Into Discourse* (Philadelphia: Temple University Press, 1990); and Peter Dews, *Logics of Disintegration* (New York: Verso, 1987).

9 Michael W. Apple, *Ideology and Curriculum*.

10   For an analysis of the strengths and weaknesses of this research program, see Daniel Liston, *Capitalist Schools* (New York: Routledge, 1988).

11   Basil Bernstein, *Class, Codes and Control.* Vol. III (New York: Routledge, 1977).

12   Michael W. Apple and Philip Wexler, "Cultural Capital and Educational Transmissions," *Educational Theory* 28 (Winter 1978): 34–43.

13   Chris Shilling, "Schooling and the Production of Physical Capital," *Discourse* (in press).

14   Basil Bernstein, *Class, Codes, and Control.* Vol. IV, *The Structuring of Pedagogic Discourse* (New York: Routledge, 1990), 113.

15   Samuel Bowles and Herbert Gintis, *Schooling in Capitalist America* (New York: Basic Books, 1976).

16   See my reanalysis of Bowles and Gintis in the light of the fifteen years of work that has succeeded them, in Michael W. Apple, "Facing the Complexity of Power," in *Bowles and Gintis Revisited,* ed. Mike Cole (Philadelphia: Falmer Press, 1988), 112–30; and Michael W. Apple, "Standing on the Shoulders of Bowles and Gintis," *History of Education Quarterly* 28 (Summer 1988), 231–41. These expand on my earlier criticisms in Michael W. Apple, *Education and Power* (New York: Routledge, ARK Edition, 1985).

17   See Bernstein, *Class, Codes and Control.* Vol. III and Bernstein, *Class, Codes and Control.* Vol. I (London: Routledge, 1971). Bernstein's sociolinguistic work has often been misinterpreted. Although some of the criticisms may be correct, in many cases they were based on only a partial reading of his theory or on the work of popularizers.

18   Bernstein, *Class, Codes and Control.* Vol. IV, 13.

19   Ibid.

20   Ibid., 13–14.

21   For a clear discussion of this, see Paul Atkinson, *Language, Structure and Reproduction* (London: Methuen, 1985).

22   For a sense of the varied types of approaches that fall under that rubric, see the special issue on the "Sociology of Curriculum" of the journal *Sociology of Education* 64 (January 1991). Of considerable interest here is Alan Sadovnick, "Basil Bernstein's Theory of Pedagogical Practice," *Sociology of Education* 64 (January 1991); 48–63.

23   Erik Olin Wright, *Classes* (New York: Verso, 1985), 9.

24   Apple, *Education and Power.*

25   For a debate on the location of these groups, see Erik Olin Wright, et al. *The Debate on Classes* (New York: Verso, 1989).

26   Here he can be rightly compared to Pierre Bourdieu. See, for example, Pierre Bourdieu, *Distinction* (Cambridge: Harvard University Press, 1984); and Pierre Bourdieu, *In Other Words: Essays Toward a Reflexive Sociology* (Stanford: Stanford University Press, 1990).

27   Bernstein, *Class, Codes and Control*. Vol. IV, 6.

28   Wright, *Classes*, 41.

29   Ibid., 60.

30   Bernstein, *Class, Codes and Control*. Vol. III, viii.

31   James Ladwig, "Comments on Education, Culture and Class Power," (unpublished personal correspondence, University of Wisconsin, October 12, 1991), 2.

32   Ibid.

33   Ibid., 3.

34   David Hogan, "Education and Class Formation," in *Cultural and Economic Reproduction in Education*, ed. Michael W. Apple (Boston: Routledge, 1983), 32–78.

35   For all its faults, one of the best examples of this approach is still Paul Willis, *Learning to Labor* (New York: Columbia University Press, 1981). See also Paul Willis, Simon Jones, Joyce Canaan and Geoff Hurd, *Common Culture* (Boulder: Westview Press, 1990).

36   What is implied by the concept of "determine" is, of course, subject to considerable debate. For an overview of part of this debate inside and outside of the context of education, see Jorge Larrain, *Marxism and Ideology*, Ernesto Laclau and Chantal Mouffe, *Hegemony and Socialist Strategy* (London: Verso, 1985); and Liston, *Capitalist Schools*.

37   Wright, *Classes*, 9–11.

38   Ibid.

39   Ibid, p. 14.

40   Basil Bernstein, *Class, Codes and Control*. Vol. IV, 13–62.

41   An insightful discussion of this can be found in Peter Stallybrass and Allon White, *The Politics and Poetics of Transgression* (Ithaca: Cornell University Press, 1986).

42   Paul Willis, et al., *Common Culture*, 2-29.

43   See, for example, Erik Olin Wright, *Classes* and Wright, et al., *The Debate on Classes*.

44   Erik Olin Wright, "Class and Occupation," *Theory and Society* 9, no. 2 (January 1980).

45   I have purposely put the concept of "black box" in inverted commas to high-light the fact that, unfortunately, we all too often associate blackness with something negative.

46   Michele Barrett, *Women's Oppression Today* (London: New Left Books, 1980).

47   I am indebted to Sue Middleton for this point. The earlier work of Madeleine Arnot was an excellent example of this.

48   Hogan, "Education and Class Formation." On the importance of the racial structuring of the state and civil society, see Michael Omi and Howard Winant, *Racial Formation in the United States* (New York: Routledge, 1986).

49   See Michael W. Apple, *Official Knowledge* (New York: Routledge, 1993); and Michael W. Apple and Linda Christian-Smith, eds., *The Politics of the Textbook* (New York: Routledge, 1991).

50   Bernstein, *Class, Codes and Control*. Vol. III.

51   Wright, *Classes*, 185.

52   Bernstein, *Class, Codes and Control*. Vol. IV, 74.

53   Ibid.

54   Some of the implications of this can be seen in Linda McNeil, *Contradictions of Control* (New York: Routledge, 1986); and Lois Weis, *Working Class Without Work* (New York: Routledge, 1990).

55   Apple, *Official Knowledge*.

56   Wright, *Classes*, 286.

57   Apple, *Official Knowledge*.

58   Bernstein, *Class, Codes and Control*. Vol. IV, 87.

59   This is discussed in considerably more detail in Apple, *Official Knowledge*.

60   Bernstein, *Classes, Codes and Control*. Vol. IV, 87.

61   See Michael W. Apple, "Social Crisis and Curriculum Accords," *Educational Theory* 38 (Spring 1988): 191–201, Roger Dale, *The State and Education Policy* (Philadelphia: Open University Press, 1989); and Martin Carnoy and Joel Samoff, *Education and Social Transition in the Third World* (Princeton: Princeton University Press, 1990).

62   Bernstein, *Class, Codes and Control*. Vol. IV, 165–218. His analysis of the ways in which recontextualizing agents work has been very useful in my own investigation of the state's complex role in the politics of official knowledge. See Apple, *Official Knowledge*, especially Chapter 4.

63   Wright, *Classes*, 201.

64   See, for example, Michael W. Apple and Lois Weis, "Ideology and Practice in Schooling," in *Ideology and Practice in Schooling*, ed. Michael W. Apple and Lois Weis (Philadelphia: Temple University Press, 1983), 3–33, and Cameron McCarthy and Michael W. Apple, "Race, Class and Gender in American Educational Research," in Lois Weis, ed. *Class, Race and Gender in American Education* (Albany: State University of New York Press, 1988), 9–39.

65   Bernstein, *Class, Codes and Control*. Vol. IV, 47.

66   Ibid.

67   Wright, *Classes*, p. 29.

68   See Apple, "Facing the Complexity of Power" and McCarthy and Apple, "Race, Class and Gender in American Educational Research."

69   See, for example, Hank Bromley, "Identity Politics and Critical Pedagogy," *Educational Theory* 39 (Summer 1989): 207–23.

70   Sadovnick, "Basil Bernstein's Theory of Pedagogic Practice."

71   Bernstein himself expressly criticizes the too-easy reliance on this term, arguing that it is so loosely defined as to have little use empirically. In many ways, his aim in some of his latest work is actually to specify more rigorously the conditions of "relative autonomy". See Bernstein, *Class, Codes and Control*. Vol. IV, 180–218. See also Daniel Liston, *Capitalist Schools*, for a similar argument, but one more based on the analytic Marxist tradition concerning appropriate forms of social explanation.

72   Basil Bernstein, *Class, Codes and Control*. Vol. IV, 133-218.

73   Ibid, 169.

74   See, for example, Mark Poster, *Foucault, Marxism and History* (New York: Polity Press, 1984); and Clarke, *New Times and Old Enemies*.

75   George Konrad and Ivan Szelenyi, *The Intellectuals on the Road to Class Power* (New York: Harcourt, Brace, and Jovanovich, 1979) and Ivan Szelenyi, "Prospects and Limits of Power of Intellectuals Under Market Capitalism," unpublished manuscript, Department of Sociology, The University of Wisconsin, Madison. See also Stanley Aronowitz, *The Politics of Identity* (New York: Routledge, 1992).

76   See Apple, *Official Knowledge* and Harvey Kaye, *The Powers of the Past* (Minneapolis: University of Minnesota Press, 1991). Some interesting points are also made in Terry Eagleton, *Ideology* (New York: Verso, 1991).

Chapter 9

Power, Meaning, and Identity: Critical Sociology of Education in the United States

Introduction

I trust that it comes as no surprise that answering the question "What is the state of sociology of education in the United States?" is not an easy task. The reasons for this are varied. First, surveying a field is itself an act of cultural production.[1] Like social and cultural activity in general, any field encompasses multiple dynamics, multiple and partly overlapping histories, and is in constant motion. Second, and equally important, what actually *counts* as the sociology of education is a construction. Academic boundaries are themselves culturally produced and are often the results of complex "policing" actions by those who have the power to enforce them and to declare what is or is not the subject of "legitimate" sociological inquiry. Yet, as Bourdieu reminds us, it is the ability to "trespass" that may lead to major gains in our understanding.[2] For these very reasons, I shall construct a picture of the state of sociology of education that is broad and that cuts across disciplinary boundaries—including important work in education in curriculum studies, history, gender studies, cultural studies, postcolonial studies, critical race theory, and so on.

Because of limitations of length, I shall only be able to give a sense of the multiple traditions and the constitutive tensions and agendas that are currently having an impact in the United States. Indeed, *each* of these traditions would require a book-length investigation to do justice to the internal controversies and conceptual, empirical, and political assumptions and arguments contained in them.[3]

Further, the development of any field is not linear. Rather, it is characterized by untidiness and unevenness. Thus, what is important in the development of a field are the breaks in which previous traditions are disrupted, displaced, and regrouped under new problematics. It is these breaks that transform the questions to be asked and the manner in which they are answered.[4] As I assess these breaks, in some ways my contribution here will by necessity take the form of something like an enhanced bibliographic essay, in essence a series of snapshots specifying what I take to be particular examples of some of the most interesting work being done. It will also require that I say something about the current political situation in the United States.

Multiple Traditions

There are very real tensions within the multiple traditions of sociology of education in the United States, in part because of the historical trajectory of what might be called the "academic/scientific project." The attempt over time to make sociology of education into something other than educational sociology—that is, to gain recognition for the field as a "science"—meant that quantitative, supposedly value-neutral orientations dominated here in very powerful ways. For some current interpreters, this had a chilling effect on those sociologists of education whose major interest was not a generalizable understanding of all schools but instead the development of thick descriptions of particularities.[5]

It also had other effects, some of which still are embodied as constitutive tensions within the field. Thus, the academic/scientific project:

> also generated the tension between knowledge production, the legitimated activity of the professorate in academe, and knowledge use as exemplified by social intervention to change and improve educational practice. . . . These tensions are at the very heart of rethinking the sociology of education. [Furthermore], questions of how best to understand how education works for different people in various settings, how best to evaluate educational outcomes, and how best to restructure schools to maximize the educational benefits for all students, must now begin with discussions concerning (a) whose knowledge is privileged most . . . and on what basis these competing knowledge bases are constructed . . . and (b) which role (observer vs. [active] participant) is most appropriate for the sociologist to adopt.[6]

In their own attempt to portray how these constitutive tensions are worked through—or ignored—Noblit and Pink point to five traditions that exist simultaneously: empirical-analytic, applied policy, interpretive, critical, and postmodern.[7] These, of course, are no more than ideal types, since some of these can at times "trespass" onto the terrain of the others. Yet it is the first two traditions that characterize much of the sociology of education in the United States. That this is so is evident in the contents of the "official" journal of the field here, *Sociology of Education*. Although the journal is a forum for some of the most technically sophisticated empirical work, and even though in the last decade and a half it has had editors such as Philip Wexler and Julia Wrigley who have themselves been part of the interpretive, critical, and/or postmodern traditions, it has been much less apt to publish ethnographic, theoretical, and critical material than, say, the *British Journal of Sociology of Education*. It has been an outlet for the empirical-analytic and applied policy perspectives, although more than before there are now occasional interpretive studies. (It would be even more unusual to find a serious article organized around more critical or postmodern frameworks.)

Speaking very generally, then, following a path that first came to wide public attention in the research of Coleman and Blau and Duncan, a large portion of research in the sociology of education continues to focus on the problematics of social stratification and status attainment. Its questions center on "the extent to which students from different social backgrounds have access to school experiences that foster academic and social success and on how success or failure in school affects later life chances."[8]

Further, a considerable portion of sociological research on education in the United States continues to devote its attention as well to systematic attempts at policy initiatives at the federal, state, and local levels, including such areas as the reform of finance, school restructuring, accountability and assessment, and governance.[9]

Elsewhere, Lois Weis and I have engaged in an analysis of the strengths and weaknesses of these traditions and of the interpretive research that grew partly in response to them.[10] My critical evaluation of their basic orientations remains the same. Therefore, I shall spend less time on them here.[11]

Even though I shall not spend much time discussing the empirical-analytic, applied policy, and interpretive perspectives here, it is important to state that I do not wish to dismiss these traditions. Take the first two as examples. Weis and I have raised crucial theoretical, political, and empirical questions about their agendas—for example, their equating of socioeconomic status with class, their focus on the atomistic individual, their sometimes acritical stance on multiple relations of power, their vision of the disinterested researcher, their neglect of what actually counts as school knowledge and of cultural politics in general, their tendency to ignore or radically simplify issues of the state, and their neglect of what actually happens in the daily lives of teachers and students inside and outside of schools.[12] Yet, having said this, it is still crucial that we recognize the importance of their analytic and empirical sophistication.

All too many critical and postmodern researchers, for example, have too easily assumed that *any* statistical questions and representations by definition must be positivist. They have ceded this terrain to conservatives or to methodological "experts for hire" who lend their technical expertise to any policy group willing to pay for it. This has proven to be disastrous in terms of our ability to raise and answer critical questions about the large-scale effects of the conservative reconstruction of education. It has also led to a partial deskilling of an entire generation of critically oriented researchers who, when they are confronted with quantitative analyses, simply reject them out of hand or do not have the analytic skills to deconstruct and criticize their specific arguments or their technical competence. Although I have no wish at all to return to the days of unbridled positivism (there were *reasons* for the decades of critiques against it), we may need to take much more seriously the losses that accompanied the largely progressive move toward, say, qualitative work.

Having raised these cautions, however, I shall devote the rest of this article to recent developments within what I take to be some of the most interesting movements in the sociology of education that occurred after the breaks with the dominant traditions. I shall begin with a discussion of representative examples within the sociology of curriculum and its concern with the politics of meaning. In essence, the issue of the politics of meaning will be the thread that guides my entire analysis of the recent development of certain tendencies in the field and of the breaks that have been made. In order to accomplish this, I shall then examine work on critical discourse analysis, identity politics, political economy and the labor process, and racial formation. Finally, I shall conclude with a discussion of the continuing tensions within and between the critical and postmodern communities methodologically, conceptually, and politically.

Official Knowledge and Popular Culture

A major question in the Noblit and Pink statement quoted above is, whose knowledge is privileged most and on what basis [are] these competing knowledge bases constructed? This question involves complex issues of cultural politics, of the relationship between cultural legitimacy and state regulation, and of the power/knowledge nexus. It has also involved tensions between different models of understanding these issues from neo-Marxist, world system, and poststructural/postmodern perspectives. In the sociology of curriculum, the relationship between culture and power has continued to receive considerable attention. What counts as "official knowledge" has been one of the foci and what does *not* receive the imprimatur of legitimacy has also been an important subject.

Thus, the tradition represented in *Knowledge and Control* in the United Kingdom[13] and first articulated in coherent form in *Ideology and Curriculum* in the United States[14] has been widened and deepened, not only in its scope and sophistication but also in the number of ways in which the relationship between knowledge and power is interrogated. One of the prime emphases has been on that most common "pedagogic device," the textbook, and other commodities actually found in classrooms. Influenced in part by Basil Bernstein's work on the processes of "recontextualization" of knowledge,[15] by the long European and American traditions of sociological studies of culture, and by newer models of textual analysis, considerably more sophisticated investigations of the political economy of texts (of various sorts), of the form and content of knowledge, and of readers' constructions of meanings have been produced.[16]

These issues have been examined historically in Teitelbaum's exceptional analysis of the development of socialist alternatives to the knowledge that was declared by the state to be official knowledge.[17] Olneck's series of studies on the symbolic crusade of "Americanization" and its influence on what was taught and on the larger politics of what schools were to do are very useful here.[18] David Labaree's investigation of class politics, credential markets, differentiated course offerings, and the contradictory pressures on schools provides an insightful discussion of the connections between curricular organization and larger political struggles in the development of secondary schools.[19] A growing concern with the role of the state is evident as well in my own treatment of the increasing role of state intervention in the process of the regulation, organization, and control of knowledge in textbooks. Here the activist state is seen as the contradictory result of social movements that were organized around class and race antagonisms and around regional politics.[20]

Although a focus on textbooks as the embodiment of official knowledge is but one example of a much larger concern for the politics of culture in schools, there are a number of reasons why such things have been seen as important. First, textbooks and other curriculum material provide levers to pry loose the complex connections among economy, politics (especially the state), and culture. They are *simultaneously* commodities that are produced for sale and representations of what powerful groups have defined as legitimate knowledge that are at least partly regulated by the state, and they speak to ongoing struggles over cultural legitimacy. In the absence of an officially recognized national curriculum—although proposals are now being promoted,[21] the textbooks provide the material basis for the construction of legitimate content and form in schools. Further, they are the results of hegemonic and counterhegemonic relations and social movements involving multiple power relations, including, but not limited to race, class, gender/sexuality, and religion.[22] Finally, the textbooks are subject to processes of interpretation as they are used and read by teachers, students, parents, and other community members. Thus, they are subject to multiple readings—in dominant, negotiated, or oppositional ways—depending on their form and content, the ways they position the reader, and on the person doing the reading.[23] In this way, such material provides one of the best examples for illuminating what Richard Johnson has called the circuit of cultural production.[24]

Yet the analysis of official knowledge has not proceeded only along such "critical" lines. Part of the research agenda in the sociology of curriculum has centered on a more world system perspective. John Meyer and his colleagues have argued that most critical sociological studies of educational systems and of their curricula have overly emphasized the determining role of specific national or local needs and interests, and have assumed too readily that the curriculum "reflects" particular social histories, problems, and requirements that are the embodiments of entrenched powers. Although they recognize that such research has contributed a good deal to our understanding of the relationship between power and school knowledge, Meyer and his colleagues emphasize the global power of the idea of modernity as a distinctive project or vision.[25] In Meyer's words, "the overall structure of this vision—organized around great conceptions of the nation-state as moving toward progress and justice—is entrenched on a worldwide basis. Both the nation-state model, and the particular professions that define the nature and content of mass education within this model, have had worldwide hegemony throughout the modern period."[26]

Thus, Meyer and his colleagues wish to advance a tradition in which the characteristics of mass education, and especially the curriculum in nations throughout most regions of the world, reflect worldwide forces. Local determinants and interests tend to be filtered through such wider world cultural forces. For this very reason, the general outline of mass education and the curricula found in most nations are remarkably homogeneous around the world.[27]

This kind of approach is partly flawed by its unfortunate stereotyping and lack of knowledge of some of the best work in the more critical tradition, by its neglect of national and international class relations, and by its treatment of the state in undertheorized ways. Yet, Meyer's analyses do raise a number of interesting issues about the internationalization of ideological visions that may cut across political economies. Though less theoretically elegant than, say, Basil Bernstein's formulations, it is similar in some ways to Bernstein's emphasis in his later work on the similarities of pedagogic devices across economic systems.[28]

A third tendency evident in the United States is organized around poststructural and postmodern forms of analysis of the power/knowledge nexus. These kinds of arguments are grounded in antiessentializing tendencies, in a mistrust of "grand narratives" and of calls for "emancipatory" curricula and pedagogy, and in efforts to broaden the traditional concern with particular kinds of power relations (in particular class, but also gender and race). Such arguments have become increasingly influential. For example, Ellsworth's analysis of the politics of meaning and pedagogy in a college classroom,[29] and of the ways in which multiple relations of power are constructed at that specific site, draws heavily on postmodern and feminist poststructural theories of multiplicity and difference. It suggests that previous critically oriented curricula and teaching smuggled in hidden assumptions about power as a zero-sum game that actually reproduced existing hierarchies and continued to privilege particular kinds of knowledge and experience centered on the power/knowledge relations of the academy and largely on white, male, heterosexual assumptions.

This was an important intervention into the debate over "the" emancipatory project in critical educational activity, one that generated considerable debate.[30] Also representative of some of these tendencies is Popkewitz, who employs one particular reading of a Foucaultian approach to the study of the politics of educational reform and the relationship between power and knowledge.[31] Although I have a number of concerns about what is lost as well as gained in the recent turn toward postmodern and poststructural theories—for example, the tendency by *some* postmodernists and poststructuralists to see *any* focus on political economy and class relations to be somehow reductive, to analyze the state as if it floats in thin air,[32] to expand the linguistic turn until it encompasses everything, to embrace overly relativistic epistemological assumptions, and the stylistic arrogance of some of its writing[33]—and shall say more about this later on in this essay, it is important to note the emerging emphasis on these approaches and to recognize that there are a number of advances in them.

By and large, the orientations toward curricula I have just discussed see official knowledge in two general ways. In the first, it is seen as the commodified result of a complex historical and political process by which particular knowledge, ways of knowing, and perspectives are made available. Hence, "legitimate" culture is seen as an object. In the second, culture is seen as lived.[34] A lived curriculum, a curriculum in use that embodies multiple and contradictory power relations is produced in the bodily and linguistic interactions among texts, students, and teachers in educational institutions and between these institutions and other sites. Among the most significant ways of understanding such productions is critical discourse analysis, which is itself the result of the tensions, and sometimes the merger, of the interpretive, critical, and often poststructural tendencies I noted.

Critical Discourse Analysis

Like sociolinguistics and ethnomethodology, critical discourse analysis begins with the assumption that language plays a primary role in the creation of meaning and that language use must be studied in social context, especially if we are interested in the politics of meaning. In a manner similar to interpretive research, it sees human subjects as constantly engaged in the negotiation of knowledge, social relations, and identity. However, it goes well beyond "mainstream" ethnographic research in that its primary focus is on how power, identity, and social relations are negotiated, are legitimated, and are contested toward political ends. In Luke's words, "Such an analysis attempts to establish how textual constructions of knowledge have varying and unequal material effects, and how these constructions that come to 'count' in institutional contexts are manifestations of larger political investments and interests."[35]

The focus here is on "systematic asymmetries of power and resources." Such asymmetries between speakers and listeners and between, say, writers and readers are then linked to the processes of the production and reproduction of stratified economic and political (in the broadest sense) interests. In essence, discourse in institutional life is viewed in a particular way. It is seen as "a means for the naturalization and disguise of power relations that are tied to inequalities in the social production and distribution of symbolic and material resources."[36]

Speaking broadly, Luke puts it this way:

> This means that dominant discourses in contemporary cultures tend to represent those social formations and power relations that are the products of history, social formation and culture (e.g., the gendered division of the workforce and domestic labor, patterns of school achievement by minority groups, national economic development) as if they were the product of organic, biological and essential necessity. By this account, critical discourse analysis is a political act itself—an intervention in the apparently natural flow of talk and text in institutional life that attempts to 'interrupt' everyday commonsense.[37]

The Bakhtinian influences here should be clear. Behind this position is the sense that critical discourse analysis should be involved in the destabilization of "authoritative discourse."[38] In the process, its task is to place at the very center of attention relations of domination, subordination, and inequality.[39]

This critical moment in critical discourse analysis is accompanied by a positive or constructive moment as well. Unlike some of the more aggressively postmodern positions that even deny its existence, one of the major aims of such critical research is to "generate agency." It wishes to provide tools to students, teachers, and others that enable them to see "texts"[40] as embodying both particular "representations"[41] of the social and natural world and particular interests. It wants to enable people to understand how such "texts" position them and at the same time produce unequal relations of institutional power that structure classrooms, staffrooms, and educational policies.[42]

Thus, some of these analyses are not only concerned with the active production of institutional power through a particular politics of meaning-making. They are also concerned with the ways in which knowledge is reconfigured, how new meanings are produced that challenge institutional regimes of power, not only in the classroom but also in the structuring of daily economic and political relations. To take but one classroom example, in an insightful study Dyson analyzes how young children in an urban primary school who are learning how to read and write construct and reconstruct stories to reveal and transform images of gender and power in their classrooms. The children constantly mediated and transformed images of gender relations that did not stand alone, but "were interwoven with race, class, and physical demeanor."[43] They reworked the material of the official curriculum and material from popular culture (for example, "superheroes" such as Ninja Turtles and the X-Men) that usually privileged male-dominated meanings and relations in ways that provided the possibility for counterhegemonic roles to be established in their classrooms.

There are many strengths in these kinds of approaches to the study of the politics of knowledge in schools, not the least of which is the activist component that takes a position on one of the tensions that Noblit and Pink have noted are deeply ingrained in the sociology of education in the United States. Yet a number of cautions that need to be taken seriously. Seeing the world as a text has a number of dangers if the practice is taken too far. It can lead to the neglect of the gritty materiality of the social world, of the materiality of the state, the economy, and class, race, and gender relations. It can ultimately embody what Whitty earlier called a "romantic possibilitarianism" in which changes in meaning and consciousness are the "new engines" of social transformation.[44] And it can make everything into a discursive construction.[45] On the other hand, when it is used well such a research agenda and perspective can provide insights that can be very helpful in efforts to illuminate and act on the complexities of the relationships between power and meaning in education.

The continuing attempt to think through the complex issue of the sociocultural "determinants" of commodified and lived culture is not limited to official knowledge or to discursive relations in schools. In fact, some of the most insightful advances have occurred in the area of popular culture. Though Giroux has recently called for more attention to be paid to popular culture,[46] an interest in this area predates this recognition and some of the best of current work goes well beyond his call in analytic and empirical sophistication.

Perhaps the best example of such work is Weinstein's analysis of the ways the "texts" of popular culture at a popular tourist museum are produced, made available, and then "read" by youth.[47] This investigation takes Johnson's earlier intuitions about the circuit of cultural production and Willis's interrogation of the multiple uses of popular culture to a new level by examining the processes by which culture is constructed, deconstructed, and "performed."[48] Its integration of material in cultural studies, political economy, and critical poststructuralist theory enables Weinstein to give us an analysis of the ways in which popular culture is produced and consumed and of the ways that young people make sense of their world in and out of schools. Koza's recent discussion of rap music in schools and the larger society is also useful here,[49] as is Giroux's deconstruction of the popular cultural productions of Walt Disney.[50]

Identity Politics and Social Movements

The intuitions that lie behind critical discourse analysis and the study of the politics of official and popular culture also underpin the recent growth of interest in various forms of narrative research in the United States. These include life histories, oral histories, autobiographies, feminist or antiracist "testimonies," work on popular memory, and narrative interviews. These approaches are distinctly interdisciplinary. Although they are socially critical in intent, they selectively integrate elements from literary, historical, anthropological, psychological, sociological, and cultural studies.

As Casey documents in her recent review of such narrative approaches, what links them together is again a powerful interest in the ways people make meaning through language. While tracing out the history and contradictions of narrative research in education, and being duly cautious of some of its possible roots in the "bourgeois subject" and in the new middle-class's seeming infinite need for self-display, Casey demonstrates how such social and cultural research attempts to defy "the forces of alienation, anomie, annihilation, authoritarianism, fragmentation, commodification, depreciation, and dispossession."[51] In her words, those forms of narrative research that are culturally and politically *committed* "announce 'I am'('we are')."[52] Perhaps one of the best examples of such work is her own research on the collective biographies of politically active women teachers who are engaged in struggles over curricula, teaching, and larger relations of power inside and outside of schools.[53]

The issue of "I am" ("we are") speaks directly to the study of identity politics. Although Casey's synthetic review of the emergence of narrative approaches is largely devoted to methodological and political issues, a considerable portion of the newest critical sociocultural work deals with the role of the school as a site for the production of identities. Here too there are benefits and problems. The poststructural emphasis on identity politics is visible in a number of areas; for example, Bromley argues for much more attention to be paid to it and Wexler criticizes its evacuation of class dynamics as *the* primary determinant of identity formation.[54] Wexler's ethnographic study of the "moral economy" of identity creation in different U.S. secondary schools is a partial return to structural forms of analysis by him, but still within a partly poststructural understanding.[55] His argument that class is primary in the production of student identities is provocative, but his volume is too brief to fully develop his arguments about this. It is not just the issue of brevity that has been a concern here. Lois Weis—whose own research on the politics of identity formation provides important connections among the political economy; identity in gender, class, and race terms; and social movements[56]—has raised a number of cautions about the centering of class as *the* fundamental dynamic.[57]

Weis's argument about Wexler's position is instructive in this regard. Both have major concerns about the loss of a structural understanding of identity formation within some of the recent poststructural material. Yet, for Weis, rather than seeing race and gender as things that students bring in after their identities are structured in class terms by schools, the very structure of these institutions compellingly reflects raced and gendered—as well as classed—practices that are deeply implicated in identity formation.[58] I have sympathy with both positions here. It is unfortunate but clear that all too often class relations have been marginalized in much of the recent work on identity politics, in part because a concern with it is seen as somehow too reductive. This position speaks more to the unfamiliarity of researchers with the best of class analysis and of the ways we might think through the contradictory tensions both within class and among multiple relations of power that include class, than to the necessarily reductive nature of a concern with class itself. There is a world of difference between taking class as seriously as it deserves to be taken and reducing everything down to it.[59]

The Wexler/Weis discussion points to an important movement in the multiple critical communities within the sociology of education in the United States. It speaks to an attempt to widen the dynamics of power that are considered to be important, to look at the contradictory histories and relations within and among them, and at the same time to include class dynamics—when thought about more elegantly—as truly constitutive.[60] In my mind, this is a crucial movement. There is perhaps a widening divide epistemologically, empirically, and at times politically between the "neos" and the "posts," with unfortunate stereotypes on both sides. Some of this is caused by, but not limited to, the rejectionist impulses, partial loss of historical memory, overstatements, and stylistic peculiarities of some postmodern and poststructural writings and some of it is caused by an overly defensive attitude on the part of some neo-Marxists.[61] In the midst of this debate, however, a tendency has begun to grow that seeks to let these traditions "rub against each other." The attempt is to let each one correct the emphasis of the other and to see the tensions caused by their differences as *productive*—always provided that there is a clear political commitment behind each position and always provided that the interest is not merely cynically deconstructive.

Let me say more about this, because I believe it provides a context for one of the more significant breaks that I noted earlier. There have been attempts to combine neo-Marxist (specifically neo-Gramscian) and poststructural theories. Thus Bruce Curtis, in a book that should be required reading for anyone involved in the history and sociology of education, integrates these two perspectives to illuminate the complex politics of state formation and the growth of school bureaucracies over time.[62] He examines the collective biographies of the groups of people who populated the newly emerging state, demonstrates the power of the conflicts over meaning and control and over the local and the more global, and insightfully shows the ethical and political nature of the search for centralization, standardization, and efficiency.

Perhaps some of my own recent work can also be useful here to provide an instance of the search for more integrative strategies. In *Cultural Politics and Education*, I demonstrate how a neo-Gramscian perspective—with its focus on the state, on the formation of hegemonic blocs, on new social alliances and the generation of consent, all within an economic crisis—and poststructuralism—with its focus on the local, on the formation of subjectivity, identity, and the creation of subject positions—can creatively work together to uncover the organizational, political, and cultural struggles over education.[63]

This work analyzes how authoritarian populist social movements are formed during a time of economic and ideological crisis and at a time when the state engages in "policing" official knowledge. By examining a textbook controversy in a polarized local community that was undergoing an economic crisis and changes in class relations, it demonstrates how people can be pushed into rightist identities through their interactions with the state. Research such as this represents not only an attempt to integrate neo and post positions, but an extension and reorientation of the material about identity politics so that it focuses on the formation of *oppositional* identities and oppositional politics—the growth of rightist social movements.

In *Social Analysis of Education*, Wexler urged researchers doing critical sociological work in education to devote more of their attention to the formation and power of social movements.[64] These social movements—both emergent and residual[65]—provide crucial elements in determining the stability and instability of the policies and practices involved in curricula, teaching, and evaluation and of beliefs about schooling, the state, and the economy in general. This insight has been explored in work on the dialectical relationship between conservative cultural, religious, and economic movements on the one hand and schooling on the other. Struggles over schooling both participate in the formation of oppositional social and religious movements and are the subjects of these movements.

My research on the role of the struggle over meaning in the formation of authoritarian populist movements is an attempt to take these issues seriously. It argues that most analyses of "the Right" assume (wrongly) a number of things. Too often they assume a unitary ideological movement, and see it as a relatively uncontradictory group rather than a complex assemblage of different tendencies, many of which are in a tense and unstable relationship with each other. Even more importantly, many analyses also take the Right as a fact, as a given. This takes for granted one of the most important questions that needs to be investigated. How does the Right get *formed*? Thus, this research demonstrates how conflicts over state-supported schooling—in particular the struggle over official knowledge and over the bureaucratic state—can lead to the formation of rightist movements that combine authoritarian populist religious elements (which in the United States are growing extremely powerful) and economic conservatism. In essence, oppositional political and cultural identities are formed among community members in interaction with local institutions such as schools, identities that are sutured into conservative movements in powerful ways.[66]

The Gramscian moment—his dictum that one must look to the role of common sense in the formation of ideologies that organize and disorganize "a people"—is more than a little visible here in these analyses, as are the poststructuralist moments surrounding issues of identity and subjectivity. It is here that the sociology of curriculum and theories of state formation meet the sociology of identity, where a concern with the politics of meaning and the formation of new conservative hegemonic blocs meets the realities of the formation of subject positions and identity at a local level.

Although I have focused on the building of oppositional identities and social movements, in no way do I wish to slight the research on identity politics inside schools in the lives of students and teachers. Although some of this research, like other elements of the postmodern and poststructural positions, is at times in danger of underplaying the very real structurally generated conditions of this society, as my comments on the Wexler/Weis positions indicate important work indeed is being done on the role of the school as a site of contested student and teacher identities along multiple dynamics such as race, class, gender, sexuality, and ability. Perhaps some of the best places to turn for examples of such research is in work by McCarthy and Crichlow, Weis and Fine, and Fine, Weis, and Wong.[67] Of considerable interest here as well is Bourgois, who has conducted a detailed and sensitive study of the complex educational, economic, and personal lives of Latino drug dealers.[68] These issues are related not only to issues such as "I am" ("we are") among students, but also have surfaced in important ways in terms of the identities of researchers as classed, raced, gendered, sexed, and differently abled people as well, although at times in ways that again marginalize class issues a bit too much.[69]

Political Economy and the Labor Process

The fact that there has been a growing interest in cultural politics and in the area of identity politics and an increasing influence (some of it warranted and some of it rather too trendy) of poststructuralist/ postmodern theories and cultural studies does not mean that research on issues surrounding political economy and the labor process have not also had a significant presence. Exactly the opposite is the case.

Even though neo-Marxist sociology of education—especially the sociology of curriculum—advanced fairly sophisticated arguments against the reductive tendencies in base/superstructure models and developed alternatives to them, the current neoliberal attempts to reorganize schooling around its ideological and economic agenda has stimulated a return to an emphasis on economic arguments. At times, this has meant a return in negative ways. That is, the material sounds not unlike the positions of an earlier generation that was influenced by the work of Bowles and Gintis in *Schooling in Capitalist America*.[70] In this situation, there has been something of a loss of collective memory of the very real conceptual and empirical advances that were made in such areas as the dialectical and contradictory relationships among the economic, political, and cultural spheres; on the nature of the state; on the "relative autonomy" of cultural practices; and so on.[71]

Yet at other times, the reemergence of political economy has been accomplished by the incorporation of some of the best newer material in critical urban studies and on the social organization of class and race in spatial terms. Thus, Rury and Mirel provide an insightful discussion of the political economy of urban education that draws on Harvey's analysis of the transformations of the political geography of space in advanced capitalism.[72] This is crucial. Rury and Mirel demonstrate how previous traditions of analyzing urban contexts are weakened in the extreme by their inability to situate the transformations of cities in the histories of class and race dynamics and by their lack of sophistication in the analysis of *political* economy.[73]

A return to political economy,[74] and an increasing focus on the tensions and conflicts generated by the crisis in the paid labor market and in income distribution, is also visible elsewhere. Thus, there have been comparisons of the claims made by neoliberals about the connections between schooling and the economy with demographic evidence about the current and future structuring of paid employment and the distribution of benefits. They show that such claims are at best based on very shaky evidence and at worst are simply incorrect.[75]

At the same time, approaches based on political economy have been used with counterintuitive results. For example, Gintis has recently argued in support of particular marketized voucher and choice plans for schools. He claims that there are political and economic justifications for such initiatives when they are incorporated into a larger program for the redistribution of economic assets.[76] As you would imagine, this suggestion has proven to be exceptionally contentious. It may document the fact that critical studies in the political economy of education may lead to surprising results. Or it may signify the loss of faith in democratic socialist alternatives among a number of scholars who were leaders in the early years of the political economy of education. It is not totally clear at this time which direction this kind of analysis will take. My own position is that such arguments may ultimately lend support to those marketized initiatives proposed under the conservative restoration that expressly *do not* have economically redistributive ends.

Although analyses of political economy have once again gained momentum—in part stimulated by the evident crisis and the climate of conservative triumphalism here—there has also been a continuation and deepening of research on the labor process of teaching. This has followed up, expanded, corrected, and made more empirically substantial previous research on intensification, deskilling, reskilling, the contradictions of professionalism, and the daily lives of teachers.

Gitlin and Margonis may serve as an example here.[77] Taking account of previous work on intensification, resistance, and the contradictory elements of "good sense" and "bad sense" in the understanding of teachers of their daily practices,[78] and situating their work within the past efforts to understand the classed and gendered nature of teaching,[79] they examine the processes by which teachers interpret administrative attempts at school "reform." Gitlin and Margonis engaged in an intensive study of a site-based management reform and the resistance of teachers to the reform. Their analysis demonstrated the ways in which both "first-wave" and "second-wave" analyzers of site-based management reform fundamentally misconstrued what is happening.[80] Both of these groups of social researchers "overlook the good sense embodied in teachers' resistant acts, which often point to the fundamental importance of altering authority relations and intensified work conditions."[81]

Although there indeed is a recognition that teaching is a gendered occupation in Gitlin and Margonis, as Acker notes in her important synthesis of the literature on gender and teachers' work in the United States, Canada, the United Kingdom, Australia, and elsewhere that the increase in feminist scholarship in education over the past three decades has led to a significant body of recent work that makes gender central to the study of teaching.[82] She cautions us about the dangers of employing simple dichotomies (male/female) and urges us to think through the complexity that lies at the heart of teaching. Thus, there is a growing recognition here that not only do we need to integrate class and race into our discussions of gender, but we need to recognize the diversity *within* each of these groups. The research challenge facing those interested in teachers' work is clear in Acker's words: "how to keep gender considerations paramount, while simultaneously deconstructing the concept of teacher and still managing to achieve some generalizability about teachers' work."[83]

While less overtly connected to political economy and to studies of the labor process, the complexities of the racial structuring of teaching have provided important insights into the historical and current construction of teaching around racial dynamics.[84] Further, Ladson-Billings's recent ethnographic study of racial dynamics at the level of teaching and curricula—a study that highlights the potential of socially committed, mostly African American teachers to connect with students of color—gives us a sense of possibility in a literature that is too often characterized by a sense of defeat.[85]

Racial Formations

My previous section concluded with a statement about race and teaching. Yet, it would be hard to overstate the constitutive role played by overt and covert racial dynamics historically and currently in the construction of teaching, evaluation, official knowledge, popular culture, identities, economic divisions, public policy, and the state itself in the United States. A sociology of education that does not recognize this lives in a world divorced from reality. For race is not an "add on." The realities and predicaments of people of color are neither additions to nor defections from American life. Rather, they are *defining* elements of that life.[86] In Omi and Winant's words, in what is considered to be one of the most impressive analysis of race and the state in the United States, "Concepts of race structure both state and civil society. Race continues to shape both identities and institutions in significant ways.[87]

Race is not a stable category. What it means, how it is used, by whom it is used, how it is mobilized in social discourse, its role in educational and more general social policy are all contingent and historical. Of course, it is misleading to talk of race as an "it." "It" is not a thing, a reified object that can be tracked and measured as if it were a simple biological entity. Race is a set of fully social relations.[88]

If race is not a thing, but what critical cultural analysts have called a "performance", neither is it an innocent concept. Real people's histories and collective memories, languages, and futures are at stake here. Understanding what race is and does has required a multidisciplinary approach that includes studies of popular culture, literature, the state, national and international political and economic structures, and the cultural politics of imperialism and postcolonialism, to name but a few areas.[89]

In fact, it has become abundantly clear that behind much of the conservative discourse about education—the supposed decline in standards, the call for a return to the "Western tradition," a reassertion of toughness and discipline, the call for privatization and marketization—lies a vision of "the other." It symbolizes an immense set of anxieties, including cultural and economic ones, that are used to build a new hegemonic alliance around conservative policies.[90]

The increasing circulation of racial subtexts is heightened by the visibility of racist and racial discourse in the popular media and in (supposedly) academic books that receive widespread publicity. The recent popularity of the genetic arguments found in Herrnstein and Murray's volume, *The Bell Curve* (of which nearly 400,000 copies were sold), is an indication of this phenomenon.[91] This has occasioned a series of critical interrogations of its conceptual, empirical, and social assumptions and of the historical reasons behind its wide circulation and acceptance as plausible.[92] The fact that there have been a considerable number of such engaged critical social and historical analyses of positions such as Herrnstein and Murray's provides yet another example of the critical sociologist as "public intellectual" during a time of conservative restorational politics.

The growing acceptance of genetic arguments about race and/or of conservative restorational positions in general has led to even greater emphasis on the issue of the politics of race in the sociology of education, especially on the issue of "whiteness," that bears on my earlier discussion of identity. An assumption that has underpinned much of the research on racial identity is the belief that "white racial hegemony has rendered whiteness invisible or transparent."[93] Thus, whiteness becomes the unarticulated normative structure. It becomes so naturalized that European Americans do not even have to think about "being white." It becomes the absent presence, the "there that is not there." As Roman puts it, race becomes a "reified synonym" that is applied only to racially subordinate groups.[94]

Yet the assumption of such invisibility is now more than a little problematic. Racial identities among, say, white students—partly formed out of a politics of common sense during a period of conservative restructuring—are becoming increasingly powerful and volatile. Gallagher's research on the construction of white identities among university students provides an important example here, one that is worth examining.[95]

Among many white working-class and middle-class students there is now a belief that there is a social cost to being white. Whites are the "new losers" in a playing field that they believe has been levelled now that the United States is a supposedly basically "egalitarian, colorblind society".[96] These students constructed identities that avow a "legitimate, positive narrative of one's own whiteness . . . that negated white oppressor charges and framed whiteness as a liability."[97] Since "times were rough for everybody," but policies such as affirmative action were unfairly supporting "non-whites," these students began to claim the status of victims.[98] As Gallagher puts it,

> Ignoring the ways in which whites "get raced" has the makings of something politically dangerous. A fundamental transformation of how young whites define and understand themselves racially is taking place. [They] have generally embraced the belief that the U.S. class system is fair and equitable. [They argue] that individuals who delay gratification, work hard, and follow the rules will succeed regardless of their color . . . For many whites the levelled playing field argument has rendered affirmative action policies a form of reverse discrimination and a source of resentment. White students who believe social equality has been achieved are able to assert a racial identity without regarding themselves as racist, because they see themselves as merely affirming their identity through language and actions—something racially defined groups do frequently.[99]

These arguments point to something of considerable moment in the politics of education in the United States and elsewhere. As it is being shaped by the political Right, whiteness as an explicit cultural product is taking on a life of its own. In the arguments of the conservative discourses now so powerfully circulating, the barriers to social equality and equal opportunity have been removed. Whites, hence, have no privilege. Thus, "this ostensibly non-racist white space being carved out of our cultural landscape allows whites to be presented as just another racial contender . . . in the struggle over political and cultural resources and self-definition"—but always with an underlying belief that history has shown the superiority of "Western" political and cultural institutions and values.[100]

The implications of all this are profound politically and culturally. For, given the Right's rather cynical use of racial anxieties, given the economic fears and realities many citizens experience, and given the historical power of race in the American psyche, many members of the next generation who are now in school may choose to develop forms of solidarity based on their "whiteness." The new identity of whiteness is not inconsequential in terms of the struggles over meaning, identity, and the very characteristics and control of schools, to say the least. It underscores the movement toward marketized schooling in the United States and points toward a crucial terrain for socially committed sociological researchers.

Critical Policy Research

Although it is not totally explained by racial dynamics, the issue of the characteristics and control of schools has played an important role in one particular part of the sociology of education. Even though I have not gone into detail about the policy-oriented tradition in the sociology of education in the United States, it should be noted that there has been an emerging focus on *critical* policy research.[101] As in the United Kingdom, the conservative restoration in the United States has attempted to redefine what is public as necessarily bad and what is private as necessarily good. The effects of this emphasis in educational policy have been predictable, and have included opening schools to even more corporate control and influence. The most powerful example is Channel One, an arrangement by which schools sign contracts with a large corporation that gives them "free" equipment and a "free" news broadcast in return for the delivery of their students as a captive audience for advertisements that are broadcast over Channel One. More than 40 percent of all private and public middle and secondary school students are currently enrolled in schools that receive Channel One. In reaction to this, research has critically examined the history, policy formation process, and ideological effects of such "reforms."[102]

Another major effect of such market-driven initiatives has been the development of voucher and choice plans. Although many of the empirical assessments are still being completed, there is growing evidence that such policies do not lead to higher achievement on the part of poor children and children of color. As Whitty has concluded in his review of what the American evidence has shown, "The stronger claims of choice advocates cannot be upheld . . . and choice needs to be carefully regulated if it is not to have damaging equity effects."[103] A number of analyses of the neoliberal efforts to make schools part of the marketplace, and of the academic discourse that supports these efforts, have been carried out. By and large, these too raise serious questions about its ideological vision of this project and its differential effects.[104]

The neoliberal emphasis on the weak state has been accompanied by a neoconservative emphasis on strong state control over values, culture, and the body.[105] Although there have been analyses of the cultural agendas of neoconservatives—especially of their visions of what and whose knowledge is legitimate[106]—it is only recently that investigations of their educational policies have been linked specifically to the ways in which they construct the meanings and histories of social problems and to the question of whether the empirical evidence supports such constructions.

Perhaps one of the more interesting examples of such an investigation is Burdell's analysis of the social and cultural construction of the problem of teenage pregnancy and of the educational responses to it.[107] Using critical feminist tools, Burdell contextualizes the growth of teenage pregnancy as a *public* problem. She shows how these largely conservative constructions take on the power of "truth" and increasingly come to dominate discussions of the causes, effects, and solutions to the "problem" of pregnant teens. In the process, she brings together historical and current evidence to counter the popular views of these causes, effects, and solutions, and suggests an alternative agenda for research and for educational policy and practice. Burdell's discussion provides another interesting example of the model of engaged research I noted earlier.

Conclusion

In this essay, by necessity I have had to be selective both in my discussion of the multiple traditions within the sociology of education and related areas in the United States and in my choice of research that exemplifies some of these traditions. I have sought to show how concerns with the politics of meaning, identity formation, the state, political economy, and the labor process intersect with concerns with multiple and contradictory dynamics of power, such as race, gender, and class.

After reviewing the vast amount of material within these multiple traditions, especially within the critical, postmodern, and poststructural elements of them, certain things become more obvious. There were clear silences, areas that were in considerable need of critical analyses of various kinds. For example, although a focus on identity politics is growing, it is much harder to find work on the best of recent theories of class. The *state* remains undertheorized and does not surface enough within critical analyses. Further, although the perspectives growing out of, say, cultural studies are growing, there is still a relative neglect of nonreductive theories of the political economy of culture. Consumption practices now too often "eat" production practices. And even though there has been a partial return to political economy, in my opinion this is still too neglected and at times is less sophisticated than it might be. Finally, it is clear that there has been a growth of interest in postmodern and poststructural approaches in the United States.

In other places, I have raised a number of questions concerning this turn.[108] Yet, while I have real worries about the relatively uncritical acceptance of some aspects of these theories—and have noted a few of them briefly here—as I also indicated among the most positive signs on the horizon are the attempts at integrating the perspectives of the neo and post traditions and letting them interact with each other. At a time when we face a period of conservative triumphalism in the United States, too many neos and posts wind up arguing with each other rather than enabling the critical impulses of each to inform the other.

A good deal of the postmodern and poststructural emphases now emerging in critical educational studies has had a positive effect. It has increased the number of voices that need to be made public. It has helped legitimate and/or generate a welcome return to the concrete analysis of particular ideological or discursive formations, as well as to the multiple sites of their elaboration and legitimation in policy documents, social movements, and institutions.[109] This focus on the concrete historical instance that does not require a search for hidden sets of determinations, does in part free us to understand the complexities of "the local" and the contingent.

Yet having said this (and it must be said), some of these studies suffer from the same silences as one of the major figures from whom they have often borrowed their emphasis—Michel Foucault. As Hall reminds us, it has proven all too easy in scholarship and theory to accept Foucault's epistemological position whole and uncritically. There is a world of difference (and no pun is intended here) between emphasizing the local, the contingent, and the noncorrespondent and ignoring any determinacy or any structural relationships among practices. Too often important questions about the state and social formation are simply evacuated and the difficult problem of *simultaneously* thinking about both the specificity of different practices and the forms of articulated unity that they constitute is assumed out of existence as if nothing existed in structured ways.[110]

In my mind, it is exactly this issue of simultaneity, of thinking neo and post together, of actively enabling the tensions within and among them to help form our research, that will solidify previous understandings, avoid the loss of collective memory of the gains that have been made, and generate new insights and new actions. A little trespassing may be a good thing here.

Notes

I would like to thank Geoff Whitty for his perceptive comments on earlier drafts of this article.

1   G. Noblit and W. Pink. "Mapping the Alternative Paths of Sociology of Education, in *Continuity and Contradiction: the Futures of the Sociology of Education*, ed. W. Pink and G. Noblit (Cresskill, NJ: Hampton Press, 1995), 8.

2   P. Bourdieu. *In Other Words* (Stanford: Stanford University Press, 1990).

3   See, for example, R. Morrow and C. Torres, *Social Theory and Education*. (Albany: State University of New York Press, 1995).

4   S. Hall, "Cultural Studies: Two Paradigms," in *Cultural Studies*, ed. L. Grossberg, C. Nelson, and P. Treicher (New York: Routledge, 1992), 520.

5   Noblit and Pink, "Mapping the Alternative Paths," 27.

6   Ibid.

7   Ibid., 25.

8   B. Rowan, "Research on School Effects and Status Attainment," in *Continuity and Contradiction: the Futures of the Sociology of Education*, ed. W. Pink and G. Noblit. (Cresskill: Hampton Press, 1995), 34.

9   See the section on "The Policy Path" in Pink and Noblit, *Continuity and Contradiction*, 233–303.

10 M.W. Apple and L. Weis, "Ideology and Practice in Schooling," in *Ideology and Practice in Schooling*, ed. M.W. Apple and L. Weis (Philadelphia: Temple University Press, 1983).

11 Those readers who wish to examine the recent empirical and social agendas of such research programs will find clear discussions in the sections on "The Empirical-Analytic Path" and "The Interpretive Path" in *Continuity and Contradiction*, ed. Pink and Noblit, 33–100, 103–73.

12 Apple and Weis, "Ideology and Practice in Schooling."

13 M.F.D. Young, ed., *Knowledge and Control* (London: Collier-Macmillan, 1971).

14 M.W. Apple, *Ideology and Curriculum* (New York: Routledge, 1979; second edition 1990).

15 B. Bernstein, *The Structuring of Pedagogic Discourse* (New York: Routledge, 1990).

16   See, for example, M.W. Apple, *Teachers and Texts* (New York: Routledge, 1988); M.W. Apple, *Official Knowledge* (New York: Routledge, 1993); M.W. Apple, and L. Christian-Smith, ed., *The Politics of the Textbook*. (New York: Routledge, 1991); L. Christian-Smith, ed., *Texts of Desire* (London: Falmer, 1993); A. Luke, *Literacy, Textbooks, and Ideology* (London: Falmer Press, 1988); and A. Luke, "The Secular Word," in *The Politics of the Textbook*, ed. Apple and Christian-Smith.

17   K. Teitelbaum, *Schooling for Good Rebels* (New York: Teachers College Press, 1995).

18   See M. Olneck, "Americanization and the Education of Immigrants, 1900–1925," *American Journal of Education* 97 (August 1989): 398–423; M. Olneck, "The Recurring Dream: Symbolism and Ideology in Intercultural and Multicultural Education," *American Journal of Education* 98 (February 1990): 147–74; and M. Olneck, "Terms of Inclusion: Has Multicultural Redefined Inequality in American Education?" *American Journal of Education* 101 (May 1993): 234–60.

19   D. Labaree, *The Making of an American High School* (New Haven: Yale University Press, 1988).

20   Apple, *Official Knowledge;* C. Cornbleth and A. Waugh, *The Great Speckled Bird* (New York: St. Martin's Press, 1995).

21   Apple, *Cultural Politics and Education*; E. Eisner, ed., *Hidden Consequences of a National Curriculum* (Washington, DC: American Educational Research Association, 1995).

22   J. Delfattore, *What Johnny Shouldn't Read* (New Haven: Yale University Press, 1992).

23   Apple, *Official Knowledge*; Luke, "The Secular Word."

24   R. Johnson, "What Is Cultural Studies Anyway?" *Social Text* 16 (1986/1987): 38–80.

25   J. Meyer, D. Kamens, and A. Benavot, *School Knowledge for the Masses* (London: Falmer Press, 1992), 1.

26   Ibid., 1–2.

27   Ibid., 2.

28   Bernstein, *The Structuring of Pedagogic Discourse*. It is unfortunate that Bernstein's work is now less well-known in the United States among students and sociologists in education. As I have argued elsewhere for a largely American audience, his work provides some of the most important elements of a serious and disciplined sociology of education. Because of the popularity—and at times trendiness—of an all-too-often uncritical acceptance of postmodern and poststructural approaches in a number of areas in the United States, too

many individuals have turned away from such work. I shall have more to say about this later. See M.W. Apple, "Education, Culture, and Class Power," *Educational Theory* 42 (Spring 1992): 127–45.

29   E. Ellsworth, "Why Doesn't This Feel Empowering?" *Harvard Educational Review* 59 (August 1989): 297–324. The focus on *pedagogy* rather than on *teaching*, in much of the new literature on "critical pedagogy," is an interesting case of the politics of linguistic usage, I believe. Because teaching is seen as a low-status occupation and taking it as worthy of scholarly criticism, hence, is also usually seen as low-status within the academy and confined to low status areas such as the field of education, higher status academic inquiries into one's teaching must be reconfigured and reorganized around more "elegant" linguistic forms. In my mind, it is not an accident that much of the recent attention being paid to "critical pedagogy" (whatever that means, since it is a sliding signifier that shifts around the linguistic map) as a theoretical enterprise is to be found among academics in the humanities [See, for example, D. Morton and M. Zavarzadeh, eds., *Theory/Pedagogy/Politics* (Urbana: University of Illinois Press, 1991)]. All of this new scholarship proceeds as if it were a new topic and as if the field of education and the very long tradition of dealing with the politics of teaching and curriculum did not exist. This phenomenon would make a fascinating study in the politics of academic discourse and the construction of "new" fields.

30   C. Luke and J. Gore, eds., *Feminisms and Critical Pedagogy* (New York: Routledge, 1992).

31   T. Popkewitz, *A Political Sociology of Educational Reform* (New York: Teachers College Press, 1991).

32   For one example of this tendency, see I. Hunter, *Rethinking the School* (Boston: Allen and Unwin, 1994).

33   M.W. Apple, *Education and Power.* 2d ed. (New York: Routledge, 1995); Apple, *Cultural Politics and Education,* L. Zipin, "Emphasizing 'Discourse' and Bracketing People," in T. Popkewitz and M. Brennan, eds., *Foucault's Challenge* (New York: Teachers College Press, 1998).

34   Apple and Weis, "Ideology and Practice in Schooling."

35   A. Luke, "Text and Discourse in Education," in M.W. Apple, ed., *Review of Research in Education.* Vol. 21 (Washington, DC: American Educational Research Association, 1996), 9.

36   Ibid.

37   Ibid.

38   M. Bakhtin, *Speech Genres and Other Essays* (Austin: University of Texas Press, 1986).

39   Luke, "Text and Discourse in Education," 9.

40 In this tradition, a "text" is not only a textbook, but is also defined as language use—that is, as any instance of written and spoken language that has coherence and coded meanings. See Luke, "Text and Discourse in Education."

41 Of course, the very concept of representation and how it is used, and overused, is contentious. See Ibid.

42 Ibid. See also K. Gutierrez, et al. "Script, Counterscript, and Underlife in the Classroom," *Harvard Educational Review* 65 (Fall 1995): 445–71.

43 A.H. Dyson, "The Ninjas, the X-Men, and the Ladies," *Teachers College Record* 94 (Winter 1994): 219–39.

44 G. Whitty, "Sociology and the Problem of Radical Education Change," in M. Flude and J. Ahier, eds., *Educability, schools and ideology* (London: Halstead Press, 1974).

45 B. Palmer, *Descent into Discourse* (Philadelphia: Temple University Press, 1990).

46 H. Giroux, "Doing Cultural Studies," *Harvard Educational Review* 64 (Fall 1992): 278–308. See also P. McLaren, *Critical Pedagogy and Predatory Culture* (New York: Routledge, 1995).

47 M. Weinstein, *Robot World*. (Ph.D. diss., University of Wisconsin-Madison, 1995).

48 Johnson, "What Is Cultural Studies Anyway," and P. Willis, *Common Culture* (Boulder: Westview, 1990).

49 J. Koza, "Rap Music," *The Review of Education/Pedagogy/Cultural Studies* 16 (Fall 1994): 171–96.

50 H. Giroux, "Animating Youth," *Socialist Review* 24, no. 3 (1994): 23–55. Giroux's analysis here does prove that he can write more clearly when he works hard enough at it. It is unfortunate that this is found much less often in the rest of the corpus of his work and in his overly defensive dismissal of such efforts to develop a less arrogant writing style.

51 K. Casey, "The New Narrative Research in Education," in M.W. Apple, ed., *Review of Research in Education*. Vol. 21, 5.

52 Ibid.

53 K. Casey, *I Answer with My Life* (New York: Routledge, 1993).

54 H. Bromley, "Identity Politics and Critical Pedagogy," *Educational Theory* 39 (Summer 1989): 207–23 and P. Wexler, *Becoming Somebody* (London: Falmer Press, 1992).

55 Wexler, *Becoming Somebody*.

56 L. Weis, *Working Class Without Work* (New York: Routledge, 1990).

57   L. Weis, "Qualitative Research in the Sociology of Education," in *Continuity and Contradiction*, ed. Pink and Noblit.

58   Ibid., 164.

59   See Apple, "Education, Culture and Class Power," and E.O. Wright, *The Debate on Classes* (New York: Verso, 1989).

60   See L. Weis and M. Fine, eds., *Beyond Silenced Voices* (Albany: State University of New York Press, 1993).

61   See Apple, *Education and Power* and Apple, *Cultural Politics and Education*.

62   B. Curtis, *True Government by Choice Men?* (Toronto: University of Toronto Press, 1992).

63   Apple, *Cultural Politics and Education*. See also, M.W. Apple and A. Oliver, "Becoming Right: Education and the Formation of Conservative Movements," *Teachers College Record* 97 (Spring 1996): 419–45.

64   P. Wexler, *Social Analysis of Education* (New York: Routledge, 1987).

65   R. Williams, *Marxism and Literature* (New York: Oxford University Press, 1977).

66   See Apple, *Cultural Politics and Education*, Apple, *Official Knowledge*, and Apple and Oliver, "Becoming Right."

67   See C. McCarthy and W. Crichlow, eds., *Race, Identity and Representation in Education* (New York: Routledge, 1993); Weis and Fine, eds., *Beyond Silenced Voices*, and M. Fine, L. Weis, and W. Wong, eds., *Off White* (New York: Routledge, 1997).

68   P. Bourgois, *In Search of Respect* (New York: Cambridge University Press, 1995).

69   A. Gitlin, ed., *Power and Method* (New York: Routledge, 1994).

70   S. Bowles and H. Gintis, *Schooling in Capitalist America* (New York: Basic Books, 1976).

71   See, for example, Apple, *Education and Power* and M. Carnoy and H. Levin, *Schooling and Work in the Democratic State* (Stanford: Stanford University Press, 1986).

72   J. Rury and J. Mirel, "The Political Economy of Urban Education," in Apple, ed., *Review of Research in Education*. Vol. 21, D. Harvey, *The Urban Experience* (Baltimore: Johns Hopkins University Press, 1989).

73   See also J. Mirel, *The Rise and Fall of an Urban School System* (Ann Arbor: University of Michigan Press, 1993).

74   Actually, "return" is not the appropriate word because although the tradition of political economy was never dominant in the United States in sociology of

education, it also was never abandoned and continued to grow and to become increasingly nuanced.

75 See Apple, *Cultural Politics and Education*, especially Chapter 4; A. Sherman, *Wasting America's Future* (Boston: Beacon Press, 1994).

76 H. Gintis, "The Political Economy of School Choice," *Teachers College Record* 96 (Spring 1995): 492–511.

77 A. Gitlin and F. Margonis, "The Political Aspect of Reform," *American Journal of Education* 103 (August 1995): 377–405.

78 See Apple, *Teachers and Texts*; Apple, *Official Knowledge*; and Apple, *Education and Power*.

79 See, especially, S. Acker, "Gender and Teachers' Work," in *Review of Research in Education*. Vol. 21, ed. Apple.

80 They particularly and appropriately refer to A. Hargreaves, *Changing Teachers, Changing Schools* (New York: Teachers College Press, 1994).

81 Gitlin and Margonis, "The Political Aspect of Reform," 379. See also, J. Anyon, "Teacher Development and Reform in an Inner-City School," *Teachers College Record* 96 (Fall 1994): 14–31; J. Anyon, "Race, Social Class, and Education in an Inner-City School," *Teachers College Record* 97 (Fall 1995): 69–94; and D. Carlson, *Teachers and Crisis* (New York: Routledge, 1992).

82 Acker, "Gender and Teachers' Work."

83 Ibid., 79. See also J. Rury, "Who Became Teachers?" in *American Teachers*, ed. D. Warren (New York: Macmillan, 1989).

84 See L. Perkins, "The History of Blacks in Teaching," in *American Teachers*, ed. Warren; and M. Fultz, "African-American Teachers in the South, 1880-1940," *Teachers College Record* 96 (Spring 1995): 544–68.

85 G. Ladson-Billings, *The Dreamkeepers* (San Francisco: Jossey-Bass, 1994).

86 C. West, *Race Matters* (New York: Vintage, 1993), 6. See also, G. Ladson-Billings and W. Tate, "Towards a Critical Race Theory of Education," *Teachers College Record* 97 (Fall 1995): 47–68.

87 M. Omi and H. Winant, *Racial Formation in the United States* (New York: Routledge, 1995), viii.

88 Ibid.

89 Among the more interesting works of note here are E. Said, *Culture and Imperialism* (New York: Vintage, 1993); McCarthy and Crichlow, *Race, Identity, and Representation in Education*; Weis and Fine, *Beyond Silenced Voices*; and Fine, Weis, and Wong, *On Whiteness*.

90 Apple, *Official Knowledge* and Apple, *Cultural Politics and Education*.

91   R. Herrnstein and C. Murray, *The Bell Curve* (New York: The Free Press, 1994). This volume basically argues that African Americans are genetically "less intelligent" on average. It had an immense advertising budget and was given considerable resources by conservative foundations to bring its case to the public. It has also been reported in the national press that the authors received as much as $1,000,000 from conservative foundations to support the writing of the book. No reputable geneticist would make such arguments. But, as is often the case, conservative movements must find ways of explaining the destructiveness of their social policies that distance their own decisions from these consequences. Social Darwinist and biological arguments are often turned to here consciously or unconsciously as part of a legitimation strategy.

92   See, for example, J. Kincheloe and S. Steinberg, eds., *Measured Lies* (New York: St. Martin's Press, 1996). Of considerable importance in situating these positions within larger historical dynamics is N. Fraser and L. Gordon, "A Genealogy of Dependency," *Signs* 19 (Summer 1994): 309–36.

93   C. Gallagher, "White Reconstruction in the University," *Socialist Review* 24, no. 1–2 (1994): 167.

94   L. Roman, "White Is a Color!" in *Race, Identity, and Representation in Education*, ed. McCarthy and Crichlow, 72. See also, b. hooks, *Black Looks* (Boston: South End Press, 1992).

95   Gallagher, "White Reconstruction in the University."

96   Ibid., 175–76.

97   Ibid., 177.

98   Ibid., 180.

99   Ibid., 182–83.

100   Ibid., 183.

101   The basis of both "mainstream" and critical policy research has been critically analyzed, using largely Bourdieuian and postmodern perspectives, in J. Ladwig, *Academic Distinctions* (New York: Routledge, 1996). Although at times Ladwig overstates his case and is not always accurate chronologically, he does make a number of interesting arguments.

102   See Apple, *Official Knowledge*.

103   This evidence is clearly synthesized in G. Whitty, "Creating Quasi-Markets in Education," in *Review of Research in Education*. Vol. 22, ed. M.W. Apple (Washington DC: American Educational Research Association, in press).

104   Among these are J. Henig, *Rethinking School Choice* (Princeton University Press, 1994); A. Wells, *A Time to Choose* (New York: Hill and Wang, 1993); and K. Smith and Meier, eds., *The Case Against School Choice* (Armonk,

NY: M.E. Sharpe, 1995). Henig, in particular, shows the importance of technical and quantitative sophistication in his critical analysis of the empirical claims by researchers of marketization and choice plans.

105   Apple, *Cultural Politics and Education*.

106   S. Aronowitz and H. Giroux, "Textual Authority, Culture, and the Politics of Literacy," in *The politics of the textbook*, ed. Apple and Christian-Smith.

107   P. Burdell, "Teen Mothers in High School," in *Review of Research in Education*. Vol. 21, ed. Apple.

108   See Apple, *Official Knowledge*; Apple, *Education and Power*, and Apple, *Cultural Politics and Education*.

109   Hall, "Cultural Studies," 537.

110   Ibid., 537–38.

Chapter 10

Freire, Neoliberalism, and Education

Knowing Paulo Freire

In every nation in the world, there are those who recognize that education is not a neutral activity, that it is intimately connected to multiple relations of domination and subordination—and very importantly to struggles to deconstruct and reconstruct these relations. In every nation in the world, there are those people who have devoted their lives to creating new visions of educational possibilities and new practices that embody them. Yet, some individuals are able to generate insights that are *so* powerful, *so* challenging, *so* compelling that they become teachers (and I use this word with the utmost respect) of hundreds, even thousands, of other people not only in their own nations but in many others as well.

I know of no one more powerful in this regard than Paulo Freire. My use of the present tense (the word *know*) here shows how difficult it is for me to think of him in the past. For he was that rare combination of teacher and friend. He was important to all of the many people in so many countries who recognize that our task is to "name the world," to collectively build an education that is counterhegemonic and is part of the larger terrain of struggle over what counts as literacy, who should control it, and how critical literacy (what he called conscientization) was connected to real struggles by real people in real relations in real communities. For him, an education that was not connected to the struggles for emancipation and against exploitation was not worthy of the label "education".

Yet all of this is too abstract for me right now. His death came at a time when I was beginning work on a lecture that was to be presented as an honor to him after his being awarded an honorary degree at the

University of Lisbon in Portugal. His death makes me wonder what I now have to say, how I can honor the person for whom the lecture was to be presented and who will never hear or read it. This void can never be filled. It is the mark of my respect for the man and what he stands (stood?) for that I can already recognize the space and already miss the eloquent voice.

Yet I do not want to simplify either Paulo or my complex relationship to him. Of course, as you know, he was the author of a number of absolutely crucial theoretical books that served as the focal point for several generations of critical educational work. In fact, he had completed a new volume, *The Pedagogy of Autonomy*, that was published last March and was in the middle of working on another, *Pedagogic Letters*, when he died.[1] Of course, as you also know, he suffered greatly; as so many, many people in Brazil, Chile, Argentina, and elsewhere did during a time of horrible repression. He also risked trying to put his ideas into practice by serving as the Secretary of Education of the city of São Paulo later in his career. He became something of a lightning rod for all of the social criticism of rightists during that period. And because of this, the social and educational activists that he brought into the Ministry of Education actually had more freedom than might otherwise have been possible. Attention was focused more on Paulo than it was on the attempts on the ground to create a more socially just education.

All this must be recognized and he deserves our utmost respect for his work. But there is something more personal that I need to say, something that speaks to why *I* respect him so much. As I read his material, there were points—sometimes entire arguments—with which I disagreed. (Indeed, there were many progressive social and educational activists and writers in Brazil and elsewhere who had similar worries.) I was fortunate enough to have had many conversations with him, sometimes in front of large audiences and sometimes in the privacy of a home or an office. Paulo wanted to discuss; he made dialogue into something of an art form. Indeed, in the time before his death, he delayed going into the hospital for a number of weeks because he simply could not bear to be cut off from conversation. The worst thing imaginable to him was to be unable to speak.

However, this did not mean that he wanted to dominate. He *always* listened carefully to my arguments. He agreed or he disagreed. He didn't wear a mask of congeniality. He *wanted* to deal with the hard questions. He fully understood that *not* dealing with the hard questions was an excuse to let the voices of the powerful work through you. He wanted (perhaps demanded is a better word) others to do the same. Hours would go by, even in those large public dialogues between the two of us—and I cannot remember wanting our conversation to end. The time we spent in those large public conversations went by too fast; too much was left to say. Even the audience felt the same. I cannot say this about too many other people. In the process of these public and private conversations, I changed—but so did he. His willingness to take a radical intellectual and political position in times of grave danger—when everything is conspiring against you— and yet to change his mind, to see where he might have been wrong, is the characteristic of all too few people. Because of this, Paulo will remain in me—as a model of radical commitment, as a model of what one does when better arguments are given than your own, as a model of combining theory and practice into a pedagogical/political praxis, and as a model of a fully *human* being.

The way to honor him is to live out the reality of what must never degenerate into an idle slogan: Don't mourn; teach and organize. Paulo would demand no less. Let us at least attempt to do the impossible— to fill the void left by his passing in a way he would want. There are hard questions to radically ask and to answer—and educational work to be done. His life may be over, but his legacy remains a living presence in all of us who demand justice.

The Politics of Class Conversion Strategies

But how are we to honor that legacy? In what follows, I shall not do what so many others are doing. I shall not write a review of Paulo's ideas; nor shall I spend much time examining the contradictions found within them.[2] This is not because I respect Paulo's ideas less than other people who have chosen to write about what he stood for. Indeed, there are few authors for whom I have greater respect than Paulo. Instead, because so many others have written or will write reviews of his arguments, I wish to change the focus. Because I assume that people are already familiar with the central core of his ideas, I want to demonstrate why—at this current historical conjuncture—his arguments and commitments are even more crucial than they ever have been. That is, I want to analyze the current ways our societies and their educational systems are being reconstructed, so that it becomes clearer why a commitment to radical social/pedagogical activity such as that embodied in Paulo Freire's life and work is of such great importance *now*.

But, in doing so, I must distance myself from some "Freireanos." There is something like a Freire industry right now. Multiple books have been written on his work and influence. Article after article appears, often restating what has been said before. This is not necessarily bad. Indeed, it is a mark of an act of political commitment on the part of these authors that they have consciously chosen to employ Freire's work as a foundation for their own. Further, even though what is written by these authors may have been said before, each new generation of critical educators must rediscover Freire's work anew to connect itself to the long history of educational struggles against exploitation and domination.

Yet, I must be honest here, especially because Paulo himself insisted on speaking the truth. I have many worries about this "Freire industry." Too many people have employed Freire as writer and person as part of mobility strategies within the social field of the academy. Bourdieu would recognize this as a set of conversion strategies in which members of an upwardly mobile fraction of the new middle class substitute linguistic activity—radical-sounding words and supposed friendship with and closeness to radical actors—for lived political action of a more substantive kind. They, thus, engage in the collection of cultural and social capital that they hope to someday convert into economic capital gained through academic advancement and prestige. For some individuals, getting close to Freire, using his books and language, was at least partly a strategy (in Bourdieu's words, a conversion strategy) of career advancement in which being seen as part of his circle gave one legitimacy in the social field of critical education.

I realize when I say this that there is a danger of overstating this claim. However, in this case I believe that Bourdieu's analysis is useful. Status is related in complex ways to markets in social and cultural capital in academic fields.[3] And too often, members of the new middle class within the academy solve their class contradictions by writing in an elaborately abstract but seemingly political manner, by being seen as a member of a critical community of academics and as someone who from the outside looks as if she or he is part of the inner circle of Freire initiates; yet their political work is limited to writing political-sounding words on a page.

One of the major elements that gave Paulo Freire such legitimacy was not only that he focused on and wrote about a particular kind of educational/political praxis, but that he himself had engaged in the hard and disciplined (and sometimes dangerous) work of putting theory and practice together. He had actually helped build programs that were not meant to be simply rhetorical. Yet, unfortunately, some parts of the Freire "industry" have recuperated much of his work into the safe haven of the academic world. In the process of supposedly politicizing the academic, one of the latent effects of this has been the opposite. They have too often succeeded in *academicizing the political*. In the process, much of what gave Freire's work its meaning—its concrete connections to lived struggles in favelas, in rural areas, among the identifiable, not abstract or anonymous groups of oppressed and exploited people, and so on—is vitiated. It is not connected to social movements in which the writer herself or himself is involved (in part because the writer is unconnected in any meaningful and organic way to large-scale social movements). It becomes something we only write about and study. Here I must admit that I am suspicious of those individuals who have appropriated Freire's language and name, but who themselves have never been engaged in putting such work into concrete practice.

I do not want to be misunderstood here. I am *not* claiming in any way that there is not crucial political/intellectual value in serious academic work; nor am I taking a vulgar pragmatist position here. Indeed, like Freire himself, I believe that we must be critical of a position that is antibook and antitheory. And like him, I "prefer knowledge that is forged and produced in the tension between practice and theory."[4] Rather, I want us to take seriously the historical conjuncture in which we live. In a time when the university is increasingly populated by possessive individuals and when forms of solidarity are being fractured ideologically and materially both within the university and between cultural workers at universities and other sites of struggle in the "real world," I want us to explore the possibility that some academics may be using Freire's ideas to create an illusion that they are politically committed to social change when they are actually unwilling to make any sacrifices that might endanger their individualistic goals of achieving status and prestige. I also want to claim that this strategy is made easier because of the *disconnection* between the persons doing the writing and the concrete historical and current struggles to put Freire's work into practice in multiple sites, from schools and communities to labor unions to other oppressed groups. Yet, this disconnection is something Paulo Freire would have never wanted. He better than anyone knew both intellectually and bodily what was at stake in the struggles over literacy, culture, economy, and power. And he more than almost anyone else I knew understood that "naming the word and the world" was part of an ongoing and never-ending struggle in which we could never be satisfied with abstract commitments. They had to be acted upon, embodied, lived. They could not be incorporated in new middle class conversion strategies, nor could they be consistent with the possessive individualism that is increasingly becoming the dominant form of subjectivity in all too many nations.

It is this very issue—the transformation of subjectivity and the ways in which schooling fits into this—that concerns me here. I shall want to claim in this essay that there are very powerful ideological transformations occurring in all of our societies. They are actually part of a large-scale educational project—a project paradoxically similar to what Paulo called upon us to do—to radically change common sense. In this case, however, these ideological transformations are aimed in directions exactly the opposite of what Freire stood for. Whereas Freire's aim was to "reawaken" the individual and collective sensibilities of oppressed people through the processes of critical literacy, there is a new and quite powerful dynamic at work today. Rather than "naming the word and the world" as a site of structures of exploitation and domination and of self-conscious struggles to alter it, we are being asked to embrace this new world. Progressive social criticism and literacy practices based on such criticism are to be replaced by what Gramsci would have called *active consent*. And such active consent will make it much harder for emancipatory educational projects such as those articulated by Freire to go on or even to seem sensible to those who are oppressed.

How this active consent is gained, and what its emerging effects are, will be my focus in the next section of this essay. In order to do this, I shall have to talk about the ways in which new ideological formations are constructed. I shall suggest that widespread transformations are now occurring inside and outside of education—ones centered largely on conservative positions—as the Right engages in its own society-wide educational project to move people's consciousness in neoliberal directions. I shall then return to Freire and the issues of political/pedagogic practice.

Education and the Conservative Restoration

Education is a site of struggle and compromise. It also serves as a proxy for larger battles about what our institutions should do, who they should serve, and who should make these decisions. This insight is especially crucial today.

The current rightward turn in education and the larger society—what I have elsewhere called the conservative restoration[5]—has been the result of the successful struggle by the right to form a broad-based alliance. This new alliance has been so successful in part because it has been increasingly able to win the battle over common sense. That is, it has creatively stitched together different social tendencies and commitments and has organized them under its own general leadership about issues relevant to social welfare, culture, the economy, and education. Its goal for educational and social policy is what might best be described as "conservative modernization."[6]

There are four major elements in this alliance. Each has its own relatively autonomous history and dynamics; but each has also been sutured into the more general conservative movement. These elements include neoliberals, neoconservatives, authoritarian populists, and a particular fraction of the upwardly mobile new middle class. I shall pay particular attention to the first of these groups here because neoliberals are currently in leadership in this alliance to "reform" education and are most concerned with the relationship between schooling and the material and ideological conditions of economic life. However, in no way do I want to dismiss the power of these other three groups and have spent considerable time on the tensions and compromises among them.[7]

Neoliberalism, Education, and the Market

Neoliberals are the most powerful element within the conservative restoration. They are guided by a vision of the weak state. Thus, what is private is necessarily good and what is public is necessarily bad. To their way of thinking, public institutions such as schools are "black holes" into which money is poured—and then seemingly disappears—but that do not provide anywhere near adequate results. For neoliberals, there is one form of rationality that is more powerful than any other, and that is economic rationality. Efficiency and an "ethic" of cost-benefit analysis are the dominant norms. All people are to act in ways that maximize their own personal benefits. Indeed, behind this position is an empirical claim that this is how *all* rational actors act. Yet rather than a neutral description of the world of social motivation, this is actually a construction of the world around the valuative characteristics of an efficiently acquisitive class type.[8]

Underpinning this position is a vision of students as human capital. In the neoliberal universe, the world is intensely competitive economically, and students, as future workers, must be given the requisite skills and dispositions to compete efficiently and effectively. Further, any money spent on schools that is not directly related to these economic goals is suspect. In fact, as "black holes," schools and other public services, as they are currently organized and controlled, waste economic resources that should go into private enterprise. Thus, not only are public schools failing our children as future workers, but like nearly all public institutions they are sucking the financial life out of this society. Partly this is the result of "producer capture." Schools are built for teachers and state bureaucrats, not for "consumers." They respond to the demands of professionals and other selfish state workers, not to the consumers who rely on them.

The idea of the consumer is crucial here. For neoliberals, the world is in essence a vast supermarket. "Consumer choice" is the guarantor of democracy. In effect, education is seen as simply one more product like bread, cars, and television.[9] By turning it over to the market through voucher and choice plans, it will be largely self-regulating. Thus, democracy is turned into consumption practices. In these plans, the ideal citizen is the purchaser, not the worker. The ideological effects of this are momentous. Rather than democracy being a *political* concept, it is transformed into a wholly *economic* concept. The message of such policies is that of what might best be called "arithmetical particularism," in which the unattached individual—as a consumer—is deraced, declassed, and degendered.[10] This ideology serves as an attack on the very basic understandings that underpin any Freirian-inspired strategy.

The metaphors of the consumer and the supermarket are actually quite apposite here. For just as in real life, there are individuals who indeed can go into supermarkets and choose among a vast array of similar or diverse products. And there are those who can only engage in what can best be called postmodern consumption. They stand outside the supermarket and can only consume the image.

The entire project of neoliberalism is connected to a larger process of exporting the blame from the decisions of dominant groups onto the state, onto workers, and onto poor people.[11] After all, it was not the government that made the decisions to engage in capital flight and to close or move factories to those nations that have weak or no unions, fewer environmental regulations, and repressive governments. And it was not working-class and poor communities that chose to lose those jobs and factories, with the loss of hope and schools and communities in crisis that were among the results of these decisions. And it was neither of them who chose to lay off millions of workers—many of whom in my own country had done rather well in school—due to mergers and leveraged buyouts.

Because of their emphasis on the consumer rather than the producer, neoliberal policies need also to be seen as part of a more extensive attack on the rights that workers have gained over decades of constant struggle. In education in particular, these policies constitute an offensive against teacher unions who are perceived to be much too powerful and much too costly.[12]

The varied policy initiatives that have emerged from the neoliberal segments of the new hegemonic alliance are varied. Most have centered on either creating closer linkages between education and the economy or placing schools themselves into the market. The former strategy is represented by widespread proposals for "school-to-work" and "education for employment" programs, and by vigorous cost-cutting attacks on the "bloated state." The latter strategy is no less widespread and is becoming increasingly powerful. It is represented by both national and state-by-state proposals for voucher and choice programs.[13] These proposals include providing public money for private and religious schools (although this strategy is highly contested in the United States). Behind these proposals is a plan to subject schools, like workers, to the discipline of market competition.

There is increasing empirical evidence that the development of "quasi-markets" in education has led to the exacerbation of existing class and racial social divisions.[14] There are now increasingly convincing arguments that although the supposed overt goal of voucher and choice plans is to give poor people the right to exit public schools, among the ultimate long-term effects may be to increase white flight from public schools into private and religious schools and to create conditions such that affluent white parents may refuse to pay taxes to support the public schools that are more and more suffering from the debilitating effects of the fiscal crisis of the state. The result may be even more educational apartheid, not less.[15]

As I noted, there is a second variant of neoliberalism. This one at times is willing to spend more state and/or private money on schools, if and only if schools meet the needs expressed by capital. Thus, resources are made available for "reforms" and policies that further connect the education system to the project of making "our" economy more competitive. Two examples can provide a glimpse of this position. In a number of states in my own country, legislation has been passed that directs schools and universities to make closer links between education and the business community. In the state of Wisconsin, for instance, all teacher education programs must include identifiable experiences about "education for employment" for all of its future teachers; and all teaching in the public elementary, middle, and secondary schools of the state must include elements of education for employment in its formal curricula.[16]

The second example is seemingly less consequential, but in reality it is a powerful statement of the reintegration of educational policy and practice into the ideological agenda of neoliberalism. I am referring here to Channel One, a for-profit television network that is now broadcast into schools, many of which are financially hard-pressed, given the fiscal crisis and the attempt to "cut the bloated state." Channel One enrolls over 40 percent of all middle and secondary school students in the nation. In this "reform", schools are offered a "free" satellite dish, two VCRs, and television monitors for each of their classrooms by a private media corporation. They are also offered a free news broadcast for these students. In return for the equipment and the news, all participating schools must sign a three- to five-year contract that guarantees that their students will watch Channel One every day.[17]

This sounds relatively benign. However, not only is the technology hard-wired so that only Channel One can be received, but broadcast along with the news are *mandatory* advertisements for major fast-food, athletic wear, and other corporations that students—by contract—must also watch. Students, in essence, are sold as a captive audience to corporations. Since, by law, these students must be in schools, the United States is one of the first nations in the world to consciously allow its youth to be sold as commodities to those corporations willing to pay the high price of advertising on Channel One to get a guaranteed (captive) audience. Thus, under a number of variants of neoliberalism, not only are schools transformed into market commodities, but so too now are our children.[18] In this way, students are seen in two different ways—both as exploitable and replaceable future workers and as current consumers who themselves can be bought and sold to the highest bidder.

As I noted, the attractiveness of conservative restorational politics in education rests in large part on major shifts in our common sense—about what democracy is, about whether we see ourselves as possessive individuals ("consumers"), and ultimately about how we see the market working. Underlying neoliberal policies in education and their social policies in general is a faith in the essential fairness and justice of markets. Markets ultimately will distribute resources efficiently and fairly according to effort. They ultimately will create jobs for all who want them. They are the best possible mechanism to ensure a better future for all citizens (consumers).

Because of this, we of course must ask what the economy that reigns supreme in neoliberal positions, most especially those positions that are used to justify many policies and programs that seek to more closely connect education to a "more competitive" economy, actually looks like. Yet, far from the positive picture painted by neoliberals in which technologically advanced jobs will replace the drudgery and underemployment and unemployment so many people now experience if we were to only set the market loose on our schools and children, the reality is something else again. As I demonstrate in a much more complete analysis in *Cultural Politics and Education*, markets are as powerfully destructive as they are productive in people's lives.[19]

Let us take as a case in point: the paid labor market in the United States to which neoliberals want us to attach so much of the education system. Even with the growth in proportion in high-tech related jobs, the kinds of paid work that are and will be increasingly available to a large portion of the U.S. population will not be highly skilled, technically elegant positions. Just the opposite will be the case. The paid labor market will increasingly be dominated by low-paying, repetitive work in the retail, trade, and service sectors. This is made strikingly clear by one fact. There will be more cashier jobs created by the year 2005 than jobs for computer scientists, systems analysts, physical therapists, operations analysts, and radiologic technicians *combined*.

In fact, it is projected that 95 percent of all new positions will be found in the service sector. This sector broadly includes personal care providers, home health aides, social workers (many of whom are now losing their jobs because of cutbacks in social spending), hotel and lodging workers, restaurant employees, transportation workers, and business and clerical services. Further, eight of the top ten individual occupations that will account for the most job growth in the next ten years include the following: retail salespersons, cashiers, office clerks, truck drivers, waitresses/waiters, nursing aides/orderlies, food preparation workers, and janitors. It is obvious that the majority of these positions do not require high levels of education. Many of them are

low-paid, nonunionized and part-time jobs that provide few or no benefits. And many are dramatically linked to, and often exacerbate, the
existing race, gender, and class divisions of labor.[20] This is the emerging economy we face, not the overly romantic picture painted by
neoliberals who urge us both to trust the market and to more closely
connect schools to the "world of work."

Neoliberals argue that making the market the ultimate arbiter of
social worthiness will eliminate politics and its accompanying irratio-
nality from our educational and social decisions. Efficiency and cost-
benefit analysis will be the engines of social and educational transformation. Yet, aside from forgetting that markets *are* a form of politics,
among the ultimate effects of such "economizing" and "depoliticizing"
strategies is actually to make it *ever* harder to interrupt the growing
inequalities in resources and power that so deeply characterize this
society. Nancy Fraser illuminates the process in the following way:

In male-dominated capitalist societies, what is "political" is nor-
mally defined contrastively against what is "economic" and what is
"domestic" or "personal." Here, then, we can identify two principal
sets of institutions that depoliticize social discourses: they are, first,
domestic institutions, especially the normative domestic form, namely
the modern restricted male-headed nuclear family; and, second, official economic capitalist system institutions, especially paid workplaces,
markets, credit mechanisms, and "private" enterprises and corporations. Domestic institutions depoliticize certain matters by personaliz-
ing and/or familializing them; they cast these as private-domestic or
personal-familial matters in contradistinction to public, political matters. Official economic capitalist system institutions, on the other hand,
depoliticize certain matters by economizing them; the issues in question here are cast as impersonal market imperatives, or as "private"
ownership prerogatives, or as technical problems for managers and
planners, all in contradistinction to political matters. In both cases,
the result is a foreshortening of chains of in-order-to relations for
interpreting people's needs; interpretive chains are truncated and prevented from spilling across the boundaries separating the "domestic"
and the "economic" from the political.[21]

For Fraser, this very process of depoliticization makes it very difficult for those with less economic, political, and cultural power to be
accurately heard and responded to in ways that deal with the true
depth of their problems. This is because of what happens when needs
discourses get retranslated into both market talk and "privately" driven
policies.

For our purposes here, we can talk about two major kinds of needs discourses. There are first *oppositional* forms of needs talk. They arise when needs are politicized from below and are part of the crystallization of new oppositional identities on the part of subordinated social groups. What was once seen as largely a private matter is now placed into the larger political arena. Sexual harassment, race and sex segregation in paid labor, exploitation on the job, the absence of paid work itself, and affirmative action policies in educational and economic institutions provide examples of private issues that have now spilled over and can longer be confined to the "domestic" sphere.[22] These kinds of oppositional needs talk lie at the heart of Freirian strategies.

A second kind of needs discourse is what might be called *reprivatization* discourses. They emerge as a response to the newly emergent oppositional forms and try to press these forms back into the private or the domestic arena. They often seek to dismantle or cut back social services, deregulate "private" enterprise, or stop what are seen as "runaway needs." Thus, reprivatizers may attempt to keep issues such as domestic violence from spilling over into overt political discourse and will seek to define it as purely a family matter. Or they will argue that the closing of a factory or land ownership issues are not political questions, but instead represent an "unimpeachable prerogative of private ownership or an unassailable imperative of an impersonal market mechanism."[23] In each of these cases, the task is to contest both the possible breakout of runaway needs and to depoliticize the issues.

Educational policies in the United States provide a number of clear examples of these processes. In the state of California, for instance, a recent binding referendum that prohibited the use of affirmative action policies in state government, in university admission policies, and so on, was passed overwhelmingly because reprivatizers spent an exceptional amount of money on an advertising campaign that labelled such policies as "out of control" and as improper government intervention into decisions that involve "individual merit." Voucher plans in education—by which such contentious issues as whose knowledge should be taught, who should control school policy and practice, and how schools should be financed are left to the market to decide—offer another prime example of attempts to depoliticize educational needs. Finally, giving primary responsibility for the definition of important "work skills" in schools to the private sector—an act that evacuates the possibility of public criticism of the ways work is actually constructed, distributed, controlled, and paid—allows a definition of work as a "private" matter and as purely a technical choice to go unchallenged. Each of these examples shows the emerging power of reprivatizing discourses. They also demonstrate how important it is for us to directly place the educational issues back into the larger reprivatizing strategies surrounding neoliberal policies.

A distinction that is useful here in understanding what is happening in these cases is that between "value" and "sense" legitimation.[24] Each term signifies a different strategy by which powerful groups or states legitimate their authority. In the first strategy (value legitimation), legitimation is accomplished by actually giving people what may have been promised. Thus, the social democratic state may provide social services, land, or jobs for the population in return for continued support. That the state will do this is often the result of oppositional discourses that have gained more power in the social arena and have more power to redefine the border between public and private.

In the second strategy (sense legitimation), rather than provide people with policies that meet the needs they have expressed, states and/or dominant groups attempt to *change the very meaning* of the sense of social need into something that is very different. Thus, when less-powerful people call for "more democracy" and for a more responsive state, the response is not to give "value" that meets this demand, especially when it may lead to runaway needs. Rather, the response is to change what actually *counts* as democracy. Neoliberal policies redefine democracy as the guarantee of choice in an unfettered market. Schools are to be driven by private needs. Education is to be a private good and is to incorporate the skills, knowledge, and values "necessary" to perform in a manner that enhances the competitiveness of the private sector. The responsibility of the "public" is limited to enhancing the project of competitiveness. Anything else, and especially anything that has its roots in social criticism and the long history of emancipatory educational projects, is inappropriate government intervention. In essence, the state withdraws. The extent of acceptance of such transformations of needs and needs discourses shows the success of the reprivatizers in redefining the borders between public and private and demonstrates how a people's common sense can be shifted in conservative directions during a time of economic and ideological crisis.

In essence, neoliberals have engaged in a vast "educational" project. They have sought to take the intuitions of criticism that many people have of education—its bureaucratic intransigence, its unequal results, its failure to listen to the voices of "the people"—and have turned these intuitions into mandates for a rightist reconstruction. They have combined both value and sense legitimation to win active consent for their agenda among many people (but certainly *not* all). They will give "value" to their allies in affluent groups and the upwardly mobile new middle class at the same time as they seek to alter the subjectivities (the "sense") of the majority. If "we" can think of ourselves as "consumers" rather than as members of collectivities, active consent can be won.[25]

By weaving together new definitions of rationality, citizenship, education, and work in quite creative ways, the new alliance may display a more thorough understanding of Gramsci than the left, unfortunately. (Of course, the fact that it is supported by millions and millions of dollars from corporations and conservative foundations certainly helps. We need to always remember that this is not a level economic playing field.) The new alliance knows that to win in the state, you must win in civil society. Any attempt to employ Freirian forms to interrupt these tendencies must face the profound transformations that are occurring in common sense honestly. Ignoring them will not make our job any easier.

Freire, Neoliberalism, and Critical Educational Practice

In reading the previous section of this essay, it is important to realize that it too was written from a particular position. Although I have spent a good deal of time living and working in what some people arrogantly call "the third world," I speak from the perspective of someone from the United States. Not only are the social and ideological conditions and history here the product of a specific constellation of race, class, and gender relations, but the ways in which education has historically been financed, controlled, organized, and struggled over are also products of that particular constellation of relations and help to reproduce and transform them. Because of this, I do not assume that everything I have said here about neoliberalism is the same elsewhere. Nor do I assume that the history of radical education[26] is the same as the United States even in those nations with similar economic patterns and histories. However, it is becoming ever more clear that neoliberal ideological positions and policies have aggressively interrupted more progressive critiques of schools and the development

of movements that seek to create more critical forms of popular education in many nations. It is equally clear that the arrogant policies of
the conservative restoration—and most especially the attacks of
neoliberal—have had a truly major impact on countries throughout the
world. Thus, although I do not assume that all the points of my analysis are generalizable, I do assume that there are enough similarities
across geographic borders that you will recognize similar tendencies
from your own experiences.

Freire himself clearly saw the dangers associated with the development and widespread acceptance of neoliberal beliefs and practices.
In his recent book, *Letters to Cristina*, he commented on what he
saw happening all around him. He wrote:

The dominant class, deaf to the need for a critical reading of the
world, insists on the purely technical training of the working class,
training with which that class should reproduce itself as such. Progressive ideology, however, cannot separate technical training from
political preparation, just as it cannot separate the practice of reading
the world from reading discourse.[27]

He then added this commentary on that statement based on what
was happening in the 1990s, a situation he called "reactionary
postmodernism":

Perhaps never before has the dominant class felt so free in exercis-
ing their manipulative practice. Reactionary postmodernity has had
success in proclaiming the disappearance of ideologies and the emergence of a new history without social classes, therefore without an-
tagonistic interests, without class struggle. They preach that there is
no need to continue to speak about dreams, utopia, or social justice.
. . . [The] postmodern reactionary . . . suggests in his pragmatic discourse that it is now the duty of capitalism to create a special ethics
based on the production of equal players or almost equal players.
Large questions are no longer political, religious, or ideological. They
are ethical in a "healthy" capitalist sense of ethics.[28]

For Freire, then, the equality promised by "we are all consumers,"
its accompanying depoliticization, and its creation of the possessive
individual, must be rejected. A pedagogy that focuses on production
and consumption "without any preoccupation about what we are producing, whom it benefits, and whom it hurts" is certainly not a critical
pedagogy.[29] But in saying this, he was not an apologist for the past.
For him, the task was clear. We need to recognize the mistakes that
progressive forces may have made in the past. By this he meant that
such things as dogmatic and overly aggressive discourse, mechanistic

proposals and analysis, an inflexible and teleological sense of history that removed or ignored historical specificity and human agency, pedagogies that limited "the marginalized classes'" universe or their epistemological curiosity about objects that have been depoliticized— all of this was to be critically and radically examined. Yet, at the same time as we were to question what we have too often taken for granted, Freire cautioned against allowing ourselves to become enchanted with the present neoliberal ideology—"an ideology of privatization that never speaks about costs, the costs are always absorbed by the working class."[30]

Freire's position raises crucial questions about critical pedagogic work. How *do* we interrupt common sense? How do we create pedagogies that are deeply connected to the daily realities of people's lives and to struggles to overcome exploitation and domination in a time when the Right has already understood how such connections might be creatively (albeit manipulatively) made? Who is this "we" in the first place? How do we avoid the possible arrogance of a position that assumes that "we" know the best and only paths to emancipation and that we will bring it to "you"?[31]

These of course are *difficult* questions. And our answers to them may be partial, flawed, contradictory, or temporary. Yet, only by asking the hard questions—as Paulo did—can we continue the never-ending struggle of what Raymond Williams (whose theoretical work was independent of but had major parallels to Freire's work) so poetically called "the long revolution."[32] Although these questions are difficult, they do have immense theoretical *and* practical implications. We should not pretend that they can be answered by one person, although Paulo Freire comes as close as anyone in our time to providing the outlines of answers to many of them. However, we do have partial answers (many of which have clear similarities to Freire's emphases) to a number of the practical issues embedded in the questions about interrupting neoliberal policies and practices in education.

For example, in the United States the increasingly popular journal *Rethinking Schools* has provided an important forum for social and educational criticism and for descriptions of critical educational practices in schools and communities. At times the journal is influenced directly by the work of Paulo Freire and by educators who have themselves elaborated on and extended his work, and at other times its contributions come directly from diverse indigenous radical educational traditions specific to the United States. *Rethinking Schools* and emerging national organizations such as the National Coalition of Educational Activists have jointly constructed spaces for critical educators, cultural and political activists, radical scholars, and others to teach each other, to provide supportive criticism of each other's work, and to build a more collective set of responses to the destructive educational and social polices of the conservative restoration.[33]

I must stress that the phrase "collective responses" does not signify anything like "democratic centrism" in which a small group or a party cadre speaks for the majority and establishes the "appropriate" position. Given the fact that there are diverse emancipatory movements whose voices are heard in publications like *Rethinking Schools* and in organizations such as the National Coalition of Educational Activists—anti-racist and postcolonial positions, radical forms of multiculturalism, gays and lesbians, multiple feminist voices, neo-marxists and democratic socialists, "greens," and so on—a more appropriate way of looking at what is happening is to call it a *decentered unity*. Multiple progressive projects, multiple "critical pedagogies," are articulated. Like Freire, each of them is related to real struggles in real institutions in real communities. We of course should not be romantic about this. There are very real political, epistemological, and/ or educational differences in these varied voices. Yet, they are united in their opposition to the forces involved in the new conservative hegemonic alliance. There *are* tensions, but the decentered unity has remained strong enough for each constituent group to support the struggles of the others.

This is not all. At the same time as these critical movements are being built, critical educators are also attempting to occupy the spaces provided by existing "mainstream" publication outlets to publish books that provide *critical* answers to teachers' questions about "What do I do on Monday?" during a conservative era. Some of these attempts have been remarkably successful. Let me give one example. One very large professional organization in the United States, the Association for Supervision and Curriculum Development (ASCD), publishes books that are distributed each year to its more than 150,000 members, most of whom are teachers or administrators in elementary, middle, or secondary schools. ASCD has not been a very progressive organization, preferring to publish largely technicist and overtly depoliticized material. Yet it has been concerned that its publications have not sufficiently represented socially and culturally critical educators. Thus, it has been looking for ways to increase its legitimacy to a wider range of educators. Because of this legitimacy problem and because of its large membership, it became clear to a number of us who were part of the critical educational traditions in the United States that it might be possible to convince ASCD to publish and widely circulate material that would demonstrate the actual practical *successes* of critical models of curriculum, teaching, and evaluation that attempted to solve real problems in schools and communities, especially with working-class and poor children and children of color.

After intense negotiations to ensure that censorship would not be an issue, a colleague and I agreed to publish a book, *Democratic Schools*, with ASCD that provided clear practical examples of the power of Freirian and similar critical approaches at work in classrooms and communities.[34] *Democratic Schools* was not only distributed to all 150,000 members of the organization, but it has gone on to sell an additional 100,000 copies. Thus, nearly 250,000 copies of a volume that tells the practical stories of the largely successful struggles of critically oriented educators in real schools are now in the hands of educators who daily face similar problems. This is an important intervention.

Although there is no guarantee that teachers will always be progressive (nor is there any guarantee that those who are progressive about class and union issues will be equally progressive about issues of gender and race), many teachers do have socially and pedagogically critical intuitions. However, they often do not have ways of putting these intuitions into practice because they cannot picture them in action in daily situations. Because of this, critical theoretical and political insights, then, have nowhere to go in terms of their embodiment in concrete pedagogical situations where the politics of curriculum and teaching must be *enacted*. This is a tragic absence and strategically filling it is absolutely essential. We need to use and expand the spaces in which critical pedagogical stories are made available so that these positions do not remain on the theoretical or rhetorical level. The publication and widespread distribution of *Democratic Schools* provides one instance of using and expanding such spaces in ways that make Freirian and similar critical educational positions seem actually doable in "ordinary" institutions such as schools and local communities.

Conclusion

I have spent time on the issue of practice in part because of what I said earlier about why Paulo Freire was so widely respected. Not only was he among the most powerful writers and theorists on "the long revolution" in the history of radical education, but he went further. He took seriously the importance of struggling (and it is a constant struggle) to answer the question of what practices come from our eloquent criticisms. He asked how his theory could be informed by the practice of critical education, the practice of conscientization. He demanded that we maintain the dialectical connections between theory and practice—in a word, *praxis*. This very word signifies one of the reasons why we must never assume that now that he is no longer among us, that Freire's work is no longer essential.

Instead, we need to return constantly to Freire—not because he provided us with "the answers," not for easily reproducible models of pedagogical techniques that can be applied in each and every case, and certainly *not* as part of a mobility strategy of the academic who seeks to convert the cachet of Freire into valued capital in the status market at the university. Rather, we need to return to Freire as part of a larger process of the restoration of collective memory. In these neoliberal times, we need to return to him to remind ourselves of the ethical and political concerns that should animate our social and ideological criticism, to remind ourselves of the importance of engaging in truly *critical* education, to reconnect with the dreams, visions, and, yes, even utopian hopes that are denied in a society in which profits count more than people. And we need to return to him both because his ideas remain so articulate and because his call for praxis sustains us in the long night of the conservative restoration.

Of course, we need to do all this with appropriate respect not only for Paulo, but also for the criticisms his work generated among other progressive movements and scholars.[35] Although some of these criticisms were overstated and were sometimes not based on a serious reading of his work, others did illuminate theoretical, political, and educational silences in his arguments. We should welcome these progressive criticisms, even when we disagree with some of them. Surely, the mark of the greatness of someone's insights is the seriousness with which people take them up, extend them, refine them, and even go beyond them at times.

Because of the seriousness of his legacy and of his project, I believe that we need to constantly take seriously a number of questions. Given the ideological transformations associated with the conservative restoration—in how people think about democracy, how they think about alternatives to dominant economic and political forms, how they think about the past and the future, how they think about themselves as historical actors and as individual and collective persons—can an unreconstructed Freirian pedagogy provide "the" answer? Given his own constant search for more adequate responses to changing historical conditions, it is safe to assume that he would not have been totally satisfied to remain still. He too might have asked something like "Given the fragmentation of a unifying discourse and project on 'the left,' what might an array of critical pedagogies look like that both rejects the subjectivities of the conservative alliance and respects the diversities and differences and identities of progressive struggles?"

Thus, in answering these questions, Freire himself provides a model. Paulo himself constantly took in, reconstructed, and reworked both his own ideas and those of others. He forged a new synthesis while standing on the shoulders of those he drew upon.[36] This, it seems to me, is our task as well. We, too, must take Paulo Freire in, with all of his work's complexities and contradictions, rework him in light of new and emerging historical circumstances, and stand on *his* shoulders. We must recapture him from the grasp of those who would make him of only academic or theoretical interest, at the very same time that we must continue on the theoretical, political, and pedagogic paths he forged.

Of course, in my mind the best way to do this is to reinsert ourselves into the daily struggles and social movements that are forming and re-forming the institutions in which we and others live and work. Utopias and dreams are crucial points of reference here. But, unless we personally commit ourselves as living, breathing actors to the multiple emancipatory projects currently underway, there can be no doubt about what will happen. Neoliberals, in concert with neoconservatives, authoritarian populists, and upwardly mobile fractions of the new middle class are already mobilizing. They are reconstructing common sense *now*. Sidelines may be comfortable places to sit during athletic events, but what is happening to millions of people in all of our nations is no game. The lives and futures of the majority of our citizens (not as "consumers" or as commodities for sale, but as Freire saw them—as agents of social and cultural transformation) are at stake here. There is work to be done.

Notes

1   P. Freire, *The Pedagogy of Autonomy* (São Paulo, Brazil: Editora Paz & Terra, 1997).

2   See P. Taylor, *The Texts of Paulo Freire* (Milton Keynes, UK: Open University Press, 1993); K. Weiler, "The Liberatory Teacher: Reading the Word and the World of Paulo Freire" (unpublished manuscript, Tufts University, Medford, Massachusetts, 1997).

3   P. Bourdieu, *Distinction* (Cambridge: Harvard University Press, 1984); P. Bourdieu, *Homo Academus* (Stanford: Stanford University Press, 1988).

4   P. Freire, *Letters to Cristina* (New York: Routledge, 1996), 85.

5   M.W. Apple, *Official Knowledge* (New York: Routledge, 1993); M.W. Apple, *Cultural Politics and Education* (New York: Teachers College Press, 1996).

6   R. Dale, "The Thatcherite Project in Education," *Critical Social Policy* 9 (Winter 1989/1990): 4–19.

7   M.W. Apple, *Cultural Politics and Education* (New York: Teachers College Press, 1996); M.W. Apple, "Under the New Hegemonic Alliance: Conservatism and Educational Policy in the United States," in *Education and Change in the Pacific Rim*, ed. K. Sullivan (Cambridge: Cambridge University Press, 1998), 79–99.

8   Apple, *Cultural Politics and Education*; T. Honderich, *Conservatism* (Boulder: Westview, 1990).

9   See M.W. Apple, *Ideology and the Curriculum*, 2d ed. (New York: Routledge, 1990).

10 See S. Ball, *Education Reform* (Milton Keynes, UK: Open University Press, 1994) and Apple, *Cultural Politics and Education*.

11 M.W. Apple, *Education and Power*, 2d edition. (New York: Routledge, 1995). Of course, there are truly constitutive gender and racial dynamics at work here as well. See for example, M. Omi and H. Winant, *Racial Formation in the United States* (New York: Routledge, 1994) and N. Fraser, *Justice Interruptus* (New York: Routledge, 1997).

12 Although perhaps this offensive does not represent a conscious effort, it needs to be interpreted as part of a longer history of attacks on women's labor because the vast majority of teachers in the United States, Canada, and so many other nations are women. See M.W. Apple, *Teachers and Texts: A Political Economy of Class and Gender Relations in Education* (New York: Routledge, 1988) and S. Acker, "Gender and Teachers' Work," in *Review of Research in Education*, vol. 21, ed. M.W. Apple (Washington, DC: American Educational Research Associates).

13   J. Chubb and T. Moe, *Politics, Markets, and America's Schools* (Washington, DC: Brookings Institution, 1990).

14   G. Whitty, "Creating Quasi-Markets in Education," in *Review of Research in Education*, vol. 21, ed. M.W. Apple (Washington, DC: American Educational Research Association, 1997), 3–47.

15   Apple, *Cultural Politics and Education.*

16   Many times, however, these initiatives are actually unfunded mandates. That is, requirements such as these are made mandatory, but no additional funding is provided to accomplish them. The intensification of teachers' labor at all levels of the education system that results from this situation is very visible.

17   Apple, *Official Knowledge.*

18   Apple, *Official Knowledge;* see also A. Molnar, *Giving Kids the Business* (Boulder, CO: Westview, 1996).

19   Apple, *Cultural Politics and Education,* 68–90.

20   Apple, *Cultural Politics and Education.*

21   N. Fraser, *Unruly Practices* (Minneapolis: University of Minnesota Press, 1989), 168.

22   Ibid., 172. See also the discussion of how gains in one sphere of social life can be transported into another sphere in S. Bowles and H. Gintis, *Schooling in Capitalist America* (New York: Basic Books, 1976); Apple, *Teachers and Texts.*

23   Ibid.

24   R. Dale, *The State and Education Policy* (Milton Keynes, UK: Open University Press, 1989).

25   For those populations who refuse this or for whom such neoliberal policies are simply a disaster, of course, the repressive apparatus of the state is always there as a potent threat and as a reality. Thus, in the United States, in many states more money is now spent on prisons than on higher education. The population of these prisons is predictable—a large and ever-increasing population of the poor and especially of poor people of color.

26   See, for example, K. Teitelbaum, *Schooling for Good Rebels* (New York: Teachers College Press, 1996).

27   P. Freire, *Letters to Cristina* (New York: Routledge, 1996), 83.

28   Ibid., 84.

29   Ibid.

30   Ibid., 84–85.

31   See, for example C. Luke and J. Gore, eds., *Feminisms and Critical Pedagogy* (New York: Routledge, 1992); Weiler, "The Liberatory Teacher." I do

not necessarily agree with all of these criticisms of Freire and of "critical pedagogy" in general. Although some of them are accurate and need to be taken very seriously, a number of them seem not to be based on a close reading of Freire himself or are themselves based on romanticized visions of teaching in which students necessarily have all of the resources within themselves that will somehow emerge with the "correct" techniques of self-disclosure. Many of the people making such claims have never spent significant amounts of time in schools, yet they assume that they can easily take pedagogies from a different context (for example, working with adults) and simply reproduce them in schools. Not only is this arrogant and naïve, but it is disrespectful of the skills of elementary and secondary teachers.

32   It would be very interesting to analyze the similarities between Williams and Friere. On Williams, see D. Dworkin and L. Roman, ed., *Views Beyond the Border Country* (New York: Routledge, 1993).

33   *Rethinking Schools* is one of the best examples of the ways in which critical academics, elementary/middle/high school teachers, students, and community activists can work together in nonelitist ways. Information is available from *Rethinking Schools*, 1001 E. Keefe Avenue, Milwaukee, Wisconsin 53212, USA. The FAX number is (414) 964-7220. The e-mail address is rethink@execpc.com.

34   M.W. Apple and J.A. Beane, ed., *Democratic Schools* (Washington, DC: Association for Supervision and Curriculum Development, 1995).

35   K. Weiler, "The Liberatory Teacher: Reading the Word and the World of Paulo Freire," (unpublished paper, Tufts University, Medford, Massachusetts, 1997).

36   Taylor, *The Texts of Paulo Freire.*

Chapter 11

Between Neo and Post in Critical Educational Studies

I began writing this chapter after I completed two recent books on which I had worked for a number of years. One of the books, *Cultural Politics and Education*,[1] was the most recent of an entire series of books that sought to answer some "simple questions": Whose knowledge is taught? Why? Whose knowledge is not taught? Why? What is the relationship between culture and power in education? Who benefits from this relationship?[2] *Cultural Politics and Education* focused on what I think are the most powerful social movements that are redefining education today—what I call the conservative restoration. It employed the questions I noted above to critically interrogate conservative proposals for national curriculum, national testing, the creation of a closer connection between schooling and the economy, and "choice plans." It unpacked their economic, ideological, and political assumptions and argued that the ultimate results of such plans will be a society that is considerably more stratified, less equal, and less just.

The second book, *Democratic Schools*, was in many ways a companion volume to the other.[3] Its basis is also in a few "simple questions": If the conservative restoration is having such a profound effect on what education is for and who it will benefit, what can educators do about it in schools? Are there more democratic possibilities in schools? What concrete practices are *now* going on that provide alternatives to the conservative policies and practices now gaining so much power? *Democratic Schools* tells the stories of four public, not private, schools that are both socially critical and educationally progressive.

These two books, then, form something of a package, complement each other, and in essence need to be read together. The first provides a critical analysis of the conservative alliance, of its economic and cultural agendas, and of what is at stake if it wins. The second turns its attention toward critical practice. Each one gives meaning to the other. Both represent a continuation of my struggle—aided by and in concert with others—to comprehend and challenge the dominant ways that education is conducted in our societies.

There were a number of tensions that stood behind these books. In this chapter, I want to employ these tensions to take a stand on some of the major conceptual and political commitments that I think are essential in critical educational studies.

I started both *Cultural Politics and Education* and *Democratic Schools* at a time when I had just returned from spending time in a Bosnian refugee camp populated by people (mostly women and children) who had somehow managed to flee the murderous situation there. What I saw in the camp and the stories the mostly Muslim Bosnian teachers told me left me with a residue of anger that will never be erased. I was also left with a feeling of gratitude and awe as an educator. For in the midst of privations, fear, despair, and uncommon courage, one of the first acts of the people in that camp was to create a school for their children. It was a powerful reminder of how important education is to the maintenance of self and community and to what Raymond Williams so brilliantly called our journey of hope.[4]

That journey of hope is not made any easier by the fact that these books were written at a time when the Right was (and is) resurgent, when it seems as if we basically have two right-wing parties in the United States, and when education and so much else is talked about as if all that counted was either competition and profit or a thoroughly romanticized return to the "Western tradition."[5] As I worked on the two books, rightist religious fundamentalism continued to grow and to have a greater influence on electoral politics, on social policy, and on what teachers will and will not teach in schools. The same was and is true about the growth of racist nativism. Such racist discourse is not limited to public debates about, say, immigration. The fact that the pseudoscience of Richard Herrnstein and Charles Murray in *The Bell Curve* is currently being treated to such sponsored mobility—even though it is utterly naive in its understanding of genetics and is overtly and covertly racist in its arguments—creates a horizon against which my own writing is constructed.[6] It is also a time when all too many of us seem to have become inured to human suffering nationally and internationally. This is a difficult period for anyone who is committed to progressive social and educational transformation.

This is a complicated and tense period intellectually as well. From the Right, the culture wars rage. Yet, equally important, these books were also produced when postmodern and poststructural theories are becoming more influential in cultural studies and in critical educational studies (a label I would prefer to use rather than the more limited one of critical theory or critical pedagogy). Significant parts of what my friends call "postie" approaches are very insightful and need to be paid very close attention to, especially their focus on identity politics, on multiple and contradictory relations of power, on nonreductive analysis, and on the local as an important site of struggle. The influences of some of this are readily visible in *Cultural Politics and Education*. I have no wish at all to widen a divide when alliances are crucial now. However, there are also significant parts of these approaches as they have been introduced into education that simply make me blanch because of their stylistic arrogance, their stereotyping of other approaches, their certainty that they've got "the" answer, their cynical lack of attachment to any action in real schools, their seeming equation of any serious focus on the economy as being somehow reductive, their conceptual confusions, and finally their trendy rhetoric that often says some pretty commonsensical things that reflexive and activist educators have known and done for years when it is unpacked. Let me hasten to add that this is true for only a portion of these approaches, but all of this gives me cause for concern.[7]

Thus, there is a fine line between necessary conceptual and political transformations and trendiness. Unfortunately, the latter sometimes appears in the relatively uncritical appropriation of postmodernism by some educational theorists and researchers. For example, there certainly are (too many) plans to turn schools over to market forces, to diversify types of schools, and to give "consumers" more choice. Some may argue that this is "the educational equivalent of . . . the rise of 'flexible specialization in place of the old assembly-line world of mass production,' driven by the imperatives of differentiated consumption rather than mass production."[8] This certainly has a postmodern ring to it.

Yet like many of the new reforms being proposed, there is less that is "postmodern" about them than meets the eye. Many have a high-tech image. They are usually guided by "an underlying faith in technical rationality as the basis for solving social, economic, and educational problems." Specialization is just as powerful, perhaps even more powerful, as any concern for diversity.[9] Rather than an espousal of "heterogeneity, pluralism, and the local"—though these may be the rhetorical forms in which some of these reforms are couched—what we may also be witnessing is the revivification of more traditional class, gender, and especially race hierarchies. An unquestioning commitment to the notion that "we" are now fully involved in a postmodern world may make it easier to see surface transformations (some of which are undoubtedly occurring) and yet at the same time may make it that much more difficult to recognize that these also may be new ways of reorganizing and reproducing older hierarchies.[10] The fact that parts of postmodernism as a theory and as a set of experiences may not be applicable to an extremely large part of the population of the world should make us be a bit more cautious as well.

In *Cultural Politics and Education*, it is clear that part, though certainly not all, of what I say there is based on a critical (and self-critical) structural understanding of education. Although it is not economically reductive, this perspective does require that we recognize that we live under capitalist relations. Milton Friedman and the entire gamut of privatizers and marketizers who have so much influence in the media and in the corridors of power in corporate board rooms, foundations, and nearly all levels of government spend considerable amounts of time praising these relations. If they can talk about them, why can't we? These relations *don't* determine everything. They are constituted out of and are reconstituted by race, class, and gender relations, but it seems a bit naive to ignore them. There is a world of difference between taking economic power and structures seriously and reducing everything down to a pale reflection of them.

I am fully cognizant that there are many dangers with such an approach. It has as part of its history attempts to create a "grand narrative," a theory that explains everything based on a unitary cause. It can also tend to forget that not only are there multiple and contradictory relations of power in nearly every situation, but that the researcher herself or himself is a participant in such relations.[11] Finally, structural approaches at times can neglect the ways our discourses are constructed out of, and themselves help to construct, what we do. These indeed are issues that need to be taken as seriously as they deserve. Poststructural and postmodern criticisms of structural analyses in education have been fruitful in this regard, especially when they have arisen from within the various feminist, antiracist, and postcolonial communities,[12] although it must be said that some of these criticisms have created wildly inaccurate caricatures of the neo-Marxist traditions.

Yet, even though the "linguistic turn," as it has been called in sociology and cultural studies, has been immensely productive, it is important to remember that the world of education and the world at large are not merely texts. There are gritty realities out there, realities whose power is often grounded in structural relations that are not simply social constructions created by the meanings given by an observer. Part of our task, it seems to me, is not to lose sight of these gritty realities in the economy and the state, at the same time as we recognize the dangers of essentializing and reductive analyses.[13]

My point is not to deny that many elements of postmodernity exist, nor is it to deny the power of aspects of postmodern theory. Rather, it is to avoid overstatement, to avoid substituting one grand narrative for another (a grand narrative that actually never existed in the United States), because the concepts of class and economy only recently surfaced in critical educational scholarship and were only rarely seen here in the form found in Europe where most postmodern and poststructural criticisms of these explanatory tools were developed. It would help if we remembered that the intellectual and political histories of the United States were very different from those castigated by some of the postmodern critics). Reductive analysis comes cheap and there is no guarantee that postmodern positions, as currently employed by some in education, are any more immune to this danger than is any other position.

Thus, in much of my recent work, it will not be a surprise that side by side with poststructural and postmodern understandings are those based on structural theories. Although they are not totally merged, each one serves as a corrective and a complement to the other. This is a point I wish to emphasize. Rather than spending so much time treating each other so warily—and sometimes as enemies—the creative tension that exists is a good thing.[14] We have a good deal to learn from each other in terms of a politics in and around education that makes a difference (no pun is intended here).

There are a number of other intellectual tensions that swirled around these books as well. As I reflected on the growth of certain styles of doing critical analysis in education, it was also clear that there had been a rapid growth of two other kinds of work—personal/literary/ autobiographical and studies of popular culture. The former has often been stimulated by phenomenological, psychoanalytic, and feminist approaches. The latter has arisen from cultural studies. Let me say something about each of these.

Much of the impetus behind personal stories is moral. Education is correctly seen as an ethical enterprise. The personal is seen as a way to reawaken ethical and aesthetic sensitivities that increasingly have been purged from the scientistic discourse of too many educators. Or it is seen as a way of giving a voice to the subjectivities of people who have been silenced. There is much to commend in this position. Indeed, any approach that, say, evacuates the aesthetic, the personal, and the ethical from our activities as educators is not about education at all. It is about training. As someone who spent years teaching in inner-city schools in a severely economically depressed community, I reject any approach that reduces education to mere training or is not grounded in the personal lives and stories of real teachers, students, and community members. Yet something remains a little too much in the background in many variants of the stories written by professional educators and academics—a biting sense of the political, of the social structures that condemn so many identifiable people to lives of economic and cultural (and bodily) struggle and, at times, despair. It is essential to make connections between what might be called the literary imagination and the concrete movements—in education *and* the larger society—that seek to transform our institutions so that caring and social justice are not just slogans but realities. Political arguments are not alternatives to moral and aesthetic concerns. Rather, they are these concerns taken seriously in their full implications.[15] And this leads me to raise a caution about some of the hidden effects of our (generally commendable) urge to employ the personal and the autobiographical to illuminate our (admittedly differential) educational experiences.

For nearly twenty years, until the publication of another recent book of mine, *Official Knowledge*,[16] I did not write about my experiences as a filmmaker with teachers and students, in part because I could not find an appropriate "voice." It would have required a fair dose of autobiography. I often find autobiographical accounts and narrative renderings compelling and insightful, and do not want in any way to dismiss their power in educational theory and practice. Yet—and let me be blunt here—just as often such writing runs the risk of lapsing into what has been called possessive individualism.[17] Even when an author does the "correct thing" and discusses her or his social location in a world that is dominated by oppressive conditions, such writing can serve the chilling function of simply saying "But enough about you, let me tell you about me" if we are not much more reflective about this than has often been the case. I am still committed enough to raising questions about class and race dynamics to worry about perspectives that supposedly acknowledge the missing voices of many people in our thinking about education, but still wind up privileging the white, middle-class woman's or man's need for *self-display.*

Do not misconstrue what I am saying here. As so much feminist and postcolonial work has documented, the personal often is the absent presence behind even the most eviscerated writing and we do need to continue to explore ways of heightening the sense of the personal in our stories about education. But, at the same time, it is equally crucial that we interrogate our own "hidden" motives here. Is the insistence on the personal that underpins much of our turn toward literary and autobiographical forms partly a class discourse as well? The personal may be the political, but does the political end at the personal? Furthermore, why should we assume that the personal is any less difficult to understand than the "external" world? I cannot answer these questions for all situations; but I think that these questions must be asked by all of us who are committed to the multiple projects involved in struggling for a more emancipatory education. (And for this very reason, later on I shall end my discussion in this chapter with a personal story that is *consciously* connected to a clear sense of the realities of structurally generated inequalities that play such a large role in education.)

My intellectual/political tensions did not end here, however. "Boom times" in academic stocks and bonds come and go.[18] In some parts of the critical educational community, the study of popular culture—music, dance, films, language, dress, bodily transformations, the politics of consumption, and so on—is also big business. And in many ways it should be. After all, we should know by now that popular culture is *partly* a site of resistance and struggle,[19] but we should also realize that for schooling to make a difference it must connect to popular understandings and cultural forms. Yet our fascination with "the popular," our intoxication with all of these things, has sometimes had a paradoxical and unfortunate effect. It often has led us to ignore the actual knowledge that *is* taught in schools, the entire corpus and structure of the formal processes of curriculum, teaching, and evaluation that remain so powerful. In many ways, it constitutes a flight from education as a field. In my more cynical moments, I take this as a class discourse in which new elements within the academy in education fight for power not only over school folks but over positions within the academy itself.

In *Cultural Politics and Education,* I talk about the importance of popular culture and make a plea for its utter centrality in our struggles

to understand cultural politics and to institute more socially just models of curriculum and teaching. Yet, many members of the critical
educational community have been a bit too trendy about this topic as
well. They seem to have forgotten about schools, curricula, teachers,
students, community activists, and so on. It's as if they feel that dealing with these issues is "polluting," as if they are afraid of getting
their hands dirty with the daily realities of education. Or perhaps they
feel that it's not theoretically elegant enough to deal with such mun-
dane realities. Although I fully understand the utter necessity of focusing on the popular, as a critical *educator* I am even more committed
to taking the reality of school matters as seriously as they deserve to
be taken.[20] For this very reason, *Cultural Politics and Education*
devotes much of its attention to matters specifically related to the
politics of curriculum and teaching, just as *Democratic Schools* is
totally devoted to describing how we can make a real difference in the
curriculum and teaching that now dominate too many schools.

I do not want to be overly negative here. Many of us have quite
ambivalent feelings about the place called school. All of us who care
deeply about what is and is not taught and about who is and is not
empowered to answer these questions have a contradictory relationship to these institutions. We want to criticize them rigorously and yet
in this very criticism lies a commitment, a hope, that they can be
made more vital, more personally meaningful and socially critical. If
ever there was a love/hate relationship, this is it.[21] This speaks directly to the situation many people in critical educational studies face
today and underlies some of the emphases of both books.

The New Right is very powerful now. It has had the odd effect of
simultaneously interrupting the progressive critique of schooling while
at the same time leading many of us to defend an institution many of
whose practices were and are open to severe criticism.[22] As someone
who has devoted years to analyzing and acting on the social and cultural means and ends of our curricula, teaching, and evaluation in
schools, I am certainly not one who wants to act as an apologist for
poor practices. Yet, during an era when because of rightist attacks we
face the massive dismantling of the gains (limited as they were) that
have been made in social welfare; in women's control of their bodies;
in relations of race, class, gender, and sexuality; and about whose
knowledge is taught in schools, it is equally important to make certain
that these gains are defended.

Thus, there is another clear tension in these volumes. I wanted
both to defend the idea of a *public* education and a number of the

gains that do exist and to criticize many of its attributes at the same time. This dual focus may seem a bit odd at first, but it speaks to a crucial point I want to make about how we should think about the institutions of formal education in most of our nations.

Here I want to say something that may make a number of educators a bit uncomfortable who are justifiably critical of existing power relations in education. The problem I shall point to may at first seem minor, but its conceptual, political, and practical implications are not. I am referring to the discourse of *change*. It stands behind all of those claims about both the autobiographical and popular culture and behind the pressures to connect schools more closely to economic needs and goals. All too often we forget that in our attempts to alter and "reform" schooling there are elements that should not be changed but that must be kept and defended. Even given my criticisms of the unequal power relations surrounding education and in the larger society, we need to remember that schooling was never simply an imposition on supposedly politically/culturally inept people. Rather, as I have demonstrated elsewhere, educational policies and practices were and are the result of struggles and compromises over what would count as legitimate knowledge, pedagogy, goals, and criteria of determining effectiveness. In a more abstract way, we can say that education has been one of the major arenas in which the conflict between property rights and person rights has been fought.[23]

The results of these conflicts have not always been settled on the terms of dominant groups. Often, democratic tendencies have emerged and have been cemented into the daily practices of the institution. As William Reese shows in his history of populist reform in schools, many things that we take for granted were the direct results of populist movements that forced powerful groups to compromise, and even to suffer outright losses.[24] Thus, before we give a blanket condemnation to what schools do and turn to what we suppose is its alternative (say, popular culture), we need a much clearer and more historically informed appraisal of which elements of the practices and policies of these institutions are already progressive and should be maintained. Not to do so would be to assume that, say, radical teachers, people of color, women, working class groups, and physically challenged groups (these categories are obviously not mutually exclusive) have been puppets whose strings are pulled by the most conservative forces in this society and have not won any lasting victories in education. This is simply not the case. Not to defend some of the ideas behind person rights that are currently embodied in schools is to add more power to conservative attacks. There *have* been gains. The forces of the conservative restoration would not be so very angry at public schools—at the supposed overemphasis on "minority culture," on feminism, on gay and lesbian rights—if educational and community activists hadn't had at least some success in transforming what was taken for granted in schools. These gains certainly aren't sufficient; but they *are* there.

I do not want to belabor this point, but it does make a major difference in how we approach education. At times, some critical educators have been so critical that we too often assume—consciously or unconsciously—that everything that exists within the educational system bears only the marks of and is only the result of domination. It's all capitalist; it's all racist; it's all patriarchal; it's all homophobic. As you would imagine given my own efforts over the past three decades, I do not want to dismiss the utter power of these and other forms of oppression in education or in anything else. Yet, in taking a stance that *assumes*—without detailed investigation—that all is somehow the result of relations of dominance, we also make it very difficult to make connections with progressive educators and community members who are currently struggling to build an education that is democratic in more than name only. (And there are many practicing educators who have been more than a little successful in such struggles.) It is all too easy for critical educators to fall into this position.

This assumption is problematic conceptually, historically, and politically. It rests on a theory of the role of state institutions that is too simplistic and on an ahistorical understanding of the power of democratically inclined groups.[25] It also bears the marks of what seems like a form of self-hatred, as if the more we distance ourselves from the history and discourse of education—and turn to other, "more academically respectable" fields for all of our perspectives—the more academically legitimate we become. The ultimate effects of this are disabling for any of us who wish to continue the long and essential struggle to have our educational institutions respond to the needs of other groups than those in power.

This is a difficult tightrope to walk for those of us involved in education. In a time of right-wing resurgence, how do we create the educational conditions in which our students can see (and teach us about as well) the very real and massive relations of inequality and the role of schooling in partly reproducing and contesting them, and at the same time jointly create the conditions that assist all of us in empowering each other to act on these realities? Gramsci had a way of saying it: Pessimism of the intellect, optimism of the will. But my point goes well beyond this. Intellect, enlivened by passion and ethical/political sensitivities—and a fine sense of historical agency—will also see victories as well as losses, hope as well as despair. That, it seems to me, is our task.

Finally, and this is directly related to what I have just said, there has been one other tension behind these books. When I began writing *Cultural Politics and Education* not only did I want to both criticize and defend much that is happening in education, I also wanted to illuminate what it actually *is* that needs to be defended. What policies and practices now exist in schools and classrooms that are socially and educationally critical? Are there what I have elsewhere called crucial "nonreformist reforms" that need to be continued?[26] This caused me no end of headaches. Although throughout *Cultural Politics and Education* I refer to such policies and practices, for political and ethical reasons (and perhaps for reasons of sanity), I ultimately decided that extensive descriptions of such critical practices clearly deserved an entire book of their own. Furthermore, they should be written by the educator/activists who actually engage in them, in their own words. It is this very reason that at the same time that I was writing the first book, my colleague and friend Jim Beane and I produced *Democratic Schools*. As I noted, it details in much greater depth what is possible in public schools now. By focusing on the stories of a number of ongoing socially and educationally committed public schools run by educators who directly link their curricula and teaching to a clear sense of the economic, political, and cultural relations of power in the world, it gives what I believe is compelling evidence that the journey of hope in education continues in real schools with real teachers, students, and community members. Thus, if you read *Cultural Politics and Education,* and afterwards you still find yourself asking something like "Okay Apple, now what? What concrete ideas do you have to practice what you preach? What alternatives would you propose, and what would you keep, to take your critical analysis seriously?", I can only reply that my answers to these questions are provided considerably more fully in *Democratic Schools.*

Memory and Experience

The first section of this chapter laid out the "balancing act" that I've tried to engage in over the past years. This has involved me (and many others) in the following: criticizing dominant educational practices while defending gains; deepening and defending crucial aspects of structural analyses of education while recognizing a number of the insights in poststructural approaches and incorporating them into my work; engaging in detailed critical analyses of schools while trying to make public more democratic educational policies and practices; and wanting to stimulate a more personal and/or autobiographical appraisal of education but not at the expense of losing our sense of the ways education is currently structured around oppressive economic/political/cultural relations.

Of course, as I have shown throughout this chapter, this balancing act has roots in debates about concepts, methods, and politics in critical educational studies. Yet it roots go much deeper than that. As with most people, they grow out of one's biography in crucial ways. In my own case, they come from a personal history of poverty and from a family who because of this was deeply involved in political action. They come from the time I spent as an activist teacher both in inner-city and more rural schools and as a president of a teachers' union. They come from my early experiences in movements opposed to the racial structuring of this society and from the fact that I am the father of an African American child, a fact that never lets me forget what race means in this society. And they come from my repeated and continuing experiences over the past three decades in my work with dissident groups, labor unions, critical educators, and others who are involved in struggling to create a more just and caring economy, polity, and culture. In essence, it is these early and ongoing activities that provide the impetus behind my work, that constantly force me to confront the fact that education is intimately connected to relations of domination and subordination—and to struggles against them—whether we recognize this or not.[27]

Perhaps I can offer one personal story to illuminate why I think we must never forget such a structural sense of these relations and why the connections between education and the larger structures of inequality need to have a central place in our thought and action in education. In many ways, this story will crystallize and make explicit many of the points I have made here about the political, theoretical, and educational tensions that lie behind my work.

Education and Cheap French Fries

The sun glared off of the hood of the small car as we made our way along the two-lane road. The heat and humidity made me wonder if I'd have any liquid left in my body at the end of the trip and led me to appreciate Wisconsin winters a bit more than one might expect. The idea of winter seemed more than a little remote in this Asian country for which I have a good deal of fondness. But the topic at hand was not the weather; rather, it was the struggles of educators and social activists to build an education that was considerably more democratic than what was in place in that country now. This was a dangerous topic. Discussing it in philosophical and formal academic terms was tolerated there. Openly calling for it and situating it within a serious analysis of the economic, political, and military power structures that now exerted control over so much of this nation's daily life was another matter. And we were on our way to a meeting with a group of young teachers in a rural area who were involved in such struggles.[28]

As we traveled along that rural road in the midst of one of the best conversations I had engaged in about the possibilities of educational transformations and the realities of the oppressive conditions so many people were facing in that land, my gaze somehow was drawn to the side of the road. In one of those nearly accidental happenings that clarify and crystallize what reality is *really* like, my gaze fell upon a seemingly inconsequential object. At regular intervals, there were small signs planted in the dirt a few yards from where the road met the fields. The sign was more than a little familiar. It bore the insignia of one of the most famous fast-food restaurants in the United States. We drove for miles past seemingly deserted fields along a flat hot plain, passing sign after sign, each a replica of the previous one, each less than a foot high. These were not billboards. Such things hardly existed in this poor rural region. Rather, they looked exactly—exactly— like the small signs one finds next to farms in the American midwest that signify the kinds of seed corn that each farmer has planted in her or his fields. This was a good guess, it turned out.

I asked the driver—a close friend and former student of mine who had returned to this country to work for the social and educational reforms that were so necessary—what turned out to be a naive but ultimately crucial question in my own education. "Why are those signs for ———— there? Is there a ———— restaurant nearby?" My friend looked at me in amazement. "Michael, don't you know what these signs signify? There's no western restaurant within fifty miles of where we are. These signs represent exactly what is wrong with education in this nation. Listen to this." And I listened.

The story is one that has left an indelible mark on me, for it condenses in one powerful set of historical experiences the connections between our struggles as educators and activists in so many countries and the ways that differential power works in ordinary life. I cannot match the tensions and passions in my friend's voice as this story was told; nor can I convey exactly the almost eerie feelings one gets when looking at that vast, sometimes beautiful, sometimes scarred, and increasingly depopulated plain. Yet the story is crucial to hear. Listen to this.

The government of the nation has decided that the importation of foreign capital is critical to its own survival. Bringing in American, German, British, Japanese, and other investors and factories will ostensibly create jobs, will create capital for investment, and will enable the nation to speed into the twenty-first century. (This is of course elite-group talk, but let us assume that all of this is indeed truly believed by dominant groups.) One of the ways the military-dominated government has planned to do this is to focus part of its recruitment efforts on agribusiness. In pursuit of this goal, it has offered vast tracts of land to international agribusiness concerns at very low cost. Of particular significance for the plain we were driving through is the fact that much of the land has been given over to a large American fast-food restaurant corporation for the growing of potatoes for the restaurant's french fries, one the trademarks of its extensive success throughout the world.

The corporation was eager to jump at the opportunity to shift a good deal of its potato production from the United States to Asia. Because many of the farm workers in the United States were now unionized and were (correctly) asking for a livable wage, and because the government of that Asian nation officially frowned on unions of any kind, the cost of growing potatoes would be lower. Further, the land on that plain was perfect for the use of newly developed technology to plant and harvest the crop with considerably fewer workers. Machines would replace living human beings. Finally, the government was much less concerned about environmental regulations than was the government of the United States. All in all, this was a fine bargain for capital.

Of course, *people* lived on some of this land and farmed it for their own food and to sell what might be left over after their own relatively minimal needs were met. This deterred neither agribusiness nor the government. After all, people could be moved to make way for "progress." And after all, the villagers along that plain did not actually have deeds to the land. (They had lived there for perhaps hundreds of years, well before the invention of banks, and mortgages, and deeds, but the government's position was no paper, no ownership.) It would not be too hard to move the people from the plain to other areas to "free" it for intensive potato production and to "create jobs" by taking away the livelihood of thousands upon thousands of small-scale farmers in the region.

I listened with rapt attention as the rest of the story unfolded and as we passed by the fields with their miniature corporate signs and the abandoned villages. The people whose land had been taken for so little had moved, of course. As in so many similar places throughout what dominant groups call the Third World, they trekked to the city. They took their meager possessions and moved into the ever-expanding slums in and surrounding the one place that held out some hope of finding enough paid work (if *everyone*—including children—labored) so that they could survive.

The government and major segments of the business elite officially discouraged this, sometimes by hiring thugs to burn the shanty towns, at other times by keeping conditions so horrible that no one would "want" to live there. But still the dispossessed came, by the tens of thousands. Poor people are not irrational, after all. The loss of arable land had to be compensated for somehow and if it took cramming into places that were deadly at times, well, what were the other choices? There *were* factories being built in and around the cities that paid incredibly low wages—sometimes less than enough money to buy sufficient food to replace the calories expended by workers in the production process—but at least there might be paid work if one was lucky. (Although, as in many instances of this type, it was women who were "preferred" for these low-paid and exploitative factory jobs, because they supposedly were more dexterous, more docile, and were "willing" to work for less.)

So the giant machines harvested the potatoes and the people poured into the cities and international capital was happy. It's not a nice story, but what does it have to do with *education*? My friend continued my education.

The military-dominated government had given all of these large international businesses twenty years of tax breaks to entice them to come to that country. Thus, there was now very little money to supply the health care facilities, houses, running water, electricity, sewage disposal, and schools for the thousands upon thousands of people who had sought their future in or had literally been driven into the city. The mechanism for *not* building these necessities was quite clever.

Take the lack of any formal educational institutions as a case in point. In order for the government to build schools it had to be shown that there was a "legitimate" need for such expenditures. Statistics had to be produced in a form that was *officially* accepted. This could be done only through the official determination of numbers of registered births. Yet, the very process of official registration made it impossible for thousands of children to be recognized as actually existing.

In order to register for school, a parent had to register the birth of the child at the local hospital or government office, few of which existed in these slum areas. And even if you could somehow find such an office, the government offically discouraged people who had originally come from outside the region of the city from moving there. It often refused to recognize the legitimacy of the move as a way of keeping displaced farmers from coming into the urban areas and thereby increasing the population. Births among people who had no "legitimate" right to be there did not count as births at all. It is a brilliant strategy by which the state creates categories of legitimacy that define social problems in quite interesting ways.[29] Foucault would have been proud, I am certain.

Thus, there are no schools, no teachers, no hospitals, no infrastructure. The root causes of this situation rest not in the immediate situation. They can be illuminated only if we focus on the chain of capital formation internationally and nationally, on the contradictory needs of the state, on the class relations, and the relations between country and city that organize and disorganize that country. And they can be illuminated only by recognizing the fact that under prevailing neocolonial forms, the people of these slums become *disposable and invisible*—the "other"—given an international division of labor in which race plays such a large part. "We" eat; "they" remain unseen.

My friend and I had been driving for quite a while now. I had forgotten about the heat. The ending sentence of the story pulled no punches. It was said slowly and quietly, said in a way that made it even more compelling. "Michael, these fields are the reason there's no schools in my city. There's no schools because so many folks like cheap french fries."

I tell this story about the story told to me for a number of reasons. First, it is simply one of the most powerful ways I know of reminding myself and all of us of the utter importance of seeing schooling relationally, of seeing it as fundamentally connected to the relations of domination and exploitation (and to struggles against them) of the larger society. Second, and equally as important, I tell this story to make a crucial theoretical and political point. Relations of power are indeed complex and we do need to take very seriously the postmodern focus on the local and on the multiplicity of the forms of struggle that need to be engaged in. It is important as well to recognize the changes that are occurring in many societies and to see the complexity of the power/knowledge nexus. Yet in our attempts to avoid the dangers that accompanied some aspects of previous "grand narratives," let us *not* act as if capitalism has somehow disappeared. Let us not act as if class relations, nationally and internationally, don't count. Let us not act as if what are arrogantly called "center/periphery" relations that are often based on racial divisions of labor don't exist. Let us not act as if all of the things we learned about how the world might be understood politically have been somehow overthrown because our theories are now more complex. It is these principles that provide the center of gravity in my work.

The denial of basic human rights, the destruction of the environment, the deadly conditions under which people (barely) survive, the lack of a meaningful future for the thousands of children I noted in my story are not only or even primarily a "text" to be deciphered in our academic volumes as we pursue our postmodern themes. It is a reality that millions of people experience in their very bodies everyday. Educational work that is not connected deeply to a powerful understanding of these realities (and this understanding cannot eliminate a serious analysis of political economy and class, race, and gender relations without losing much of its power) is in danger of losing its soul. The lives of our children demand no less.

Postscript

I started out to do something that I thought was relatively simple in this chapter. My original intent was to put on paper some of the reasons why *Cultural Politics and Education* and *Democratic Schools* took the shape that they did. Yet this seemingly simple task soon got more complex. It caused me to delve more deeply into a set of theoretical, political, and educational tensions and to be a bit more of a storyteller than I had originally planned.

Although a good deal of what I have said here is expanded in *Cultural Politics and Education*, I do want to add one other thing. I ended the story of my drive through that plain with a call to connect our work as educators to a serious understanding of power, but an understanding that doesn't get so complicated that it forgets that many times it really "ain't that hard" at times to recognize who benefits from the ways our societies are now organized. Yet, such recognition is more than a theoretic or academic task.[30] This recognition requires that we live our lives *differently*—for example, that we build alliances with, support, and learn from both the teachers and community activists represented in *Democratic Schools* and from those young teachers I was driving to meet on that hot flat plain. Boycotting cheap french fries might help a little too.

Notes

Parts of this chapter appear in Michael W. Apple, *Cultural Politics and Education* (New York: Teachers College Press, 1996 and London: Open University Press, 1996).

1   M.W. Apple, *Cultural Politics and Education* (New York: Teachers College Press and London: Open University Press, 1996).

2   The following books made up the series and were written in the order of their listing: *Ideology and Curriculum* (1979; second edition 1990); *Education and Power* (1982; revised ARK edition 1985; second edition 1995); *Teachers and Texts* (1986); and *Official Knowledge* (1993).

3   M.W. Apple and J.A. Beane, ed. *Democratic Schools* (Washington, DC: Association for Supervision and Curriculum Development, 1995).

4   R. Williams, *The Year 2000* (New York: Pantheon, 1983), 243–69.

5   M.W. Apple, *Official Knowledge* (New York: Routledge, 1993).

6   R. Herrnstein and C. Murray, *The Bell Curve* (New York: The Free Press, 1994). For criticisms of the conceptual, empirical, and ideological agendas of *The Bell Curve,* see J. Kincheloe and S. Steinberg, eds., *Measured Lies* (New York: St. Martin's Press, 1996).

7   See M.W. Apple, "Cultural Capital and Official Knowledge," in *Higher Education Under Fire,* ed. C. Nelson and M. Berube (New York: Routledge, 1994). I say *approaches* here because it is too easy to stereotype postmodern and poststructural theories. That would be unfortunate, because the political differences, for example, among and within the various tendencies associated with both are often substantial.

8   G. Whitty, T. Edwards, and S. Gewirtz, *Specialisation and Choice in Urban Education* (New York: Routledge, 1994), 168–69.

9   Ibid., 173–74.

10 Ibid., 180–81.

11 L. Roman and M.W. Apple, "Is Naturalism a Move Beyond Positivism?" in *Qualititive Inquiry in Education,* ed. E. Eisner and A. Peshkin (New York: Teachers College Press, 1990).

12 See, for example, C. Luke and J. Gore, ed. *Feminisms and Cultural Pedagogy* (New York: Routledge, 1992); C. McCarthy and W. Crichlow, ed. *Race, Identity, and Representation in Education* (New York: Routledge, 1993).

13 M.W. Apple, "Education, Culture, and Class Power," *Educational Theory* 42 (Spring 1992): 127–45.

14   See M.W. Apple and A. Oliver, "Becoming Right: Education and the Formation of Conservative Movements," *Teachers College Record* (in press).

15   T. Eagleton, *Literary Theory* (Minneapolis: University of Minnesota Press, 1983).

16   Apple, *Official Knowledge.*

17   M.W. Apple, *Ideology and Curriculum,* 2d ed. (New York: Routledge, 1990); Apple, *Official Knowledge;* M.W. Apple, *Education and Power,* 2d ed. (New York: Routledge, 1995).

18   J. McGuigan, *Cultural Populism* (New York: Routledge, 1992), 61.

19   P. Willis, S. Jones, J. Canaan, and G. Hurd 1990, *Common Culture* (Boulder: Westview, 1990); H. Giroux, "Doing Cultural Studies," *Harvard Educational Review* 64 (Fall 1994): 278–308; J. Koza, "Rap Music," *The Review of Education/Pedagogy/Cultural Studies* 16 (Fall 1994): 171–96.

20   That one can deal with popular culture and school culture together in elegant ways is very nicely documented in M. Weinstein, "Robot World: A Study of Science, Reality, and the Struggle for Meaning" (Ph.D. diss., University of Wisconsin-Madison, 1995).

21   Ian Hunter in fact argues that critical educational researchers are so wedded to schools that their criticisms function as part of the mobility strategies of an intellectual elite. This is a provocative thesis, but is essentialist in the extreme. See I. Hunter, *Rethinking the School* (St. Leonards, Australia: Allen and Unwin, 1994). See also my response to his book in M.W. Apple, "Review of Ian Hunter, *Rethinking the School,*" *Australian Journal of Education* 39 (April 1995): 95–96.

22   Education Group II, ed., *Education Limited* (London: Unwin Hyman, 1991), 33.

23   Apple, *Official Knowledge;* Apple, *Education and Power.*

24   W. Reese, *Power and the Promise of School Reform* (New York: Routledge, 1986).

25   M. Carnoy and C. Levin, *Schooling and Work in the Democratic State* (Stanford, CA: Stanford University Press, 1985); D. Jules and M.W. Apple, "The State and Educational Reform," in *Continuity and Contradiction: The Futures of the Sociology of Education,* ed. W. Pink and G. Noblit (Cresskill, NJ: Hampton Press, 1995).

26   Apple, *Education and Power.*

27   These more autobiographical points are laid out in more detail in an interview with me published as an appendix in Apple, *Official Knowledge.*

28   I shall not name this country here, because to do so could put the teachers and my colleague at risk.

29   See N. Fraser, *Unruly Practices* (Minneapolis: University of Minnesota Press, 1989); B. Curtis, *True Government by Choice Men?* (Toronto: University of Toronto Press, 1992).

30   I do not want to dismiss the important of theoretical or academic work, if such work is *overtly* connected to movements for social justice. For further discussion of this see M.W. Apple, "Power, Meaning, and Identity," *British Journal of Sociology of Education* (in press).

Chapter 12

Epilogue

The essays brought together in this volume trace both synchronic (spacial) and diachronic (historical) paths. They work synchronically by giving examples of my arguments across a range of areas, from studies of curriculum, teaching, and evaluation to concerns with the larger arenas that deal with the complexities of the relationship between education and cultural, political, and economic power. They work diachronically by giving a sense of the history of some of the transformations of my thinking over the years that they were written. What they do not do, however, is lay out what I claimed in both *Official Knowledge*[1] and in the previous chapter here to be equally essential to understanding my development: the connections between the issues I raise in my critical writings and the concrete and continuing work I have done in schools, in working with teachers' unions and dissidents here and abroad, and in other political/cultural movements. Perhaps I will try to lay out these kinds of mutual influences in more detail in future work. But right now, I would hope that this volume gives enough of a picture of the synchronic and diachronic relations to make sense of a major portion of my concerns over the years. It should complement and perhaps deepen the picture of what I'm about that is available in the series of books I've written over the past two to three decades.

As I did at the very beginning of this volume of essays, I want to close it in a relatively unconventional, partly autobiographical, way since it bears directly on my agenda over the years. After having spent a number of years as a primary and secondary school teacher in the impoverished neighborhoods of a dying deindustrialized city and in a poor rural area on the east coast of the United States, I decided to go on to graduate school. The subjects that I originally chose to study (which were replaced later by curriculum studies and critical sociology) were philosophy and the philosophy of education. It seemed to me at the time that, in addition to the very evident causes so deeply rooted in the structures of domination and exploitation in this society, one of the major reasons that the educational institutions in which I had worked were so deadening both for students and teachers was our utter inability to step back and critically examine the means and ends of what was taken for granted about education. Philosophy seemed a good place to begin.

I was more than a little naive about what the philosophy of education was concerned with and what it had to offer. But on looking back, I do not regret this original choice, for the "knowledge that, how, and to" that I learned there has stayed with me and has provided important analytical tools for my later work.

At the time (it was the mid-1960s), both philosophy and philosophy of education were dominated by the analytic tradition.[2] Israel Sheffler, James McClellan, Jane Roland Martin, B. Paul Komisar, and Jonas Soltis, among others, were those whom one read on the western side of the Atlantic.[3] And, of course, R.S. Peters was seen as the major figure on the eastern side.[4] There was some philosophical flexibility within this tradition. This is seen in the fact that Ryle, Wittgenstein, and Hampshire were also influential in philosophy itself.[5] But the logical analysis of concepts held sway. Dewey was invisible, as were any of the "great names" in the more programmatic tradition of philosophy of education. The task of analytic philosophy was to find clarity, to search out all unacknowledged, illogical claims and hidden assumptions. It was extremely rigorous, and at times alienating and depersonalizing. But it did make one (including me) impatient with educational rhetoric and superficial arguments. In many ways, such rigor has not outlived its usefulness.

Such rigor, however, was often applied to less than consequential problems. The personal, ethical, and political "density" of education was too often ignored. Larger questions of justice, of political economy, of cultural politics, and of similar difficult (and intellectually and politically "dangerous") issues were usually eschewed. For some of us, there were traditions that compensated for these lacks. Existential and structural phenomenology—Heidegger, Merleau-Ponty, Sartre, Ricoeur, Schutz—provided dense but alternative voices.[6] The powerful work of those within the critical theory tradition(s)—from Adorno, Horkheimer, and Benjamin to Marcuse and especially Habermas—enabled many of us to see the connections between our theoretical questions and intuitions and those pressing and "dangerous" political issues and struggles so many of us were engaged in and that so many of us felt were ignored within the program and agenda of analytic philosophy.[7] The fact that so many of us were deeply engaged in antiracist and anticorporate work and later on in antiwar mobilizations gave these kinds of intellectual issues more political salience.

Any examination of the current situation in educational theory in general demonstrates that the current situation is much more fluid and fragmented; no one theory clearly dominates. To take but one example, over the past two decades the area of what I have here called critical educational studies has rapidly grown both in size and sophistication. It is an extremely diverse area, including tendencies drawn from neo-Marxisms, critical pragmatism, multiple feminisms, postmodernism, poststructuralism, critical race theory, postcolonial emphases, queer theory, and cultural studies—as well as work that offers a rich mix of many of these. Truly major gains in our understanding of the relationship between education and power have arisen out of this work. The same kinds of political intuitions about the relationship between education and power and about the nature of the institutions in which we live that drove me and many of my friends and colleagues stand behind much of this emerging work as well.

As I noted in a number of the essays in this book, this has brought about an exciting diversity of new theoretical and political lenses and possibilities, ones that need to be supported and taken very seriously. Yet having said this, these gains have been accompanied by a number of worrisome tendencies. In my essay on Paulo Freire, I remarked that the best way to show one's respect for a person's work is to take it seriously enough to criticize. Thus, although I want to support these theoretical and political gains (they certainly have had a very important and positive influence on my own work), I believe that it is equally essential not to support things blindly or uncritically. For me, among the most important of these worrisome tendencies has been the development of private language systems in which it is increasingly difficult to participate unless one is a specialist (perhaps initiate is a better metaphor) in the metatheories that stand behind the language.

I am equally worried that some of this work has lost its connections with what is happening in real schools, populated by real people, in real communities. When connected with the concern I expressed at the end of the previous paragraph, this can lead to a situation in which people engaged in critical educational studies are not as subject as I think we should be to the critiques (and perhaps affirmations) of educators, community activists, cultural workers, and others who toil every day in the difficult and uncertain conditions of these same institutions some of us write about. I do not think that this is a healthy tendency in the long run. As I said earlier, it can lead to a life "on the balcony."

In the end, I am left with a revitalized realization of the difficult paths before us. Working hard to rename the word and the world, criticizing each other's possible weaknesses and yet supporting each other at the same time, building coalitions across differences, engaging in the difficult task of thinking and acting critically with the full realization of the fallibility of our understandings, and finally doing all this in a way that *lives out* our political commitments in our own lives—all of this seems necessary to me.

This hasn't been easy in the past and it surely won't be any easier in the future. But we can continue, knowing the long history of other educators who have opened some of the many trails we will need to travel. Paulo Freire points to one of these paths in his discussion of the ways a critical and dialogic education might best proceed.

> It is a permanent, critical approach to reality in order to discover it and discover the myths that deceive us and help us maintain the oppressive, dehumanizing structures. It leaves nobody inactive. It implies that people take on the role of agents, makers and remakers of the world.[8]

Although this book provided part of the record of my own trip, our collective journey of critical discovery, making, and remaking still has quite a ways to go. But then education itself—and especially critical education—is a never-ending journey, isn't it?

Notes

1   Michael W. Apple, *Official Knowledge* (New York: Routledge, 1993), 163–81.

2   See J.O. Urmson, *Philosophical Analysis* (London: Oxford University Press, 1963).

3   See Jonas Soltis, *An Introduction to the Analysis of Educational Concepts* (Reading, Mass.: Addison-Wesley, 1968).

4   Richard S. Peters, *Ethics and Education* (Glenview, IL: Scott, Foresman, 1967).

5   See, for example, Gilbert Ryle, *The Concept of Mind* (New York: Barnes and Noble, 1949); Ludwig Wittgenstein, *Philosophical Investigations* (New York: Macmillan, 1952); and Stuart Hampshire, *Thought and Action* (New York: Viking, 1959).

6   See Herbert Spiegelberg, *The Phenomenological Movement* (The Hague: Martinus Nijhoff, 1982).

7   For an overview of the political and conceptual history written at the time, see Trent Schroyer, *The Critique of Domination* (New York: George Braziller, 1973).

8   Paulo Freire, "A Few Notions About the Word Conscientization," *Hard Cheese* 1 (January 1973), 24.

Index

Studies in the Postmodern Theory of Education

General Editors
Joe L. Kincheloe & Shirley R. Steinberg

Counterpoints publishes the most compelling and imaginative books being written in education today. Grounded on the theoretical advances in criticalism, feminism and postmodernism in the last two decades of the twentieth century, Counterpoints engages the meaning of these innovations in various forms of educational expression. Committed to the proposition that theoretical literature should be accessible to a variety of audiences, the series insists that its authors avoid esoteric and jargonistic languages that transform educational scholarship into an elite discourse for the initiated. Scholarly work matters only to the degree it affects consciousness and practice at multiple sites. Counterpoints' editorial policy is based on these principles and the ability of scholars to break new ground, to open new conversations, to go where educators have never gone before.

For additional information about this series or for the submission of manuscripts, please contact:

Joe L. Kincheloe & Shirley R. Steinberg
637 West Foster Avenue
State College, PA 16801

Studies in the Postmodern Theory of Education